Plymouth University
Charles Seale-Hayne Library
Subject to status this item may be renewed
via your Primo account

http://primo.plymouth.ac.uk
Tel: (01752) 588588

New Media Archaeologies

The book series RECURSIONS: THEORIES OF MEDIA, MATERIALITY, AND CULTURAL TECHNIQUES provides a platform for cuttingedge research in the field of media culture studies with a particular focus on the cultural impact of media technology and the materialities of communication. The series aims to be an internationally significant and exciting opening into emerging ideas in media theory ranging from media materialism and hardware-oriented studies to ecology, the post-human, the study of cultural techniques, and recent contributions to media archaeology. The series revolves around key themes:
- The material underpinning of media theory
- New advances in media archaeology and media philosophy
- Studies in cultural techniques

These themes resonate with some of the most interesting debates in international media studies, where non-representational thought, the technicity of knowledge formations and new materialities expressed through biological and technological developments are changing the vocabularies of cultural theory. The series is also interested in the mediatic conditions of such theoretical ideas and developing them as media theory.

Editorial Board
- Jussi Parikka (University of Southampton)
- Anna Tuschling (Ruhr-Universität Bochum)
- Geoffrey Winthrop-Young (University of British Columbia)

New Media Archaeologies

Edited by
Ben Roberts and Mark Goodall

Amsterdam University Press

Cover illustration: Cassette (James Stencilowsky); ASCII CNC 22 (Windell Oskay)

Cover design: Suzan Beijer
Lay-out: Crius Group, Hulshout

ISBN	978 94 6298 216 1
e-ISBN	978 90 4853 209 4 (pdf)
DOI	10.5117/9789462982161
NUR	670

Printed and bound by CPI Group (UK) Ltd, Croydon, CR0 4YY

Contents

Part 1   Experimental Media Archaeology

Part 2   Media Archaeological Theory

Part 3   Media Archaeology at the Interface

Acknowledgements

The inspiration for this collection first came from the conference *Archaeologies of Media and Film* held at the University of Bradford in September 2014. We are grateful to Ian Palmer of the University of Bradford and Iain Logie Baird of the National Science and Media Museum (then the National Media Museum) for their assistance in arranging this event and Mike Best of the Royal Television Society for providing financial support. We would also like to thank Rachel and Angela Barraclough and Roxy van der Post for helping to organize and run this conference.

Our interest in media archaeology emerged partly out of the Media Archaeologies module that we devised and ran at the University of Bradford from 2012 to the present. We would like to thank our colleague and co-tutor, Karen Thornton, and all students for their contribution to this module and the development of our ideas in this area. We are also grateful to Toni Booth of the National Media Museum for delivering support and handling collection access for this module.

In addition to those already named, we would like to thank colleagues at the University of Bradford and, in particular, Peter Excell, Ali Rashid, Charlie Meecham, and Winifred Taylor. In September 2015, Ben took up a new post at the University of Sussex where he would like to acknowledge the support of all his colleagues in Sussex Humanities Lab but, in particular, David M. Berry, Caroline Bassett, Beatrice Fazi, Alban Webb, Rachel Thomson, Sally-Jane Norman, and Alice Eldridge.

We are also grateful to the Recursions series editors, Jussi Parikka, Annie Tuschling, and Geoffrey Winthrop-Young, as well as our editors at Amsterdam University Press (AUP), Jeroen Sondervan, and Maryse Elliott. We would like to thank AUP for agreeing to allow Thomas Elsaesser's chapter to be reprinted from his *Film History as Media Archaeology: Tracking Digital Cinema* (AUP, 2016).

Introduction

Ben Roberts and Mark Goodall

This collection of essays highlights innovative work in the developing field of media archaeology. It builds on the conference *Archaeologies of Media and Film* organized by the editors in collaboration with the UK National Media Museum and Royal Television Society in September 2014. The volume includes essays by some of the contributors to that conference and it focuses, in particular, on the relationship between theory and practice and the contribution that experimentation can make to our understanding of media archaeology.

In the last decade, a growing number of volumes dedicated to the topic of media archaeology have been published, notably Siegfried Zielinski's *Deep Time of the Media* (2006 [2002]), Jussi Parikka's *What is Media Archaeology?* (2012), Erkki Huhtamo's *Illusions in Motion* (2013), and Wolfgang Ernst's *Digital Memory and the Archive* (2013). We would highlight here two very recent and notable contributions: Thomas Elsaesser's *Film History as Media Archaeology: Tracking Digital Cinema* and Wolfgang Ernst's *Sonic Time Machines: Explicit Sound, Sirenic Voices, and Implicit Sonicity* (both 2016).

In *Sonic Time Machines*, Wolfgang Ernst argues that media archaeology needs to be understood not only as a way of understanding media technology, but also as 'a form of technical perception in which the technological device itself turns into a listening organ' (Ernst, p. 31). This 'sonic' dimension of time-based media allows the media archaeologist to access the past in ways distinct from the interpretative methods of historiography, because these media preserve 'technological knowledge of the material past' (*Ibid.*, p. 113). This technological knowledge can be analysed using tools quite distinct from those of traditional hermeneutic interpretation. Fourier analysis can be used to break down sound into its constituent waveforms. Computational methods equally allow us to break down and understand audio in new ways. For example, the algorithms developed for music recognition software may lead to new forms of searching and sorting audio archives.[1] Ultrasound

---

1   See the 'Humanizing Algorithmic Listening' project, an AHRC research network that considers 'the technical, epistemological and creative possibilities, as well as cultural and ethical

Roberts, B. and M. Goodall (eds.), *New Media Archaeologies*, Amsterdam University Press, 2019
DOI: 10.5117/9789462982161_INTRO

monitors provide the metaphor here: they emit, measure, and manipulate human inaudible sound into an image that is legible to the human eye (*Ibid*., p. 31). What Ernst calls 'sonicity' is not confined to the audio domain, but opens up time-based media technology in general to new forms of analysis. Sonicity thus extends and reworks the 'symbol' and 'signal' distinction from his earlier *Digital Memory and the Archive*. For Ernst, sonicity marks a new investment in 'signal', that is, the non-cultural dimensions of media as opposed to their 'symbolic' cultural content.

A second major intervention can be seen in Thomas Elsaesser's *Film History as Media Archaeology: Tracking Digital Cinema*. Media archaeology, as Elsaesser observes, can be seen as being divided between its French and German roots. These two recent texts fully instantiate that divide: on the one hand, we have Ernst's German media theory with its emphasis on materiality and the inhuman (non-cultural) logic of the machine. On the other hand, we have the Foucauldian influence described in Elsaesser's new film history, that is, an interest in the discontinuous, in the connections between apparently divergent fields and practices in relation to the moving image (Elsaesser suggests Jonathan Crary's *Techniques of the Observer* (1992) as a media archaeological text *avant la lettre*). Both writers view media archaeology as challenging traditional narrative history. In Elsaesser's case, this comes from posing alternative narratives, such as one in which cinema and the digital find a common origin; Ernst, on the other hand, sees the sonic time machine as providing a new technical method of engaging with the past.

Although his book gathers much material that has been previously published elsewhere, the volume clearly highlights the trajectory of Elsaesser's thinking on the relationship between new film history, the digital, and media archaeology. In particular, the final chapter, 'Media Archaeology as Symptom', can be seen as a 'state of the field' address from a writer who has been intimately involved in defining, debating, and redefining media archaeology over the years. In this chapter, Elsaesser proposes the question 'why media archaeology (now)?' as well as, or rather than, 'what is media archaeology?'. He therefore pushes back a little against the idea of justifying media archaeology as a research programme and suggests that we understand that programme itself as a symptomatic response to philosophical crises in relation to the idea of progress, causality, memory, narrative, and representation (Elsaesser, pp. 360–361). In particular, Elsaesser suggests a

implications, of listening with algorithms': (Accessed 2 June 2017) http://www.algorithmiclistening.org/.

more sceptical account of media archaeology's 'radical' challenge to linear history and teleological accounts of progress. He argues that we could see one facet of a contemporary 'ideology of the digital' in media archaeology's interest in obsolete technologies, one that offers a convenient historical counterweight to digital memory loss and the constant embrace of the 'new'. As Elsaesser suggests, 'obsolescence is a term that not only belongs to the discourse of capitalism and technology, but speaks from the position of relentless innovation and "creative destruction"' (*Ibid.*, p. 384). From this perspective, one might see media archaeology's interest in media history as 'merely the flip side of the general appropriation of the past for the benefit of our corporate future'.

One possible response to this complicity with the ideology of the digital is to look further at the relationship between theory and practice. Here, one might add a further question to Parikka's ('what is media archaeology?'), and Elsaesser's ('why media archaeology?'): how is media archaeology? What does media archaeology mean in practice? Of course, posing the question of practice is not entirely new: the question of media archaeology as/in art practice is raised in almost every discussion of the field. Indeed, in her influential overview of media archaeological theory, Wanda Strauven suggests that art practice is one of the three branches of media archaeology. However, there has perhaps been significantly less discussion of media archaeology as educational and academic practice. For us as editors, one of the motivations for this book (and, indeed, the conference that preceded it) was our experience of teaching media archaeology to undergraduates at the University of Bradford. In our teaching, we tried to engage not only with media archaeology as a new way of doing media studies, but also on the experiential and experimental level. Traditional lectures were supplemented with 'hands on' experience of everything from nineteenth-century optical toys (courtesy of the UK National Media Museum) through 8 and 16mm amateur film making to the 1980s and 1990s dial-up bulletin boards that were a precursor to the internet. This educational process required us to constantly question the relationship between theory and practice.

Since its inception, the field of media archaeology has engaged with and advocated experimentation. Theorists and practitioners have done this by rediscovering and promoting avant-garde writings and methodologies from the past and reinterpreting the meanings and potential uses of these works (which in themselves have often been marginalized by conventional academic and scientific rationalist 'wisdom') whilst at the same time encouraging that contemporary writers, artists, and creative thinkers devise their own experimental theories and practices to drive the discipline forward.

Also critical is the combining of theory and practice, something that has long been common in arts schools and emerged in early media departments from the 1980s as a way of developing better 'media workers' (see for example Len Masterman's foundational text *Teaching the Media* (1985) where the term 'critical practitioner' appears central). In experimental media archaeology, theory and practice are intrinsically linked and follow on from each other, overlapping and dissolving in interesting and diverse ways. Media archaeologists, especially *experimental* media archaeologists, see the potential for work that is engaging with the historical past to be transformed into new ideas for the future. This, in turn, can influence a range of practices inside and outside of the field relating to arts projects, museum and curatorial practices, textual production, and extra-disciplinary areas of study (actual archaeology for example).

The key formal texts thus far on the subject of media archaeology have also emphasized the experimental and playful dimension to the field (whilst also noting that there should be no 'correct principles or methodological guidelines' (Huhtamo and Parikka, p. 3). The field itself has indeed been developed out of a complex mixture of theoretical works from history, cultural studies, philosophy, and media studies from modernity to post-modernity and back again. Parikka's notion of 'alternative histories' encourages us to seek out and develop approaches to media technology that may be unusual and different, not to mention bizarre and provocative, following the credo of 'it could have been otherwise' as Parikka, referencing Elsaesser and Burch, puts it (Parikka, pp. 12–13). As Parikka argues, in order to 'rethink our current visual and media field' an open and experimental approach is required, in fact is necessary; these are '*epistemological perversions*' that offer a non-mainstream approach to culture and media (*Ibid.*).

Perhaps the most famous example of this kind of approach is Walter Benjamin's *Arcades Project* with its playful, abstract, and poetic anti-narrative about the modern industrial world. Benjamin's project is referenced with notable frequency because it still remains a high point of the kind of methodology made possible by the application of experimental, avant-garde (surrealist) techniques to a study of geography, landscape, and history. Benjamin's method of 'tearing fragments out of their context and ranging them afresh in a way that they illustrated one another and were able to prove their *raison d'être* in a free-floating state' (Arendt, p. 47) is a practice that we imagine could still bear fruit in the early twenty-first century. Benjamin's approach, to borrow archaeological terminology, of 'drilling' rather than 'excavating' (*Ibid.*, p. 48) leads to inference and poetics as opposed to causal or systematic interpretation. Yet, as some of the essays in this suggest, this difficult but provocative approach can yield interesting results for media archaeology.

It is noticeable that a number of recent, high-profile academic projects have engaged with the debate around what we might call 'experimental media archaeology'. One example is ADAPT, a five-year research project, funded by the European Research Council and based at Royal Holloway, University of London. The aim of the project, which runs from 2013 to 2018, is to 'research and document the history of British broadcast television technology between 1960 and the near-present' (ADAPT, n.d.). Aside from the usual outputs, such as conferences and symposia and PhD theses, recreation/restaging/reconstruction is an important aspect of the ADAPT project. One example was the attempt in May 2016 to recreate the experience of 1970s BBC Outside Broadcasting (OB). The aim of this was to supply: 'convenient contextual material for the many websites and agencies that are now offering archival TV material to various categories of users' (ADAPT, n.d.). This resonates with reconstruction approaches taken in history, for example, the recent 'Hands on History' project hosted by the BBC, the UK National Trust, and English Heritage, designed to immerse (mostly young) learners in historical reality with the opportunity to 'give our audience the chance to become part of the action by seeing, feeling and trying the materials, weapons and activities from their chosen historic era' (Hands on History, n.d.).

A perhaps more strident and provocative set of ideas about experimentation in media archaeology is offered by Anders Fickers and Annie van den Oever (2014). They praise the 'discourse-orientated method' of the discipline thus far deployed, but suggest that more focus be aimed at the material aspect of media. They propose 'historical re-enactment as a heuristic methodology' (*Ibid.*, p. 272), an approach they note is located within certain dimensions of experimental archaeology and some histories of science. Re-enactment and 'experiencing history' are fine, but we can and must go further: '[i]n engaging with the historical artefacts, we aim at stimulating our sensorial appropriation of the past and thereby critically reflecting the (hidden or non-verbalized) tacit knowledge that informs our engagement with media technologies', they argue (*Ibid.*, p. 273). The 'transparency' dimension to media, as noted by Bolter and Grusin in their theory of 'Remediation', must be resisted in experimental media archaeology so that we can encourage a 're-sensitization of expert observers', which is required to 'construct the epistemic object' or 'to define what a "medium" is more precisely' (Ibid., p. 274; Bolter and Grusin, 1999). Fickers and Van den Oever argue that experimental media archaeology must open the black boxes and turn museums and archives into laboratories for experimental research (Fickers and Van den Oever, p. 277). This work involves a mixing together of curators, practitioners, and researchers in new and creative ways. Importantly, Van den Oever also advocate a dialogue between amateurs who increasingly 'wish to share their expertise and knowledge in online platforms and home pages' (*Ibid.*, p. 26); the possibilities opened up by the digital and 'crowd sourcing' in this area have yet to be exploited to their fullest potential.

The Network of Experimental Media Archaeology exists to promote experimental and playful ways of 'thinkering' with past media technologies. In facilitating collaborations between university scholars and cultural heritage institutions, such as museums and archives, the network aims at turning the archive or museum into a laboratory space, turning researchers (historians, media archaeologists) as well as archivists and curators into experimenters' (NEMA, n.d.). One of NEMA's aims: the creative disconcertion of available knowledge (education through failure) is notable. Experimental work will not always yield 'productive' outputs and 'results' and the process of exploring and playing with media technologies and the subsequent understanding of those as presented textually (or in another form) is as important as the results. NEMA is at the forefront of the promotion of experimental approaches to media archaeology and its practices. One is also reminded here of the experimental process of the discipline of archaeology itself, especially the 'fragmented heritage' approach where, in a potential application of Gustav Metzger's concept of 'auto-destructive' art, objects can be completely destroyed in order to understand how they are constructed in the first place, and may be reconstructed again in the future.[2]

The adoption of experimental media archaeology allows theorists and practitioners to go beyond 'the literary study of the "expert users" (as found in technical and consumer association journals and professional publica-tions)' (Fickers and Van den Oever, p. 277). More unusual or diverse fields of thinking and working are possible. Hence, it is useful perhaps to investigate experimental poetics or artistic practices from the avant-garde (although not necessarily exclusively) in order to rework theory and practice. Ap-proaches as diverse as Derrida's early experimental texts, various surrealist methodologies, and the theories and poetics of art cinema can come into play to help us better understand and shape the media landscape of the future.

2   See the 'Lithic Lab' project at the University of Bradford (Mennear). Also 'Manifesto for Auto-Destructive Art' (1960) by Gustav Metzger.

What is important and significant about experimental practices is that they hold the potential to keep the field of media archaeology vibrant and open – open to interpretation and open to all available possibilities. One of the most exciting aspects of media archaeological theory has always been its willingness to divert from and challenge 'path-dependent' thinking. Thus, the first part of the book is concerned with *Experimental Media Archaeology*.

For Wanda Strauven, media archaeology creates a new laboratory for writing and history. Strauven's chapter looks at how theory can become, and to some extent already is, a form of creative practice. Referring back to the provocative, revolutionary ideas of the late 1970s developed by the likes of Gene Youngblood in cinema, Bruno Munari in design, and Buckminster Fuller in architecture, the author updates this thinking for the digital epoch. Drawing also on earlier fascinations with 'outsider art' and alternative practices of play and experimentation, the essay in essence proposes new ways of *doing* media archaeology. It is the way that media archaeology draws on the creative arts and collective practice that sets it apart from a purely technical or socio-political mode of theory.

Annie van den Oever and Andreas Fickers are interested in moving away from using the archive simply as a means of telling timelines of narrative histories and instead using the archive as a means of re-creating processes. Their contribution, 'Doing Experimental Media Archaeology', is a provocative call for change, formed by a discussion of a series of media archaeological experiments executed by the authors in search of alternative ways to draft historical statements on past media practices. By working with certain media objects (for example, domestic film technologies) they explore the 'heuristic possibilities offered by an experimental approach to those devices'. The authors focus on *re-enactment* as an experimental practice. We know that a variety of different and diverse 'users' engage with media objects and thus a practice more reflective of this complex audience is necessary to better understand the media world of the present and the future.

Mark Goodall's contribution to the volume, 'The Ghosts of Media Archaeology', is also focused on the experimental arts and vanguard practices and theories of the past, and is suggestive of ways in which such radical ideas could be applied to current media archaeology practices and theories. This can work towards new ways of engaging with the archive, but could also be adopted in order to potentially avoid the stasis from which so many theoretical movements of the past have suffered. Goodall confirms that even the most avant-garde works can offer methods for creative adoption by established organizations, individuals, and groups.

Alison Gazzard, in '(game)(code): re-playing program listings from 1980s British computer magazines' (in this volume), extends this idea of play and experimentation with a practical application devoted to a specific collection of media artefacts. Importantly, the chapter shows that it is not just the playing or replaying of actual games in the laboratory themselves that can yield interesting results, but how play can be applied effectively to *secondary* materials connected to media technologies (printed manuals, magazines, etc.). This extends what archives and museum spaces can and should be doing to develop usage of their often vast and varied holdings.

The second section of this volume is concerned with *Media Archaeological Theory*. In 'Motion, Energy Entropy: Towards Another Archaeology of the Cinema', Thomas Elsaesser draws our attention to the tendency of media theory to focus as a paradigm on the photographic image. To move away from this dependency, during a phase we can identify as the 'death of cinema', theorists would be advised to adopt the 'multiple agenda' knowledge developed by media archaeology. Elsaesser argues that this shift 'better reflects the contemporary epoch but also acknowledges the changing function of the moving image for our information society, our service industries, our memory cultures, and our "creative industries" more generally'. Theories devoted to the 'persistence of vision', while certainly valuable for describing the manner of twentieth-century media, must be superseded in the twenty-first century. This needs to manifest in an experimental manner that is typical of media archaeological thinking: by moving forward and backwards in time to integrate ideas more innovatively to produce new knowledge.

Both Peter Buse and Ben Roberts revisit the work of Walter Benjamin, arguably one of the totemic founding figures of media archaeology theory. In 'Collector, Hoarder, Media Archaeologist: Walter Benjamin with Vivian Maier', Buse draws our attention to the important practice of collecting, reflecting on Benjamin's famous text on his own library and comparing this with contemporary examples of (photographic) archives, collections, and bodies of found work. Buse notes the complex relationships we develop with collections and collecting. On the one hand, it is a fetishist consumption of objects as consumer capital; on the other, it is a passionate and highly emotional engagement with things, of attachments. The potential parallels Buse discusses between the antiquarian and the archivist provide food for thought for the expansion of more vibrant museum and curatorial practices going forward. Ben Roberts meanwhile, in 'Media Archaeology and Critical Theory of Technology', updates Benjamin's theories in relation to more recent debates located within the work of Bernard Stiegler and Wolfgang

Ernst. Roberts suggests that we need to understand the specific contribution media archaeology makes to a critical theory of technology.

The final section of the book, *Media Archaeology at the Interface*, looks at the relationship between media archaeology and other practices.

Angela Piccini and the Cube Collective's essay 'The Cube: A Cinema Archaeology' provides a vivid case study on how media archaeology can be used not just to gain a better, deeper understanding of a historical site, but a clear demonstration that media archaeology and traditional archaeology may have more in common than at first seemed evident. The imaginative practices utilized by the author and her team on the site of The Cube arts space in Bristol offer insights for a wide potential application of experimental and poetic practices allied with more traditional techniques of (re)discovery. By using the 'full range of promiscuous methods developed and practised by both academic and developer-funded archaeologists', the project reveals the ways in which a range of these techniques can intersect.

Finally, in 'Inventing Pasts and Futures: Speculative Design and Media Archaeology', Jussi Parikka continues his work exploring the new possibilities of media archaeology. In drawing again from the realms of art and design, and by suggesting that we follow the dreams of a 'political imaginary' through 'imaginary design' (and a pedagogy of such), it is media archaeology, of all the twenty-first century theoretical models, Parikka argues, that can best divine the future, the science-fiction even, of the media landscape yet to arrive.

Works Cited

ADAPT, 'About ADAPT', Accessed 17 May 2017, http://www.adapttvhistory.org.uk/what-will-adapt-do/.

ADAPT, 'Researching the History of Television Production Technology', Accessed 17 May 2017, http://www.adapttvhistory.org.uk/.

Hannah Arendt, 'Introduction', in *Illuminations*, Walter Benjamin (New York: Harcourt, Brace & World, 1968), pp. 1–53.

Jay David Bolter and Richard Grusin, *Remediation: Understanding New Media*. (Cambridge, MA: MIT Press, 1999).

Jonathan Crary, *Techniques of the Observer: On Vision and Modernity in the Nineteenth Century*. (Cambridge, MA: MIT Press, 1992).

Thomas Elsaesser, *Film History as Media Archaeology*. (Amsterdam: Amsterdam University Press, 2017)

Wolfgang Ernst, *Digital Memory and the Archive*. J. Parikka (ed.). (Minneapolis, MN: University of Minnesota Press, 2013).

Wolfgang Ernst, *Sonic Time Machines: Explicit Sound, Sirenic Voices, and Implicit Sonicity*. (Amsterdam: Amsterdam University Press, 2016).

Anders Fickers and Annie van den Oever, 'Experimental Media Archaeology: A Plea for New Directions', in A. van den Oever (ed.) *Technē/Technology: Researching Cinema and Media Technologies: Their Development, Use, and Impact*. (Amsterdam: Amsterdam University Press, 2014), pp. 272–277.

Hands on History, 'About Hands on History', Accessed 2 June 2017, http://www.handsonhistory.co.uk/about-us.

HAL, 'Humanizing Algorithmic Listening', Accessed 2 June 2017, http://www.algorithmiclistening.org/.

Erkki Huhtamo, *Illusions in Motion: Media Archaeology of the Moving Panorama and Related Spectacles*. (Cambridge, MA: MIT Press, 2013).

Erkki Huhtamo and Jussi Parikka (eds.), *Media Archaeology: Approaches, Applications, and Implications*. (Berkeley, CA: University of California Press, 2011).

Len Masterman, *Teaching the Media*. (London: Comedia Pub. Group, 1985).

David Mennear, 'A Brief Photo Essay: The Lithic Lab at the University of Bradford', *These Bones of Mine*, 4 December 2014, Accessed 2 June 2017, https://these-bonesofmine.wordpress.com/category/fragmented-heritage-project/.

Gustav Metzger, *Auto-Destructive Art/Manifesto Auto-Destructive Art* (London: Destruction/Creation, 1965).

NEMA (n.d.) 'About the Network of Experimental Media Archaeology', *Media Heritage*, Accessed 2 June 2017, http://media-heritage.org/index.php/about.

Annie van den Oever (ed.), *Technē/Technology: Researching Cinema and Media Technologies: their Development, Use, and Impact*. (Amsterdam: Amsterdam University Press, 2014).

Jussi Parikka, *What is Media Archaeology?* (Cambridge: Polity, 2012).

Siegfried Zielinski, *Deep Time of the Media: Toward an Archaeology of Hearing and Seeing by Technical Means*. (Cambridge, MA: MIT Press, 2006).

About the authors

Mark Goodall is Head of Film and Media at the University of Bradford. His research interests include cult, horror and experimental cinema, popular music and the avant-garde, and the mondo films of the 1960s and 1970s. His publications include *Sweet and Savage: The World through the Shockumentary Film Lens* (Headpress 2006, 2nd ed. 2017), *Crash Cinema: Representation in Film* (Cambridge Scholars, 2007) and *Gathering of the Tribe: Music and*

Heavy Conscious Creation (Headpress, 2013). Forthcoming books are *Music and Fascism* (Routledge) and *The Beatles' White Album* (Headpress). He is the producer and director of the feature film *Holy Terrors* (2017) and plays in the indie chamber folk band Rudolf Rocker.

Ben Roberts is Lecturer in Digital Humanities at the University of Sussex. He has published widely on philosophy of technology, particularly the work of Bernard Stiegler. He is currently completing a monograph for Manchester University Press entitled *Critical Theory and Contemporary Technology*. He is also leading an AHRC research network on automation anxiety.

Part 1

Experimental Media Archaeology

1. Media Archaeology as Laboratory for History Writing and Theory Making

Wanda Strauven

Abstract

As suggested in 1996 by Siegfried Zielinski, media archaeology should be considered as a "form of activity" (or Tätigkeit), as something that you do or execute. In this essay, I propose to think of media archaeology as a laboratory for history writing and theory making, by engaging with various hands-on media-archaeological methods, such as creative hacking, non-narrative modes of presentation, media bricolage and play. The central aim of such a media-archaeological enterprise is to rethink media's temporality, materiality and potentiality.

Keywords: Media Archaeology, Laboratory, Creative Hacking, Creative Thinking, Zielinski, Munari

> *Die Philosophie ist keine Lehre, sondern eine Tätigkeit.*[1]
> — Ludwig Wittgenstein, *Tractatus Logico-Philosophicus* (1921)

More than two decades ago, Siegfried Zielinski already suggested thinking of media archaeology as a practice, or a continual performance, as something that you do or carry out. More specifically, in an essay published in July 1996 in *CTheory* as part of the special section on Global Algorithm, the German media theorist called media archaeology his 'form of activity', adopting Ludwig Wittgenstein's notion of *Tätigkeit*. In Zielinski's words, Wittgenstein 'adhered to the premise that philosophy is not something to be sat out on a professorial chair, but should be a continuous action of clarification in its very own medium, language' (Zielinski, 1996). As philosophy should

---

[1]   'Philosophy is not a body of doctrine but an activity.' (4.112): (Wittgenstein 2002, p.29).

Roberts, B. and M. Goodall (eds.), *New Media Archaeologies*, Amsterdam Universsity Press, 2019
DOI: 10.5117/9789462982161_CH01

consist of clarifying sentences (and not just of the sum of 'philosophical sentences'), so media archaeology could be thought of as the 'continuous action' of excavation into the media's past(s) and future(s), that is, as the *process* of digging, discovering, rediscovering, rethinking, etc., rather than as the final results of such actions. In 1996, Zielinski tentatively defined media archaeology as an 'approach [...] which in a pragmatic perspective means to dig out secret paths in history, which might help us to find our way into the future' (*Ibid.*).

This early media-archaeological definition/proposition by Zielinski resonates with two mottos formulated in the 1970s that are influential for my current research and my own take on media archaeology. The first motto is from American architect and systems theorist Richard Buckminster Fuller, as cited by Gene Youngblood in his 1970 book *Expanded Cinema*: 'I think the way to see what tomorrow is going to look like is just to look at our children.' (Youngblood, p. 45). Not only does this Fuller quote reveal an optimistic view of the future, but it also hints at the intertwining of historical layers, of different temporal experiences and perspectives, of the past (adult) opening up towards the future through the present (child). The second saying belongs to Italian designer and self-made educator Bruno Munari, who, in the second half of the 1970s, initiated art ateliers for children in museums and elementary schools for which he formulated the most basic didactic principle: 'tell how, and not what, to do' (*non dire cosa fare, ma come fare*) (Restelli, p. 35; my translation). Clearly, as I will discuss further below, Munari was more concerned with the process (the tools, the techniques, the method, etc.) than with the final results of the art labs.

In this essay, I want to focus on the shift from 'what' to 'how', by looking at some old and new ways of *doing* media archaeology. I propose to think of media archaeology as an experimental method, that is, as a method of trial and error, of hands-on exercises, of creative thinking. Yet, as I will stress throughout my chapter, I am mostly interested in the conceptual dimension and implication(s) of such a laboratorial approach. Firstly, I will introduce different notions of laboratory to make clear what is at stake. Secondly, I will discuss some historical experiments that I have engaged with in my teaching, before turning, thirdly, to child's play as an inspirational lab for media archaeologists. This last section is part of the ongoing research project '#kinderspiel' that I am developing with Alexandra Schneider. It is the fruit of our collaboration, our collective thinking process, which I consider another good example of laboratorial activity. In fact, while for scientists it is perfectly normal to work together and conduct research in a group context, for humanities scholars such an approach is still rather 'disruptive'.

Laboratories as Sites of Creative Thinking

Within the growing field of media archaeology as a new subdiscipline of media studies, the notion of the lab is not entirely new. One could mention here the multiple laboratory activities of someone like Garnet Hertz, who, together with Jussi Parikka, organized a so-called zombie media workshop at Transmediale 2011 in Berlin. According to Hertz and Parikka, a medium never dies, but instead 'decays, rots, reforms, remixes, and gets historicized, reinterpreted and collected' (Hertz and Parikka, p. 430). Zombie media are the living dead of both the past and the present, that is, of media history and today's electronic waste. They are not dead, but simply 'out of use' and can be 'resurrected to new uses, contexts and adaptations' (*Ibid.*, p. 429). Participants of a zombie media workshop are initiated, at their own risk (!), in the electronic DIY practice of circuit bending, which consists of breaking open battery-powered toys and modifying their circuits, transforming them, for instance, into noise-making instruments. Besides the very practical aspect of hardware hacking, the idea behind this type of workshop (or mini-laboratory) is to resist the planned obsolescence of the media industry. On a more conceptual level, one could also say that Hertz and Parikka are hacking media archaeology itself, by turning it not only into an artistic method, but also into a political strategy and thus safeguarding it from its own canonization.

At Transmediale 2016, Parikka introduced and moderated a panel titled 'The Persistence of the Lab', drawing attention to, among other things, the interweaving of the disruptive and the corporate in the recent phenomenon of university labs within the (Digital) Humanities. These 'intellectual start-ups', as Parikka calls them, are often operating with funding from companies. In order to trace the possible origins of the media lab, Parikka proposes looking not only into the history of the science lab (such as the Edison Laboratory at Memlo Park for its invention of the modern R&D and Bell Labs for its principle of co-working), but also into the tradition of art studios as sites where old and new methods are explored. The media lab is a specific 'site of invention', located at the intersection between liberal arts and scientific experiments, between humanities and sciences (Parikka, 2016). While an early example of media lab is the MIT Media Lab born in the 1980s, a more specifically media archaeology oriented lab is the Media Archaeology Lab (MAL), founded by Lori Emerson at the University of Colorado at Boulder in 2009. Both Parikka and Emerson, together with Darren Wershler, are involved in the research project 'What is a Media Lab?' that will result in *The Lab Book*. On the project's website, which cites many more examples of media labs, the media lab is defined in Foucauldian terms as a 'heterotopic space', because of its ambiguity as 'inextricable mix of complicities and revolutionary potential'. Moreover: 'Whether as a discourse or as an actual place, "the lab" occupies an increasingly important role in the renegotiation of disciplinary borders, practical humanities methods, and relations to conceptual, economic and critical work.' (Emerson, Parikka, and Wershler, 2016).

Before getting into the notion of the discursive lab, I want to briefly mention here another proposition to turn media archaeology into a research laboratory, formulated in 2014 by media scholars Annie van den Oever and Andreas Fickers. In their text titled 'Experimental Media Archaeology: A Plea for New Directions', the two authors explain how they want to re-sensitize media scholars by letting them physically engage with old media technology. Their approach is very much centred on the method of historical re-enactment, which should allow us to relive the past with all our senses. For this, they refer to Michel Serres's notion of the 'second tongue':

> In doing experimental media archaeology, we want to plead for a hands-on, ears-on, or an integral sensual approach toward media technologies. As the French philosopher Michel Serres argued in *The Five Senses*, we need a 'second tongue' in order to grasp the complex meaning of things. (Fickers and Van den Oever, p. 273)

While the simulation of historical effects (and 'historical practices of use'[2]) seems to be a major concern here, I would like to revalue the method of re-enacting or restaging as a critical intervention, that is, as a reflection not so much on the past, but rather on our (laboratorial) presence in the present, because what we 'really' experience in re-enacted situations is primarily an experience of the present. For instance, when we are put in front of an early black-and-white cathode ray tube in a living room that looks like a living room of the 1960s,[3] we will watch it with our (altered) knowledge of

---

2   See Giovanna Fossati and Annie van den Oever's introduction to the edited volume *Exposing the Film Apparatus: The Film Archive as a Research Laboratory* (2016), where the laboratory is defined as 'a place where old media can be tested and where historical practices of use can be taken into consideration by simulating them in order to study effects as part of research' (Fossati and Van den Oever, p. 24).

3   Andreas Fickers, together with Susan Aasman and her research team, performed such a historical re-enactment at the 9th Orphan Film Symposium, which took place at the EYE Film Institute Netherlands, in Amsterdam, 30 March - 2 April 2014.

colour TV, flat TV, internet TV, etc. That is to say, we will be re-sensitized as twenty-first century TV viewers.

Whereas Fickers and Van den Oever envision the creation of media-archaeological labs as physical places to which museum and archive objects are transferred, de-auratized, and de-aestheticized, to be explored for their material historicity (that is, as 'historical sources') (Fickers and Van den Oever, p. 275), I suggest thinking of the lab as a conceptual site, as a process of creative thinking. Such a laboratorial activity ideally takes place in a group context, favouring a collective/collaborative effort, for which the classroom, as a physical site, offers itself very well. Even if I do not eschew historical re-enactments, as my own teaching examples will show, I consider these types of activities not as *historical*, but as *conceptual* exercises. By physically engaging with old artefacts or apparatuses, the intention is not so much to bring the students in contact with the past, but rather to make them think differently, to make them question what is taken for granted, to 'unsettle' them – all this with regard to their present, that is, to their contemporary media use and their actual training as media scholars (and therefore also to their knowledge of media history).

Besides circuit bending, one can think of fun exercises with old programming languages such as BASIC or obsolete software programs, with game programming, and game hacking, or even – as I propose to do – with very low-tech or non-tech devices. The basic technique we as humanities scholars need, is (human) language, to hack but also to be hacked. For instance, how can we break with the linearity of argumentation and get closer to the non-linear process of our inner thoughts? How can we write history in a non-narrative way? How can we disengage from academic formats and writing styles?

But then, the academic discourse is a laboratory on its own. Akin to such a conception are Sean Cubitt's plea for the use of the anecdote and Jacques Derrida's notion of critical language as *bricolage*. To start with the latter, in his reading of Claude Lévi-Strauss's notion of *bricolage*, Derrida points out that, in contrast to the engineers' creative thinking, which proceeds from goals to means, the *bricoleur* re-uses available materials in order to solve new problems – which is pretty much what every discourse does. Referring to an article on literary criticism by Gérard Genette, Derrida states that every discourse can be said to be *bricoleur* for its 'necessity of borrowing one's concepts from the text of a heritage which is more or less coherent or ruined' (Derrida, p. 231). Cubitt is more explicit in considering the anecdotal method as a laboratory. He writes: 'The anecdote is the laboratory in which we can observe the interaction of the rival claims of the disciplines and their consort professions, whether the anecdote takes the form of a novel or an anthropological observation.' (Cubitt, p. 7) Yet, the anecdote is a site not only of observation, but also of theory making. It is a conceptual laboratory where claims of others are countered or disputed, and where (unsuspected) connections are made. In Cubitt's own words:

> Since recounting an anecdote is always a re-versioning, the teller has to recognise that their telling (and any interpretations and connections they offer) forms another anecdote to be pored over by another analyst in another time seeking other relevance. Relevance, another term for 'connection', ties anecdotes together. When a researcher has amassed enough anecdotes – read enough poetry, seen enough films, observed enough informants – connections always emerge, and each anecdote can be searched for its relevance to another. This is both how we form theories and how, drawing on counter-examples, we dispute them. (*Ibid.*, p. 11)

Whereas statistics tend to hide the exceptional, the anecdotal method brings the exceptional to the fore. One could also say it is a kind of disturbance, a unique instance that creates 'noise' and therefore becomes relevant. According to Cubitt, it is a form of failure, or rather a response to failure: 'The exception is precisely the focus of the anecdotal method which seeks out the circumstance where an expected result fails.' (*Ibid.*, p. 9)

Both methods – Cubitt's anecdote and Derrida's *bricolage* – can be seen as examples of discursive laboratory: focused on the process of theory making, they consist of appropriating and repurposing existing notions, of adopting the technique of trial and error to come to new notions, and of experimenting (or promoting) creative thinking.

Creativity as a mental process is at the core of Bruno Munari's educational laboratories for children. According to Munari, imagination is a visual process that nevertheless depends on our body of knowledge; that is, the more we know, the more we see and the more we can develop our creativity. Hence, he insists on offering to (school) children as much data as possible to be stored/memorized in view of future creativity. The educator or conductor of a children's lab should also offer the necessary tools and explain the basic techniques. He or she should 'tell how, and not what, to do' (see above). Munari was influenced by ideas of active learning through his connections with the Italian children's writer Gianni Rodari and the pedagogue Giovanni Belgrano, who were both related to the Movement of Cooperative Educa-tion (*Movimento di Cooperazione Educativa*), a secular movement inspired by the pedagogical principles of the American philosopher and educator

John Dewey. Unlike Dewey, however, Munari was less focused on teaching craftsmanship and more driven by the idea of stimulating creativity and activating divergent thinking.

This becomes most clear in Munari's visual communication experiments, which can all be considered as low-tech media labs: from vegetable printmaking activities to experimenting with different sizes and shapes of paper, cut on the spot, in order to alter children's drawing patterns, from using the Xerox machine to make originals instead of copies to the technique of 'direct projections' with the mechanical slide projector. In *Fantasia* (1977), Munari lists six rules that are valid for the presentation of all kinds of visual communication techniques:

> First: make [the children] familiar with the tool that is used, so that the use is appropriate and that every exploitable possibility is known.
> Second: make the best technique for this specific tool understood.
> Third: let everyone choose and decide what to do with what he or she has learned.
> Fourth: analyse and discuss together the individual results, not to decide who is the best, but to give everyone the possibility to explain their work.
> Fifth: provoke and coordinate teamwork towards a show.
> Sixth: destroy everything and repeat in order to continuously update and not romanticize the work. (Munari, p. 143; my translation[4])

Before starting with the experiment, it is fundamental, in Munari's view, to explain the mechanism of the (media) device and show all its possible techniques. For instance, for the experiment of the so-called direct projections – which consists of putting little pieces of cheap materials or debris between the two glass plates of a slide mount and projecting them directly, without the intermediate of photography, onto the wall – educators should start by demonstrating the multiple operations of the slide projector: projecting, focusing, changing slides, etc. But Munari also encourages teachers to open up the device as far as possible and show the children what it looks like inside, or to hold and operate the slide projector as a flashlight. In

---

4   'Primo: far conoscere bene lo strumento che si usa in modo che l'uso sia appropriato e che ogni possibilità strumentale sia nota. Secondo: far capire la tecnica più giusta per quello strumento. Terzo: lasciare che ognuno scelga e decida che cosa fare con ciò che ha imparato. Quarto: analizzare e discutere assieme i risultati dei lavori, non per decidere chi è il più bravo ma per dare una ragione a ognuno secondo il lavoro fatto. Quinto: provocare e coordinare il lavoro di gruppo per uno scopo spettacolare. Sesto: distruggere tutto e rifare per aggiornare continuamente e per non mitizzare il lavoro.'

other words, children are challenged to think beyond the 'proper' use of the device, or, rather, to think of all its possible uses.

As important as the first rule is the sixth and last rule: after the experiment everything has to be destroyed. As Munari explains further: 'The destruction of collective work [...] is necessary in order to avoid creating models to imitate, and turning the work into a museum piece or the author into a star. It is not the object that should be conserved but the procedure, the design method, the experience that can be modified and repeated according to the problems that arise.' (*Ibid.*, p. 144; my translation[5]) Here, again, it becomes clear that the Italian art educator is more concerned with the process (or the testing of a method) than with the final result. The idea of repeating an experiment corresponds to the technique of trial and error, which, in the case of direct projections, also has to do with unmet expectations or disappointments (as I will discuss in the following section).

In short, Munari is not promoting a *laissez faire* approach. On the contrary, his teaching method is aimed at the practical learning of tools and specific techniques. From an artistic point of view, his intention is double: that is, on the one hand, to demystify the sacrality of art and, on the other, to democratize art by teaching 'secret' techniques so that everyone can use them in their own creations. From a media-archaeological point of view, the main interest lies in the laboratorial dimension of his approach as well as in the creative hacking (or repurposing) of basic media devices, such as the photocopy machine and the slide projector (Strauven, 2015).

Historical Hands-on Experiments in the Classroom

The technique of direct projections was first explored by Munari as an artistic method in the late 1950s, when the mechanical slide projector was a novelty. In the 1970s, especially within the context of the Italian school system, the device was still regarded as a piece of new technology. When, in 2015, I decided to re-enact Munari's elementary school experiment with college students at Goethe University Frankfurt, I encountered some practical problems: first of all, it was not simple to find and buy slide

---

5   'La distruzione dell'opera collettiva [...] va intesa come modo di non creare modelli da imitare, una non museificazione dell'opera, un non divismo dell'autore. Non è l'oggetto che va conservato ma il modo, il metodo progettuale, l'esperienza modificabile pronta a produrre ancora secondo i problemi che si presentano.'

mounts with glass (at least not offline), but then, more problematically, it proved rather difficult to get hold of a slide projector at the university. In the end, I started the hands-on workshop with a malfunctioning Kodak Carousel and another basic model with a single slide changer allowing only two slides to alternate. Yet, the best evidence that the mechanical slide projector, in the 2010s, is a piece of obsolete technology is the trouble the students had locating the on-off switch. After starting the machine(s), the classroom would fill with a penetrating mechanical hum and a slight burning smell – the ideal circumstances for letting the students cultivate their 'second tongue', as Fickers and Van den Oever would agree. However, my point was elsewhere.

By getting my students in touch with the materiality of an outdated media device, I wanted to make them rethink the notion of hacking. Munari's experiment is an illustration of low-tech hacking because of its very simple repurposing of the slide projector: used for the projection of *slide-less* slide mounts filled with tangible materials in order to reveal their 'hidden' materiality. The conceptual aim of the historical re-enactment is thus twofold: not only to rethink media's operationality (from photographic projection to direct projection), but also to rethink the projected images in terms of materiality, that is, material concreteness. As I know from experience, it is especially the latter that is more difficult to achieve.

The hands-on workshop consists of at least six steps, inspired by Munari's six rules. First, the students are asked to bring to class small material particles they can find in their home or on the street. Without further explanation about the experiment itself, I usually give them some examples of 'found material' (seeds, sugar, dust, flowers, leaves, etc.) and insist that it should be quite flat. The range of selected materials tends to grow during the second step, which is the moment of composition. Each student makes his or her slide-less slides adding 'things at hand', such as tobacco, hair, wool fluff, etc. By this point, I will have explained the basics of the original experiment, so the students know that their slides will be projected. The most typically encountered problems in this phase are difficulties closing the slide frame because of the literal/material thickness of the composition and its non-stability/non-fixity after closing the frame. Expectation grows during this second step, and some students will hold their frames against the light to check out the expected result. The third step consists mainly of demonstrating the basic functions of the slide projector and of letting students 'play' with the empty device, that is, without slides. They also need to start thinking about a possible order for presenting their

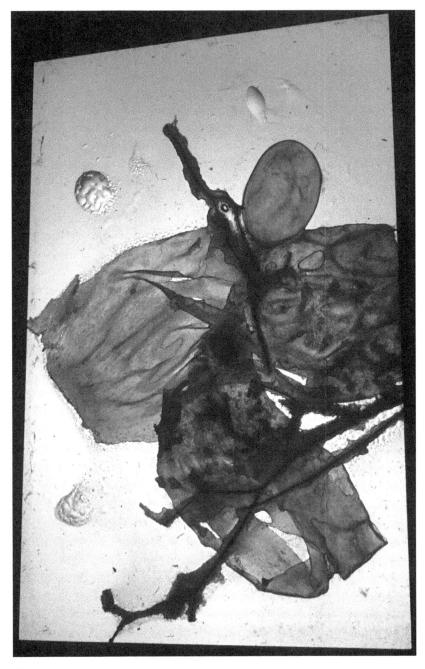

1.1

slides as a collective show and maybe about some 'special effects', like overlapping projection by using both projectors. Then, during the show, everyone needs to comment on his or her own slide(s), to explain what is in there. What is revealing about this fourth step is the astonishment and/or disappointment about the projected result. The near colourlessness of the slides is especially striking (and disillusioning), even if, at the same time, the result is surprisingly beautiful. Some students are truly in awe of their own slides, and shout: WOW! Other students join in and start commenting or pointing out certain details; it soon becomes a collective work of reflection, interpretation, and narration. The fifth step is the explanation of Munari's final rule, giving them the opportunity to repeat the experiment before destroying everything. Interestingly, there are always enough students who want to try again, to 'correct' where they failed, to make the 'transparency' more transparent, to work less figuratively, and to bring the materiality of their material more to the fore. On at least one occasion this led to a true revelation: the thin skins, pulp, and juice of a mandarin segment not only showed that less is more (the less opacity the more material details), but also that direct projections can result in 'moving pictures', since during projection the mandarin juice was evaporating and therefore in continuous motion (see Figure 1.1). Finally, the sixth step is the destruction of the work, the emptying and cleaning of the slide mounts, which is not that easy for everyone. Indeed, some students would prefer to keep their composition (and, of course, rules are made to be broken).

The most significant moment of failure of this specific experiment happens during the fourth step, when students are explaining their own 'creations' and commenting on the 'creations' of their fellow students. I deliberately put creations in scare quotes here, because students tend to think about their slides as little artworks, and not without reason: some slides are aesthetically very successful. More problematic, however, is the association that almost everyone makes with Rorschach tests and the fact that one cannot escape interpretation. They comment: 'There's a street full of traffic', 'There's a man with a hat', 'There's a skeleton', etc. Whereas the original idea behind Munari's school experiment was to reveal the 'hidden' material structure of a leaf, a flower petal, etc., or to show that sugar consists of minuscule cubes, the students all end up formulating complex associations. Of course, that is what I want to make them aware of – the fact that they are 'imprisoned' by interpretation and abstraction, which somehow blinds them to materiality and concretization. So, to some extent, the failure of this experiment is its success.

A similar mechanism is at work in the second classroom experiment that I want to discuss here and that has a direct connection to Munari's early career. The experimental designer and self-made educator started off as a Futurist artist. In 1926, at age nineteen, he moved to Milan where he joined the group of Milanese Futurists. In the early 1930s, Munari invented the 'useless machine' (*macchina inutile*), a humorous hacking of the Futurist machine as celebrated by the founder of Futurism, F.T. Marinetti, which was supposed to be very useful. In those same years, Munari also made some 'tactile tables', another Futurist concept and technique invented by Marinetti.

In 1920, Marinetti made his first tactile table, titled *Sudan-Paris*, to illustrate his concept of 'hand travel', which he further explained in his Tactilism Manifesto, published in 1921 (see also Strauven, 2018). Tactilism is the art of touch, intended to develop sensitivity in the fingertips by means of very simple tactile exercises, such as wearing gloves for several days, swimming underwater in the sea, or enumerating and recognizing, in complete darkness, all the objects in your bedroom. According to Marinetti, the main problem in human interaction, at the beginning of the twentieth century, was the lack of sensitivity in the skin. Tactile education could, in his view, help to overcome this problem. In the Tactilism Manifesto, he narrates how he submitted his own sense of touch to 'intensive therapy, localizing the confused phenomena of will and thought on the different parts of [his] body, and especially on the palms of [his] hands' (Marinetti, p. 266).

During his public lectures on Tactilism in the early 1920s, Marinetti used to circulate *Sudan-Paris* among the audience as a sample. It consisted of a wooden board on which different types of material were attached, divided into three horizontal areas or sections: top (Sudan) – middle (sea) – bottom (Paris). As Marinetti explains in his Tactilism Manifesto:

> In its *Sudan* part this table contains tactile values that are crude, greasy, rough, sharp, burning (spongy material, sandpaper, wool, pig's bristle, and wire bristle). In the *Sea* part the table contains tactile values that are slippery, metallic, cool (different grades of emery paper). In the *Paris* part the table contains tactile values that are soft, delicate, caressable, warm and cool at the same time (silk, velvet, and large and small feathers). (*Ibid.*, p. 267)

In Marinetti's tactile evaluation, material qualities like softness or smoothness do not automatically imply positive tactile experiences, while sharp or rough surfaces can trigger pleasant feelings. Art historian Caro Verbeek has tested this thesis of tactile values with contemporary audiences. In 2010,

1.2

she created, with the help of artist Edward Janssen, a replica of Marinetti's tactile board. Verbeek writes:

> I have used it in many lectures and let it be passed around audiences, just like Marinetti did, always curious about the reactions of the public. Unexpectedly, the rough and sharp parts at the top often seemed to evoke positive associations, in contrast to the smooth, elaborate textures at the bottom, which frequently made people giggle, squeak, and sometimes even shiver, especially when pausing at the feathers. (Verbeek, p. 229)

In other words, it seems that to increase our sensory perception, we need surfaces that are rougher, coarser. This is perhaps the tactile problem of today's media devices: when touching their very smooth screens without buttons, protrusions, or roughness, we don't 'feel' anything.

In 2014, following Verbeek's example, I have made my own, very freely inspired replica of Marinetti's *Sudan-Paris* for teaching purposes. But before circulating my poorly made tactile table among the students, I would first submit them to other basic tactile exercises. For instance, I would ask them to describe with tactile adjectives their mobile screenic devices, like smartphones or tablets, by merely looking at it. The most commonly used terms are 'cold', 'smooth', and 'silky'. Then, I ask the students to close their eyes, touch the device very carefully and describe it again. Usually, they discover the device is actually not so cold and also not so smooth. Finally, they are divided into pairs and take turns in being blindfolded and tactilely subjected to my self-made *Sudan-Paris* and other objects, things they are carrying with them (like a scarf, a lighter, or an apple) – see Figure 1.2. The hardest part of this hands-on experiment is always finding the right words to describe what they actually feel, because the exercise is not to recognize the object they touch ('This is an apple'), but to name the sensation of the surfaces they are touching ('This is knobbly').

Clearly, despite the non-stop manual operation of all kinds of media devices, young adults are not well trained in terms of tactile sensitivity. We could say that they are still caught in the predominantly visual regime of the twentieth century. The purpose of re-enacting Marinetti's tactile exercise is mainly to make the students aware of their double 'failure', that is, their limitation in both sensory and linguistic terms, and then, hopefully, to turn their tactile media usage into a more active and more conscious process.

The Word-Playing and Object-Oriented Child

As emerges from the hands-on workshops inspired by Munari's direct projection experiment and Marinetti's tactile exercise, a major role is assigned to verbal expression. Creative thinking happens while searching for the right words, which can, of course, be extended to experimental writing assignments. What I want to reiterate here is that language is our basic tool for laboratorial activities (within the humanities, at least), and that speaking, or uttering concepts by means of words, should be considered a very concrete activity. This brings us back to Wittgenstein and his notion of 'language-game' (*Sprachspiel*). According to the philosopher, the meaning of the word depends on the language-game in which it is used; that is, the same word can change meaning when becoming part of a different 'activity'. In Wittgenstein's own words, 'the term "*language-game*" is meant to bring into prominence the fact that the *speaking* of language is part of an activity, or of a form of life' (Wittgenstein, p. 11).

In connection with today's media use, we can think of the introduction of a new (or renewed, repurposed) vocabulary for our touchscreen gestures. In particular, I want to mention here the expression 'to pinch', introduced by Steve Jobs during the launch of the iPhone in 2007. To pinch, in Apple language, means to touch the screen very softly or tenderly; with two fingers, usually the thumb and the index, which move either towards each other or away from each other. This counters, of course, the more common association of pinching with pain. As Alexandra Schneider observes: 'The idea of being "pinched" does not necessarily evoke the sense of a tender touch, and the etymology of the corresponding French verb *pincer* (from which the English word derives) confirms this intuition.' However, as Schneider explains further, the French verb *pincer* originally also meant *saisir d'amour*, referring to 'a state of being touched (or moved) by a feeling of love' (Schneider, p. 54). So, interestingly, Job's twenty-first century language-game capturing the tenderness of pinching the touchscreen is related to a language-game of centuries ago.[6]

An equally tender wordplay was conceived some years later, in 2011, by a three-year-old girl in connection with the iPad.[7] The girl, whose mother tongue is Dutch, used to call Apple's tablet the '*aaienpet*'. Regarding the last part of the term, there is no connection to be made with the English noun 'pet' (or 'animal'), since a *pet* in Dutch means 'cap'. The language-game, which only works in Dutch, is actually limited to the first part of the term: the 'i' of iPad does not refer to the first-person singular, but rather to the verb 'to caress', which in Dutch is *aaien* (pronunciation: [ajə]). It is likely that the girl, because of the phonetic similarity between the English 'I' and the Dutch '*aai*', gave her own interpretation to Apple's name for the electronic tablet, namely: a screen to caress. Yet, such an interpretation is also confirmed by the activity of caressing itself. In other words, it is a good example of how language is woven into an action.

That it is worthwhile paying attention to children's creative minds is also suggested by Douglas Hofstadter and Emmanuel Sander in *Surfaces and Essences: Analogy as the Fuel and Fire of Thinking* (2013), a large study on the human capacity of making analogies. The following sentences made by two-year-olds, cited from the observational work by developmental psychologist Karine Duvignau, are revealing: 'I undressed the banana!', 'Gotta nurse the truck!', and 'Come on, Mommy, turn your eyes on!' (Hofstadter and Sander, p. 39). According to Hofstadter and Sander, these children's sentences contain 'hidden analogies', allowing a connection to be made between the banana skin and a piece of clothing, between a broken truck and a sick person, and between your mother and a (electrical or electronic) device that can be turned on and off. Similar to the media-related wordplay of 'turning your eyes on' is the

6   The French verb *pincer* is still used, informally, in the sense of 'to love, to be in love with'.
7   This and the other anecdotes that follow belong, unless otherwise specified, to the #kinderspiel database that Alexandra Schneider and I have put together during the last three years. We collected data (videos, still images, self-made toys, drawings as well as field observations) from around fifteen families across Europe. The social background of the children's families is rather homogeneously middle class. For privacy and child protection reasons, the names of the children involved are not revealed in our published texts.

following anecdote from a five-year-old girl who shouts to the frozen image on the computer screen during the video stream of one of her favourite cartoons: 'Come on, wake up!' Here, one could say that children not only make intelligent analogies between humans and machines, more specifically between the human activity of opening your eyes and the mechanical activity of switching on, but also understand, quite intuitively, the notion of the sleep mode.

The principle of making connections between two different semantic spheres is, to some extent, also at stake in children's repurposing of ordinary objects, which, in their play, can become all kinds of 'artefacts', from inanimate playthings to living dolls, from edible fruits to fully operational media devices. Without going into too much detail about the mechanisms of the pretend game, the 'baking' of sand cakes on the beach can serve as an example: besides the 'hidden analogy' between the dough and the sand, between cake moulds and beach moulds, the game mainly consists of eating the sand cakes, or better still, of making the others (pretend to) eat them. Many adults will have experienced situations where children insist that their sand cakes are not just nibbled at but completely eaten up. The same logic is applicable in children's media plays. When a four-year-old boy turns a flat stone, about 5 x 5 cm, into a game console by drawing a screen and some buttons on it, this becomes a fully functioning new media device not only in the hands of the little boy, but also when passed on to adults, who must then pretend that they are agreeing to the terms of the contract that they are pretending to play (or, even better, that they are pretending they know how to play). Children understand this rather complex mechanism often better than their parents. This point was made by Dutch anthropologist Johan Huizinga in his ground-breaking study *Homo Ludens* (1938). He asserted that play is:

> [...] a stepping out of 'real' life into a temporary sphere of activity with a disposition all of its own. Every child knows perfectly well that he is 'only pretending', or that it was 'only for fun'. How deep-seated this awareness is in the child's soul is strikingly illustrated by the following story, told to me by the father of the boy in question. He found his four-year-old son sitting at the front of a row of chairs, playing 'trains'. As he hugged him the boy said: 'Don't kiss the engine, Daddy, or the carriages won't think it's real.' (Huizinga, p. 103)[8]

---

8   Twenty years later, Roger Caillois comments in his study *Les jeux et les hommes* (1958) on this particular scene as follows: 'The child who is playing train may well refuse to kiss his father while saying to him that one does not embrace locomotives, but he is not trying to persuade his father that he is a real locomotive.' (Caillois, p. 21)

1.3

But why insist on child's play in these notes on media archaeology as a laboratory? Because children, I believe, often capture the essence of a certain activity (or situation) in their role-playing games or pretend games: a half-eaten sand cake is no compliment to the baker, a small portable game console is played individually, but can also be passed on to another player, a locomotive must be reliable for its carriages, etc. The same goes for their wordplays: an iPad is a caressable surface and, like any other electronic device, it can be put to sleep and wake up again.

Since media are always more present in the life of young children, it is no surprise to see them as a recurrent element in their play. One of the most common DIY media devices, for instance, is the smartphone, usually made of paper, provided with full keyboard, all manner of icons (drawn or made with stickers) and, most prominently, the Apple logo. The anecdote concerning two second-graders who created a Samsung paper phone, writing the brand's name clearly on both sides, but then adding the unmistakable apple-with-bite trademark on its back – a remarkable mixed brand strategy – is telling (see Figure 1.3).

Some kids will also make phone calls with their DIY smartphones, although other repurposed objects seem to be more effective: for instance, a collectible card with a shiny silver picture (resembling the smartphone because of its flatness and its all screen-ness), a couple of glasses, one held against the ear and one under the mouth (evoking the vintage candlestick telephone with transmitter and receiver), or the showerhead (allowing for long-distance calls thanks to its wire and maybe also its liquidity). The stone pops up again in the telephone genealogy. The same four-year-old boy who repurposed a stone into a game console, also once used an oblong stone, more or less the size of a cordless phone for landlines, to call his parents when he was visiting his grandparents. What is so striking in all these phone creations/situations, is the way children really engage in the phone conversation, by making, for instance, enough pauses to let the interlocutor have his or her say. This is, of course, partly due to their observation and imitation of adults, but also, I would argue, to their understanding of the medium's minimal condition to be operative: you just need (to pretend there is) another person on the other side of the line.

One could object that, in child's play, a stone can become anything, not only a game console or a telephone, but also an apple or an orange. Yet, there is an important difference, which is precisely the media dimension, often revealed by a very specific gesture (or activity). An apple stone will not be held in one hand close to the ear, but will instead be sold by the greengrocer and eaten by the shopper. An orange stone might be peeled or pressed, but will not be passed on from one player to the next to be thumbed. In other words, children do not mix up things. When appropriating or repurposing ordinary objects like stones into media devices, they tell us something about the media, about their essence, their minimal conditions, and their promises. This is precisely the lesson that media-archaeological scholars may draw by looking closely at children's intuitive media interactions and by considering their play as a laboratory for rethinking media.

Two Specifications to Conclude

For me, the 'new' in 'new media archaeologies' does not necessarily connote 'media', but rather invites us to think about new forms or ways of doing media archaeology. But even as qualifier for the term 'media', the adjective 'new' should not be thought of only in the narrow sense of 'digital' or 'high-tech'. On the contrary, a new media practice can also refer to new uses of already existing media, to the excavation and exploration of old media's materiality, or to the action of 'manipulating circuits and changing the taken-for-granted function of the technology' (Hertz and Parikka, p. 426). It is in this spirit that I have proposed elsewhere to call Italian experimental filmmaker Paolo Gioli a 'new media practitioner', because he explores the potentialities of the cinematic medium by pushing the camera to its lowest conditions for making images (Strauven, 2014). As a real DIY practitioner, he builds his own pinhole movie cameras out of old photographic devices. Yet, he is not only a cinema hacker, but also a history hacker, insofar as he is resurrecting a technological past that did not really take place. He reinvents a form of pre-cinema (the stenopeic or pinhole cinema), which never existed before the 'birth' of cinema. In other words, with his experimental film practice he is rewriting cinema's history.

A second specification I want to make by way of conclusion concerns the notion of 'history writing', as used in the title of this chapter. Whereas the companion notion of 'theory making' more clearly refers to the conceptual dimension of the lab, it must be stressed that 'history writing' is also proposed here as a process, as something that is carried out. To put it differently, I am not suggesting that we think of the lab as a historical method, even if, in the end, it is a form of writing into history. The ultimate goal of such a process is, of course, to rethink history, to rethink its linearity, its temporality, and its potentiality. This is why the child's play is such an interesting terrain to explore, since it teaches us how to think differently about the history of a medium, about its outdated uses (past), its minimal conditions (present), and its promises (future).

Works Cited

Roger Caillois, *Man, Play, and Games*, trans. by Meyer Barash (Urbana and Chicago, IL: University of Illinois Press, 1961).

Sean Cubitt, 'Anecdotal Evidence', *NECSUS: European Journal of Media Studies*, 2/1 (2013), pp. 5–18.

Jacques Derrida, 'Structure, Sign, and Play in the Discourse of the Humanities', in *A Postmodern Reader*, ed. by Joseph Natoli and Linda Hutcheon (New York: SUNY Press, 1993), pp. 223–242.

Lori Emerson, Jussi Parikka, and Darren Wershler, 'What is a Media Lab? Situated Practices in Media Studies', 2016, Accessed 12 April 2016, http://whatisamedialab.com.

Andreas Fickers and Annie van den Oever, 'Experimental Media Archaeology: A Plea for New Directions', in *Technē/Technology. Researching Cinema and Media Technologies – Their Development, Use, and Impact*, ed. by Annie van den Oever (Amsterdam: Amsterdam University Press, 2014), pp. 272–278.

Giovanna Fossati and Annie van den Oever, (eds.), *Exposing the Film Apparatus: The Film Archive as a Research Laboratory* (Amsterdam: Amsterdam University Press, 2016).

Garnet Hertz and Jussi Parikka, 'Zombie Media: Circuit Bending Media Archaeology into an Art Method', *Leonardo*, 45/5 (2012), pp. 424–430.

Douglas Hofstadter and Emmanuel Sander, *Surfaces and Essences: Analogy as the Fuel and Fire of Thinking* (New York: Basic Books, 2013).

Johan Huizinga, 'Nature and Significance of Play as a Cultural Phenomenon', in *The Game Design Reader: A Rules of Play Anthology*, ed. by Kate Salen Tekinbaş and Eric Zimmerman (Cambridge, MA: The MIT Press, 2006), pp. 96–120.

Filippo Tommaso Marinetti, 'Tactilism', in *Futurism: An Anthology*, ed. by Lawrence Rainey, Christine Poggi and Laura Wittman (New Haven, CT and London: Yale University Press, 2009), pp. 264–269.

Bruno Munari, *Fantasia* (Rome: Laterza, 1977).

Jussi Parikka, 'The Persistence of the Lab', panel moderation at Transmediale (2016), Accessed 12 April 2016, https://www.youtube.com/watch?v=_4Qp_x88mwo.

Beba Restelli, *Giocare con tatto. Per una educazione plurisensoriale secondo il metodo Bruno Munari* (Milan: Franco Angeli, 2002).

Alexandra Schneider, 'The iPhone as an Object of Knowledge', in *Moving Data: The iPhone and the Future of Media*, ed. by Pelle Snickars and Patrick Vonderau (Berkeley, CA: Columbia University Press, 2012), pp. 49–60.

Wanda Strauven, 'Paolo Gioli as (New) Media Archaeologist', in *Paolo Gioli. The Man Without A Movie Camera*, ed. by Alessandro Bordina and Antonio Somaini (Milan: Mimesis International, 2014), pp. 17–24.

Wanda Strauven, 'The (Noisy) Praxis of Media Archaeology', in *At the Borders of (Film) History*, ed. by Alberto Beltrame, Giuseppe Fidotta and Andrea Mariani (Udine: Forum, 2015), pp. 33–41.

Wanda Strauven, 'Marinetti's *Tattilismo* Revisited: Hand Travels, Tactile Screens and Touch Cinema in the 21st Century', in *Futurist Cinema: Studies on Italian Avant-Garde Film*, ed. by Rossella Catanese (Amsterdam: Amsterdam University Press, 2018), pp. 69–87.

Caro Verbeek, 'Prière de toucher! Tactilism in Early Modern and Contemporary Art', *Senses & Society* 7/2 (2012), pp. 225–235.

Ludwig Wittgenstein, *Philosophical investigations* (Oxford: Basil Blackwell, 1986).

Ludwig Wittgenstein, *Tractatus Logico-Philosophicus*, translated by D.F. Pears and B.F. McGuinness and with an introduction by Bertrand Russell (London & New York: Taylor & Francis e-Library, 2002).

Gene Youngblood, *Expanded Cinema* (New York: Dutton & Co, 1970).

Siegfried Zielinski, 'Media Archaeology', *CTheory* (1996), Accessed 12 April 2016, http://www.ctheory.net/articles.aspx?id=42.

About the author

Wanda Strauven is Privatdozentin of Media Studies at Goethe University Frankfurt. Her research interests include early and avant-garde cinema, media archaeology, and children and media. She is the author of *Marinetti e il cinema: tra attrazione e sperimentazione* (Campanotto, 2006) and has (co-)edited several volumes including *The Cinema of Attractions Reloaded* (Amsterdam University Press, 2006). Her essays have been published in *Cinémas, Cinéma & Cie, Iluminace, Maske und Kothurn, New Review of Film and Television Studies, and NECSUS.*

2.   Doing Experimental Media Archaeology

Epistemological and Methodological Reflections on
Experiments with Historical Objects of Media Technologies[1]

Andreas Fickers and Annie van den Oever

Abstract

The aim of this chapter is to outline experimental media archaeology
as an alternative method to a sense and object-oriented technology and
media historiography. The epistemological potential of an object and
sense-oriented experimental access to the field of the history of media
and technology will be discussed here on the basis of experiences in the
history of science and historically informed music performances. The heart
of the chapter is formed by a discussion of a series of media archaeological
experiments executed by the authors in search for alternative ways to draft
historical statements on past media practices. In these experiments, they
focus on the materiality of past-media devices, beyond their function as

1   This chapter follows up on our 2013 article 'Experimental Media Archaeology: A Plea for
New Directions', which appeared in *Technē/Technology*. Expanded and amended versions of
this plea were written by Andreas Fickers in 2015 in 'Hands-on. Plädoyer für eine experimentelle
Medienarchäologie, in *Technikgeschichte* 82. Annie van den Oever expanded on the plea with
further reflections on hands-on experiments with devices in the film archive in her book with
Giovanna Fossati, *Exposing the Film Apparatus. The Film Archive as a Research Lab*. We would
like to thank Dr. Jo Wachelder, Dr. Susan Aasman, Tim van der Heijden, and Tom Slootweg for the
fruitful discussions that were held on the type of experimental media archaeology in the context
of the project 'Changing Platforms of Ritualised Memory Practices: The Cultural Dynamics of
Home Movies', funded by the Netherlands Organization for Scientific Research (known by the
Dutch initials NWO), in which Andreas Fickers was involved. We would also like to thank the
members of the Network for Experimental Media Archaeology (NEMA) for their contributions to
discussions on the topic, in particular Prof. Giovanna Fossati, Head Curator of Eye Film Institute
the Netherlands in Amsterdam; and Prof. Benoît Turquety of the University of Lausanne, for sharing
his expertise on the complex history of film technologies with us, and Bernd Warnders and André
Rosendaal of the pilot project on Curating Media Heritage at the University of Groningen.

Roberts, B. and M. Goodall (eds.), *New Media Archaeologies*, Amsterdam Universsity Press, 2019
DOI: 10.5117/9789462982161_CH02

sign and evidence of the past, and on the heuristic possibilities offered by an experimental approach to these devices.

Keywords: Experimental Media Archaeology, Hand-on History, sensorial-focused history of technology, user perspectives

Initial Considerations: In Search of the Past User

Working on the apparatus collections in technology museums and media archives may create a growing awareness of the epistemological and methodological problems confronting researchers in the fields of technology and media history.[2] Paradoxically, the acute awareness of the historical gap between now and then is clearly deepened by the material presence of the 'leftovers' of past media practices: magic lanterns, cameras and projectors, radio sets, video recorders, and television sets with old manuals taped on the back. One reason we seek a physical, sensual engagement with these historical artefacts is to stimulate our imagination of the past: to reflect critically on the hidden or non-verbalized, sensorial, corporal, and tacit knowledge that informs our engagement with media technologies. In this chapter, we will reflect on ways of doing experimental media archaeology, to plead once again for an integral and sensual approach towards media technology.

The point of departure of the present approach is the search for alternative ways to draft historical statements on past media practices. The main question is how historical objects of media technology can be used as sources for a sensorial-focused history of technology and the media. This chapter focuses on the materiality of past media devices, beyond their function as a sign and evidence of the past, and on the heuristic possibilities offered by an experimental approach to those devices.[3] Although the approach to the material leftovers falls under the traditional craft of the historian of technology, especially when reappraising and presenting scientific and

2   The authors of this chapter have worked in technology museums and film and media archives respectively. Andreas Fickers worked in the *Deutsches Museum* in Munich and Bonn with a long-standing tradition of tinkering with technical devices. He is currently Director of the *Centre for Contemporary and Digital History* at Luxembourg University. Annie van den Oever is Head of the Film Archive at the University of Groningen; the archive has a long history of hands-on experiments developed for educational purposes; see (Accessed 8 September 2016) http://filmarchief.ub.rug.nl/root/?pLanguage=en.

3   Cf. Fickers, 'Design als "mediating interface"', pp. 199–213.

technical heritage in a museum context,[4] the sensual and experiential potential of technical objects, which we have argued in our plea for a new research agenda in media appropriation histories,[5] has hardly been broached hitherto in technology or media historiography beyond a purely aesthetic consideration.[6]

On the other hand, in recent years, media and technology historiography has frequently put the question of forms of appropriation and ways of using media technologies at the forefront of research. Instead of concentrating on production and invention narratives, technology historiography has focused increasingly on the processes of social construction, social appropriation or rejection, and on the symbolic significance of technology and technological artefacts.[7] Similar changes of perceptions in media historiography resulted in

4   Cf. 'Zwischen Inszenierung und Zeitgeist – Technikmuseen', Chapter 4.3, pp. 92–110.

5   See Fickers and Van den Oever, *Technē/Technology*. For a reflection on the perceptual imprint of 'technische Medien' in the sense of Kittler, see also a dialogue between Geoffrey Winthrop-Young and Annie van den Oever in *Technē/Technology*. See also Van den Oever, 'The Medium-Sensitive Experience and the Paradigmatic Experience of the Grotesque, "Unnatural" or "Monstrous"', pp. 88–89.

6   This dimension is not addressed in the classical introductions to the history of technology in the German-speaking world at least. Cf. Heßler, *Kulturgeschichte der Technik*; König, *Technikgeschichte*. Already in 1958, the French philosopher Gilbert Simondon attempted to sketch a philosophy of the history of technology beyond the duality of form and function. However, Somondon's works were scarcely appreciated outside France. Simondon, *Du monde d'existence des objets techniques*. For the history of the media, Jochen Hörisch presented a study motivated by the history of the senses entitled 'Der Sinn und die Sinne', which, albeit inspiring, is often restricted to associative outlines. In the Anglo-Saxon world, an interest in the experiential and aesthetic effects of film technologies (as opposed to film per se) emerged from early film studies and New Film History, in particular in reflections on the early sensations created by the cinematograph and the phonograph (e.g. see Gunning, 'Re-newing Old Technologies'. Read online (Accessed 8 September 2016): http://web.mit.edu/m-i-t/articles/index_gunning.html). We will return to this later in this chapter. In France, since the 1920s, philosophy and the sub-discipline of aesthetics (e.g. Paul Valéry c.s.) nourished an interest in the aesthetic impact of technological devices following the so-called birth of the cinema. Valéry's perceptual-aesthetic perspective famously affected Walter Benjamin's seminal essay *The Work of Art* (see *Technē/Technology*, pp. 29–50), whereas Benjamin's experiential perspective fed into the re-conceptualization of the early film era in terms of an investment in the experiential dimensions of early film technologies performed in early film shows as 'attractions' in their own right (see Gunning and Gaudreault, 1986). A new and noteworthy branch on the French tree in this context was proposed by Edmond Couchot in the late 1990s under the label of 'techno-aesthetics' (see *Technē/Technology*, pp. 29–50). See also the reflections on media art experiments assembled in Noordegraaf *et al.*, *Preserving and Exhibiting Media Art. Challenges and Perspectives*, touching upon the aesthetic experiments of (media) artists with media technologies; we will return to these reflections below.

7   Cf. representative of this trend, albeit in a more polemical undertone than others, Edgerton, *The Shock of the Old. Technology and Global History since 1900*.

describing and analysing users of media technology with the more assertive, action-oriented concept of 'user', instead of the socio-economic and media studies categories of 'audience' and 'consumer'.[8]

The keen awareness of the 'user' in media research was partly created by the changes in media use in the 1990s: the term 'new media' (which now seems a bit corny) was aptly coined in opposition to the old (news) media – television and newspapers – whose practices of use were, to a large extent, automated: the materiality of these old media technologies and the strategies of use had become so familiar they were more or less invisible (or 'transparent', if you will) to the user themselves. In sharp contrast, the new (social) media of the 1990s were remarkable, visible, exciting, and material for debate. These new social media triggered new forms of use, which needed new forms of media research, including a shying away from 'the milkshake mistake'. The term refers to a type of research mistake named after a failed research project on McDonald's milkshakes: while focusing solely on the product and how to improve it, all but one expert completely failed to observe that commuters had started to buy milkshakes as breakfast on the go. With respect to social media research, the shift in focus from product to usage was crucial, as Clay Shirky argues in his 2010 book on how the digital technologies of the 1990s first turned consumers into social users, then into collaborators.[9]

A challenge for all approaches to reception and user history – both for the history of the media in the broad sense and a history of media technologies in the narrow sense – is the question of sources and, by implicit extension, historical hermeneutics: how are historically relevant statements on ways of appropriation, ways of use, or rejection strategies of media technologies constituted in retrospect?[10] And how constitutive are certain types of sources in the semantic construction of certain types of users or categories of ways of use? Monika Röther addressed this issue systematically in her dissertation 'The Sound of Distinction' (2012), where she linked four different

8   Ellis, 'TV and Cinema: What Forms of History Do We Need?' pp. 12–25; Oudshoorn and Pinch, (eds.), *How Users Matter: The Co-Construction of Users and Technologies*; cf. also the contributions in *Technikgeschichte* 3, no. 76 (2009) which deal with the relationship of the history of design and of technology.

9   See Clay Shirky on the milkshake mistakes in social media research in his book *Cognitive Surplus. How Technology Makes Consumers into Collaborators*, pp. 12–20.

10   There is, of course, a long tradition of reception research in the history of the media, which focuses on consumer behaviour or the appropriation of media products (programmes, formats). However, the question of technological requirements and the conditions of media appropriation usually play no role in this research tradition. On the history of reception research, cf. Méadel, *Quantifier le public*; Butsch, 'Audiences. Publics, Crowds, Mass', pp. 93–108.

dimensions of sound technologies to the analysis of certain types of sources: first, the analysis of the materiality of the object itself; second, the interpretation of sources, in which manufacturers and professionals enact potential appropriation strategies (e.g. in advertising); third, the analyses of expert discourse found in product-test magazines and consumer magazines; and fourthly, those documents and sources that provide information on the actual appropriation and use of media technologies – e.g. ego documents and oral history interviews.[11]

In developing Röther's systematization further, eight (user) perspectives will be presented below, under which the relationship with different types of sources and specific user categories and discourses can be further differentiated and broadened. These eight perspectives are intended to provide a more complex vision of the diverse and alternative constructions of users in specific types of sources, and thus an increasingly effective approach to the actual historical complexity in the (scholarly) historical re-enactment of past ways of using media technologies. Only one of the suggested user perspectives will be explored in greater depth here, namely that proposed by experimental media archaeology under the label of 're-enacted users', since it is expected to make an interesting contribution to a media and technology historiography that draws inspiration from the *sensing* of the past.

Needless to say, the 'types of users' presented here are ideal-typical constructions, which may (and should) fall victim to historical re-enactments in individual cases. In spite of the different semantic meaning, 'user' and 'use' are not differentiated in the typology that follows, but these terms are used as synonyms, as in the source material. The following 'types of users' will be discussed here: first, the 'imagined users'; second, the 'configured (or prefigured) users'; third, the 'expert users'; fourth, the 'amateur users'; fifth, the 'remembered users'; sixth, the 're-enacted users'; seventh, the 'artificial (or artistic) users'; and eighth, the 'simulated users'.

If we look at the types of sources used in previous studies for the historical reconstruction of users, expert sources are clearly dominant in historical technology oriented reconstructions (e.g. *Technikgeschichte*). Expert-made sources, such as perception reports, laboratory reports, (production) logbooks, and publications in expert journals are typically driven by production-oriented and purpose-oriented questions and they tend to be directed at other expert users.[12] However rich in terms of their wealth of test

11   Röther, *The Sound of Distinction*, pp. 34–62.
12   For example, see the chain of expert discussions in the field of the production, dissemination, implementation, and use of expert projections facilities, being tested in follow-up experiments

User perspectives	Characterization of user types	Types of sources
Imagined users	Imaginative, utopian, or dystopian projections of past and future ways of use	Science fiction and fantasy literature and film, comics and cartoons, radio plays, television series, games
Configured (or prefigured) users	Strategies of use configured and prefigured, pre-planned and promoted by the industry, manufacturers, and marketers	Advertisements, posters, billboards, commercials, manuals, patents apps ('applications')
Expert users	Possible ways of use based on a scientific, empirical, and experimental assessment conducted by expert discussion (promises of performance based on testing)	Technical literature, test reports, perception reports, logbooks, laboratory records, product-test magazines, (online) expert publications
Amateur users	Forms of the actual appropriation and user tactics discussed in exchange-oriented publication media	Popularizing periodicals, fan sites, blogs and vlogs, how-to manuals, videos, club magazines
Remembered users	Remembrance of certain ways of use constructed in oral history interviews, e.g. subjective description of user experiences recorded in ego documents	Oral-history interviews, diaries, ego documents, surveys, historical and ethnographic documentation/ documentaries
Re-enacted users	Ways of appropriation and use generated by re-enactment in experiments; or teasing out tacit knowledge within experience through re-enactment	Objectives, devices, re-enactments, ethnographic records, scripts, laboratory records
Artificial users (or Artists)	Media technologies re-enacted and repurposed by artificial appropriation; usually focused on the perceptual and mimetic potential (reality construction dimension) of media devices	Artificial installations, objects, devices, audio and video installations
Simulated users	Re-enactment of user behaviour through computer aided simulations and statistical assessment of possible scope for actions and processes	Simulation software, statistical data, user profiles

material, an expert's main focus, or expertise, is not at all the *actual use* of a technology in the socio-cultural context of the day, or its actual place in technology or media history. If this is a concern to them at all, expert and expert inventors may be rather too positive, if not utopian, about the future of their device. Needless to say, this is a problem for media history. The many

in cinemas by teams of projectionists suggesting technical amendments to the expert producers/ inventors.

milkshake mistakes made by expert inventors predicting the futures of a technology in utopian terms are abundant in media history, and they are indicative of the theory-induced blindness of the expert-technicians with regard to actual user practices, and the 'conceptual fog' surrounding this problem: 'imperfectly defined explanatory notions [...] so loosely derived and so mutually irrelevant that they mix together to create a sort of conceptual fog that does much to delay the progress of science', in the words of Gregory Bateson.[13]

Ironically, the milkshake mistakes created exquisite material for alternative and amusing media archaeologies; moreover, they begged for a critical take on expert-induced blindness. In many ways, media archaeology responded to this, not so much by theorizing actual user practices, but rather by an epistemological critique of the knowledge produced in a media historiography leaning on production-driven narratives and utopian fantasies; and by constructing alternative narratives and quirky and marginal media histories (plural) or what Siegfried Zielinski emblematically and programmatically called 'variantology'.[14] The 'alternative' sources are most often used to describe the historical and contemporary potentiality of media and communication technologies, but not to reconstruct their actual dissemination or appropriation or historical use. Therefore, many media archaeology studies are primarily interested in those types of sources that allow the imagined or configured users to come to the fore, as is the case, for example, in literary presentations, advertising,[15] or patents.[16] This media archaeology of the imaginary or even utopian potential, which is ascribed to all new media and communication technologies, has led to numerous historical-discourse studies, which have made an important contribution to the cultural history of the media and media technologies.[17] Reflection in terms of media archaeology is also encountered in the field of the artistic

---

13   See Bateson, *Steps to an Ecology of Mind*, pp. xxiii–xxxii (quotation from p. xxvi).

14   See Zielinski, 'Media Archaeology', published online in *CTheory* (1996), Accessed 8 September 2016, http://www.ctheory.net/articles.aspx?id=42. See also the discussion of approaches and methods assembled under the name of media archaeology in an overview article by Strauven, 'Media Archaeology: Where Film History, Media Art, and New Media (Can) Meet', pp. 59–80.

15   Interesting examples are to be found in studies by Huhtamo, e.g. 'From Kaleidoscomaniac to Cybernerd. Towards an Archeology of the Media', pp. 221–224 and 'Elements of Screenology: Toward an Archaeology of the Screen', pp. 31–82.

16   As an example of a media archaeological study, which is, in essence, based on patents as a type of source, see: Kümmel-Schnur and Kassung (eds.), *Bildtelegraphie. Eine Mediengeschichte in Patenten (1840–1930)*.

17   See e.g. Sconce, *Haunted Media*; Sturken, Thomas, and Ball-Rokeach (eds.), *Technological Visions*; Flichy, *The Internet Imaginaire*; Buschauer, *Mobile Räume*; Huhtamo, *Illusions in Motion*.

appropriation of past and present media technologies.[18] A shared feature of most works on the history of technology and media archaeology study is that they use almost exclusively textually and visually argued types of sources in their reconstruction of media practices.

In sharp contrast to the expert users, amateur users typically provide valuable source material to historians of technology and media historians interested in *actual user practices*. Regardless of the amount of technical skills these two groups tend to have in common, the big difference between them is that experts focus on the product, amateurs on the actual use. Furthermore, amateur source material is easily accessible, whereas expert sources may be protected from rivals eyes by big commercial companies. Contrary to this, amateurs typically share their insights into the actual appropriation of all sorts of technologies as they discuss user tactics in exchange-oriented publication media.[19] They form social communities for sharing their love for and knowledge of technologies and they use and produce a 'cognitive surplus'[20] that is valuable for society at large, as Clay Shirky argued.[21] As such, amateurs produce ready and rich source material, highly relevant for technology and media historians interested in the actual user and appropriation strategies and shifts in the actual use of media technologies, including 'breaking practices' and 'failures' in use, which will be discussed below.[22]

Sources that favour more of an event-historical or phenomenologically oriented analysis perspective, such as mnemotechnical ego documents,

---

18   See Parikka, 'Practising Media Archaeology', pp. 136–158.

19   See the cascade of examples provided by Lori Emerson in the context of her Lab at the University of Colorado, Boulder: (Accessed 8 September 2016) http://mediaarchaeologylab.com/about/.

20   The term 'cognitive surplus' has two meanings: extra or spare time (surplus) gained from skipping passive activities such as watching TV; and the creation of cognitive extras (surplus) from the extra time gained. See Shirky, *Cognitive Surplus*.

21   Shirky, pp. 161–183.

22   A lot of historiographical research work has been done in the field of early film studies since the late 1980s, partly in a constructive cross-over with media archaeology, reframing the epistemological underpinnings of the field of film history, caught in a narrative on the primitive and poor storytelling capacities of silent cinema, a narrative inherited from the heyday of narratology in film studies in the 1970s and 1980s. Theories can also become history, as André Gaudreault and Tom Gunning famously argued in their seminal 'Early Cinema as a Challenge to Film History' (published in French in 1989). This has resulted in a readdressing of the role technologies played in the history of (early) cinema. See New Film History, a term coined by André Gaudreault. See also Gunning, 'The Cinema of Attraction: Early Film, Its Spectator and the Avant-Garde', first collected in the volume *Early Cinema: Space Frame Narrative* (1990). For an overview, see the anthology: Strauven (ed), *The Cinema of Attractions Reloaded*.

devices, installations, or simulations, have largely been neglected hitherto in historical research.[23]

Re-enactment: Grasping the Materiality and Sensuousness of Historical Objects

What is the epistemological potential of an experimental approach to media historiography with an interest in sensing the past? Our main aim here is to explore and outline the heuristic added value of an experimental expansion of the methodological repertoire of media archaeology, which is geared to discourse analysis. As valuable as these studies are for the historical reconstruction of past-expectation horizons, which, according to Charles Bazerman's concept of 'heterogeneous symbolic engineering'[24] or Mikael Hård's and Andrew Jamison's concept of 'intellectual appropriation',[25] are always the result of a complex interplay of imagination, invention, and marketing strategies, they have very little to say about the complex process of the concrete appropriation and use of devices and objects in people's everyday life.

Drawing from our plea, we will briefly outline the conceptual and methodological features of re-enactment, to leave room for discussion of a series of small experiments, suggestions, and lessons learned. The discussion is focused on the practical and epistemological consequences of such a hands-on approach and the value of re-enactments as a heuristic tool for a technological history of the media. Instead of the intellectual or mental appropriation, at issue in what follows is a search for methods and possibilities to 'grasp' media and communication technologies in their concrete materiality and tangibility. Grasping is to be understood here as a hermeneutical act in the sense given to it by Ernst Cassirer, which comprises both the intellectual process of comprehending as well as the sensory-physical appropriation of getting a grip on things.[26]

In our view, one possibility of methodologically implementing Cassirer's hermeneutic concept of 'grasping' (within the meaning of a critical and self-reflective historical scholarship) lies in the transposition of the concept

---

23   A recent example of use of such documents is the ADAPT research project on the history of television technology initiated by John Ellis. See online (Accessed 2 June 2017) http://www.adapttvhistory.org.uk/.

24   Bazerman, *The Language of Edison's Light*.

25   Hård and Jamison (eds.), *The Intellectual Appropriation of Technology*.

26   Cassirer, 'Form und Technik', p. 52.

of historical re-enactment in experimental practice. The idea of making re-enactment useful as a heuristic concept for historical scholarship stems from the British philosopher Roger Collingwood:

> Historical knowledge is the knowledge of what mind has done in the past, and at the same time it is the re-doing of this, the perpetuation of past acts in the present. Its object is therefore not a mere object, something outside the mind which knows it; it is an activity of thought, which can be known only in so far as the knowing mind re-enacts it and knows itself as doing so.[27]

If Collingwood's idea is expanded to a concrete, hands-on – experimental dimension of knowledge generation, however, then the historian who is interested in objects and sensory aspects can gain concrete experiences with the physiological and sensory qualities of communication and media technologies: through experimental access, these technologies can be grasped in their technical, material, and sensory dimension. In line with this, experimental media archaeology proposes a playful construction of its epistemic object[28] to be put in the hands of the historian/experimenter who 'becomes sensitive to everything which evades pure description', as Michel Serres suggests in his plea for a history of the senses.[29]

Drawing inspiration from experiences in the experimental history of science,[30] experimental archaeology,[31] and historically informed performance in music,[32] experimental media archaeology is geared to generating 'knowledge that provides a springboard for action', which underscores the performative dimension of media and communication technical objects in practice. This means that the intrinsic performative quality of devices

---

27   Collingwood, *The Idea of History*, p. 218. On the epistemological dimension of the concept of 're-enactment', see Dray, *History as Re-Enactment. R.G. Collingwood's Idea of History*; also Gerber, *Analytische Metaphysik der Geschichte*, pp. 39–48.

28   On the construction of epistemic objects, see Rheinberger, 'Experiment: Präzision und Bastelei', pp. 52–60.

29   Serres, *Die fünf Sinne. Eine Philosophie der Gemenge und Gemische*.

30   For a detailed reflection on the methods, concepts, and findings of the experimental history of science, see Breidbach, Heering, Müller, and Weber, 'Experimentelle Wissenschaftsgeschichte', pp. 13–72.

31   Schiffer and Skibo, 'Theory and Experiment in the Study of Technological Change', pp. 595–622; Saraydar, *Replicating the Past*; Ferguson (ed), *Designing Experimental Research in Archaeology*; Schiffer, *The Archaeology of Science*.

32   Lawson and Stowell, *The Historical Performance of Music*; Butt: *Playing with History*; Bithell and Hill (eds.), *The Oxford Handbook of Musical Revival*.

(which tends to be plastic in media devices) and the interaction between user(s) and object become perceptible in the experiment and are then described and reflected upon. Described by Breidbach et al. as the cognitive mode of 'heuristic groping', this process expounds, in a playful and reflective manner, the relationship between the knowledge that provides a springboard for action, theoretical knowledge, and ignorance.[33] The aim of this experimental approach can, by definition, never be to reconstruct an authentic historical experience of whatever nature. On the contrary, the aim is to create a situation in which inventories of knowledge available can be unsettled in a creative manner. Only such artificially generated tension between exploratory and experimental knowledge can lead to an experience that Sönke Ahrens refers to as 'education' (as opposed to 'learning' as a process of appropriating inventories of knowledge available and of facts considered certain).[34]

The Archive as Laboratory: 'Thinkering' as Style of Thinking in Education

Since 2010, we have done some small tests, in research as well as education, with experimental media archaeology as a heuristic method, trying to find out whether it can function as a tool that provides new access to the study of past media practices and appropriation in assigning to the historian or archaeologist the role of an experimenter instead of that of a reader or a passive observer. A prerequisite for this change in roles is the creation of an experimental space where it is possible to experiment either with communication and media originals or with replicas in a creative and playful manner – what Erkki Huhtamo has designated as 'thinkering'.[35] The approach is not used by us as a replacement of conventional media archaeology or media history methods, but rather as a methodological supplement, whose greatest heuristic potential may well lie on the didactic, educational front, as we found out.

As a space for one of the experiments with students, we used the Film Archive & Media Archaeology Lab, embedded in the University of Groningen.

---

33 Breidbach *et al.*, *Experimentelle Wissenschaftsgeschichte*, p. 18.
34 The experience of failure or not succeeding acquires an exceptional function in this process – an insight that is of central importance for the planning or the structure, and organization of experiments. See Ahrens, *Experiment und Exploration*, pp. 17–21 and 266–275.
35 Huhtamo, 'Thinkering with Media: On the Art of Paul DeMarinis', pp. 33–39.

It is one of the prerogatives of such collections that most objects may actually be touched and manipulated in hands-on experiments, as they are neither unique, nor rare, nor valuable.[36] On and off, the archive's educational space is used as a *laboratory*: what Simone Venturini called a 'handmade environment for using the technology available and the human and corporal reclaiming of the technology'.[37] (At other moments, the space is used for seminars.) After a tour through the archive, we present a series of devices to students as part of their introduction to film and media studies. They are invited to touch, operate, and 'play' with some of the historical devices in the archive, e.g. a magic lantern, lantern slides, a Zeiss Ikon 35 mm projector, an anamorphic lens; a replica of a nineteenth-century stereoscope; and a series of optical toys, a view master among them (see Figure 2.1–2.5). The invitation to tinker with the Zeiss Ikon 35 mm projector (or what is left of it), with a hand crank that still functions, allows students the fun of hearing the (to some familiar) sound of the sewing machine when the pull-down mechanism goes up and down, and the dry clicks of the Malthezer cross and the flapping of the projector's double-bladed shutter, which is relatively loud and, without failure, raises questions about film's silent era: silent? Really?! We have been doing these experiments annually since 2010, with 100 to 200 hundred students divided into small groups of about 20 students from all over the world (the language of instruction is English). Often, a quiz-like buzz of asking and guessing is triggered amongst the students by these small hands-on operations. Where do these funny sounds come from? Was the machine meant to make such noises? What is that repulsive smell coming from the film reel? (vinegar syndrome). What is this?! An anamorphic lens? (see Figure 2.6) What does an anamorphic lens *do*?

It should be stressed here that most of the actions by the students in this specific introductory class are not framed to experience the technology's proper place in history or to learn how to operate it in terms of former use. Students are simply invited to touch, smell, hear, look, experience, and play with the device; indeed, most of the students' actions look beyond the normal use or purpose of the device. It is in no way a technology class for students who need to learn how to make or repair technologies. In many ways, our educational experiments are much closer to what artists and

36   The collection of apparatuses was donated by Tjitte de Vries and Ati Mul with the explicit objective of use in education. The full collection was a donation from the Vrienden van het Nijmeegs Filmarchief, Catholic University of Nijmegen (now Radboud University), and the collection was used for film projection mainly in days when DVD and video were rare.
37   Venturini, 'Technological Platforms', p. 202.

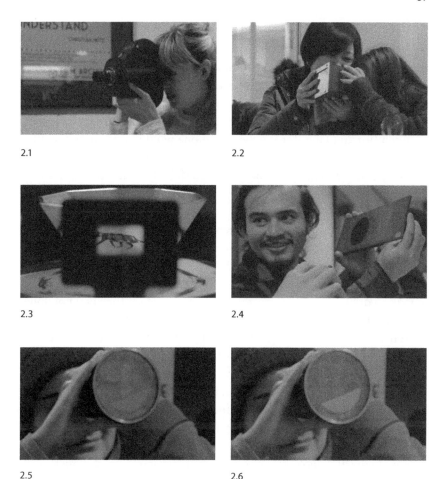

2.1

2.2

2.3

2.4

2.5

2.6

artist-amateurs, or art-students do in their studios (e.g. the students of the Amsterdam Rietveld Academy for the Arts, Department for Unstable Media, with whom we have started doing experiments too): they do tinkering experiments with media technologies that are not useful for a technician, but are highly interesting for an artist in terms of testing the sensorial and expressive, performative potential of a device. Such 'aesthetic experimentations' with media devices are described by Simone Venturini as 'practical operations on the technology and material of a reflective nature'.[38] Emilio Garroni typifies them as 'a mainly meta-operational activity'.[39]

38 *Ibid.*
39 Emilio Garroni 1977, cited in Venturini, p. 202.

What makes these small operations so effective in educational terms is the strong aesthetic and performative impact of media devices. The first thing students experience and comment on are the sensorial, tacit, and expressive dimensions of the experience. As a result, the smallest hands-on experiment already triggers the imagination and indeed helps the students to reclaim technology corporally (Venturini 2013, p. 202). In fact, there is so much fun and laughter involved that one would forget that, usually, students claim to suffer from technophobia when asked to read a chapter on historical technology. In the hands-on didactic context, we also use drawing as an additional tool to explore experiences. Once the tinkering stops and the devices leave the lab, the students are invited to draw from their memories, to re-imagine and then draw a picture of one of the devices (often the Zeiss Ikon 35 mm projector). What we learned from this is that there is an additional element of regressive pleasure in all these activities; for example, being invited in an academic context to play with toys and to make a drawing, two things, many students told us, they had not done since their childhood. From these small introductory experiments, we have come to understand that these additional pleasures, too, make the hands-on experiments a valuable educational tool, and in some ways kick-start reading about technology and media history.

If experimenting is understood in the sense of Sönke Ahrens's differentiation of the exploratory and experimental form of discovering the world as a style of thinking, which, instead of relying on a certain theory is characterized by processes of collecting, tinkering, and translating, experimental media archaeology can make a contribution to (media) historical *education*, which expands the conventional forms of historical learning to a dimension of sensing the past and theoretical-perception perspectives.[40] Learning as an 'explorative form of discovering the world' and education as an 'experimental form of discovering the world' constitutes a complementary relationship of necessity, according to Arens: 'The frequently encountered intellectual separation of the learning of facts and playful experimenting as an activity, which occurs independently from those facts, entails an essential separation of what structurally belongs together, namely: learning as facts considered certain so be able to open up an unforeseen event in an educational process.[41]

As many studies in the field of the experimental history of science have shown, the epistemological added value of an experimental approach to

40   Arens, *Experiment und Exploration*, p. 271.
41   Op. cit.

the history of the sciences also lies in exposing the complex interaction of objects, practices, ideas, and participants involved on the one hand, and the experience of failure on the other.[42]

Reflections on Experimenting in Home Mode

If laboratories or workshops are seen as spaces of action, where different actors and actants engage in a complex interaction, the question arises how this space is to be designed for media archaeology experiments in which the focus of attention is, apart from the technical devices themselves, the place where these devices are appropriated and used, as well as the social constellation in which this occurs. Since the home can be considered as the privileged locus for the appropriation and use of communication and media technologies, the arrangement of a domestic environment seems entirely appropriate for conducting media archaeology experiments. As the 'central integration power' (Gaston Bachelard)[43] and the 'museum of the soul' (Mario Praz),[44] the home is the symbolic place for experiencing the whole of life, and, as such, often also the place for the 'domestication' of new communication and media technologies.[45] The living room has a special role to play as a material and social ensemble, according to Hans Peter Hahn, as the privileged space of conspicuous consumption.[46] The biographies of objects and their users are intertwined in the living room and are thereby consolidated into a socio-technical topography.[47] According to this hypothesis, this special topography should be taken into consideration in the experimental re-enactment, in order to not only analyse the 'language of things', but also to try the playful 'dialogue with things'.[48]

An initial media archaeology experiment in the domestic appropriation of family films in different media technology devices has shown the importance of understanding the experiment also as a social, communicative, and

---

42   Heering, Markert, and Weber (eds.), *Experimentelle Wissenschaftsgeschichte didaktisch nutzbar machen*; Heering and Witje (eds.), *Learning by Doing*.

43   Bachelard, *Poetik des Raumes*, p. 33.

44   Praz, Histoire de la décoration d'intérieur, p. 19.

45   On the concept of domestication, see Silverstone and Hirsch (eds.), *Consuming Technologies*.

46   Hahn, 'Von der Ethnografie des Wohnzimmers', p. 13.

47   See Woodward, 'Material Culture, Narratives and Social Performance. Objects in Contexts', pp. 151–168.

48   Hahn, 'Von der Ethnografie des Wohnzimmers', p. 16. See also Riggins, 'Fieldwork in the Living Room. An Autoethnographic Essay', pp. 101–147.

collective practice. This experiment was conducted as a 'performance' at the International Orphan Film Symposium 2014 in Amsterdam, and stemmed from a research project on the history of family films.[49] This media archaeology experiment featured three scenes of domestic use of amateur film technology, based on a prepared script, representing the different possible amateur film dispositifs: first, the '8 mm dispositif' (with 8 mm camera, projector, and projection screen), second the 'video dispositif' (with video camera, video recorder, and television set), and, third, the 'mobile telephone dispositif' (with the mobile telephone as camera, recorder, and playback medium). The purpose of this experiment was to attempt to confront the theoretical considerations of experimental media archaeology with practical experiences. In other words, to juxtapose explorative speculation with experimental-practical knowledge. A short film montage of the experiment is available on Vimeo.[50] Perhaps the greatest cognitive value of the public staging of the experiment lay in what one of the researchers of the project, Susan Aasman, described as the 'art of failure' in her review of the performance:

> One of the biggest lessons was in fact a major failure. In the first scene, at a particular moment, the father failed to wind the reel in the projector. And even worse: when the film was finally in the projector, the lamp broke and we were unable to screen our home movie. Bad luck, but [...] the audience laughed. And even more surprisingly, they accepted this moment as part of the screening practice. They thought it was a moment that was scripted! That moment of laughter made us aware of the importance of people's relation with technology. And this becomes most clear at those moments when technology fails. Or better put: when people's interaction with technology becomes a struggle.[51]

Furthermore, the staging also aimed to leave behind the conventional forms of the transfer of knowledge at academic conferences (lecture) by a theatrical staging of the topic. A 'lecture-performance' was chosen to

49   This NWO-supported research project with one postdoc and two PhDs was headed by Andreas Fickers; three books on the project, by Susan Aasman, Tom Slootweg, and Tim van der Heijden, respectively, are forthcoming.
50   A short film montage of the experiment/'performance' produced by Tim van der Heijden is available at: (Accessed 8 September 2016) http://vimeo.com/95314562.
51   Details on the project, a documentary film sequence of the experiment, and a critical review by Susan Aasman are available at: (Accessed 8 September 2016) http://homemoviesproject.wordpress.com/report-staging-the-amateur-dispositif/.

enable the audience to take part in the research process – and partake in findings through sensory perception. In her study entitled 'Der Vortrag als Performance' [The lecture as performance], Sibylle Peters argues that the lecture-performance makes it possible to subvert the scientific scheme of research versus presentation and to make audiences participate in research projects by performancing experiments *on-stage*.[52] In other words, the idea of the media archaeology experiment as a medium for the generation of knowledge is combined with the situation of the performance as the actual transfer of knowledge through the lecture-performance format.

If the social dimension of historical ways of media appropriation and use are to be investigated in the case of the experiment with the different home-movie dispositifs described here, role plays (as in academic seminars) provide an opportunity to assign specific roles to actors participating in the experiment and thus have them experience how the production as well as consumption of family films frame 'the home' and 'the family' in equally large measure. As 'formatted spaces of participation', these spatial as well as socio-cultural factors shape the habits and rituals of all participants: those in front and those behind the camera, as well as on the projection screen or monitor.[53] The complex social interactions played out in the background of the production and consumption practices nonetheless influence the 'result' – in this case the family film – which Martina Roepke has designated as 'ensemble play'.[54] Our experiment has clearly shown that the re-enactment method can make an essential contribution to becoming aware of this 'ensemble play' and thus to reflect thereon as a significant experience. This post-experimental reflection on the experiences through one's own body and senses certainly changes the analytical perspective on traditional types of sources, which, as argued at the start of this chapter, reflect certain types of users and user experiences each time. In this way, the media archaeology experiment is not only the producer of a new type of knowledge inventory for the historical reconstruction of past media practices, but it also changes the analytical perspective through its phenomenological-experience dimension.[55] Thanks to experimental education, the historian's attentiveness easily changes and with it the critical perspective on traditional types of sources: the historical interpretation attains a new degree of complexity.

---

52 Peters, *Der Vortrag als Performance*, p. 187.
53 Müller, 'Formatted Spaces of Participation: Interactive Television and the Reshaping of the Relationship between Production and Consumption', pp. 47–61.
54 Roepke, *Privat-Vorstellung*, 2006.
55 See Waldenfels, *Phänomenologie der Aufmerksamkeit*.

Conclusion

Experimental media archaeology is not about the reconstruction of authentic historical experiences. Instead, it is geared to raising the awareness of participants in the experiment about the functionalities ascribed to the materiality of the object (what can and cannot be done with a device), as well as the symbolic nature (design, semantics, interfaces); the explication of implicit inventories of knowledge and ignorance (knowledge that provides a springboard for action); the creative disconcertion of available knowledge (education through failure); the reflective analysis of the performative dimension of technical objects (object as medium) and the reflective analysis of the tactile; the sensorial dimension of technical objects (object as art work); as well as the critical reflection of the situation dynamics in the experimental space (between the object and the experimenter as well as between different actors).

The heuristic re-enactment method can be used to gain new insights into the temporality ascribed to the communication and media-technology devices – the intriguing noises produced by old film projectors, the repulsive smell of corrupted film reels, the magic created by optical toys, the limited shooting time of 8 mm amateur film reels, the short playing time of a shellac record, or the long exposure times of photographic cameras, the tacit knowledge of the weight of magic lanterns and lantern slides: all this is grasped altogether differently through the experimental approach to the object than through explorative readings of user's instructions or how-to manuals. Re-enactments re-sensitize experimenters to the sensorial and performative dimensions of media use and sharpen their attention to such aspects (or lack thereof) in the source material. Furthermore, re-enactments, such as in makeshift laboratory spaces in the living room, enhance the reflexive awareness of the spatial and topographic dimension of past media practices – as regards to both the production and consumption of contents transmitted through media technology. This practical insight into the space-time conditionality of past objects and equipment provides a better historical and critical understanding of the expressive, constructivist nature of communication and media-technology content (photographs, films, audio recordings), though the perceptual imprint of the materiality of technical media (Kittler) is mostly obscured on the level of the representation and easily escapes attention. The knowledge that provides a springboard for action generated by the experimental approach thus makes an important contribution to historical-source criticism and raises awareness among media and technology historians about the significance of the senses in the cognitive process as well as the sensory nature of technical objects.[56]

Acknowledgements

The authors would like to thank Klaas Lommerse and Tim van der Heijden for providing the illustrations for this chapter.

Works Cited

Sönke Arens, *Experiment und Exploration. Bildung als experimentelle Form der Welterschließung* (Bielefeld: Transcript Verlag, 2011), pp. 17–21, 266–275, 271.

Gaston Bachelard, *Poetik des Raumes* (Frankfurt: Fischer Verlag, 1987), p. 33.

Gregory Bateson, *Steps to an Ecology of Mind* (Chicago, IL: Chicago University Press, 2000) [first published in 1972], pp. xxiii–xxxii (p. xxvi).

Charles Bazerman, *The Language of Edison's Light* (Cambridge, MA: MIT Press 1999).

Caroline Bithell and Juniper Hill (eds.), *The Oxford Handbook of Musical Revival* (Oxford: Oxford University Press, 2014).

Olaf Breidbach, Peter Heering, Matthias Müller, and Heiko Weber, 'Experimentelle Wissenschaftsgeschichte', in *Experimentelle Wissenschaftsgeschichte* ed. by Olaf Breidbach, Peter Heering, Matthias Müller and Heiko Weber (Munich: Wilhelm Fink Verlag, 2010), pp. 13–72.

Regine Buschauer, *Mobile Räume. Medien- und diskursgeschichtliche Studien zur Tele-Kommunikation* (Bielefeld: Transcript Verlag, 2010).

John Butt, *Playing with History: The Historical Approach to Musical Performance* (Cambridge: Cambridge University Press, 2002).

Richard Butsch, 'Audiences. Publics, Crowds, Mass', in *The Handbook of Communication History*, ed. by P. Simonson, J. Peck, R. Craig, and J. Jackson (London: Routledge, 2013), pp. 93–108.

Ernst Cassirer, 'Form und Technik', in *Symbol, Technik, Sprache. Aufsätze aus den Jahren 1927–1933*, ed. by Ernst Wolfgang Orth and John Michael Krois (Hamburg: Meiner Verlag 1995), pp. 39–89 (p. 52).

Dominique Chateau, 'The Philosophy of Technology in the Frame of Film Theory: Walter Benjamin's Contribution', in *Technē/Technology: Researching Cinema and Media Technologies – Their Development, Use, and Impact*, ed. by Annie van den Oever (Amsterdam: Amsterdam University Press, 2014), pp. 29–50.

---

56   For a plea for a sense-sensitive historiography, see Smith, *Sensing the Past*.

Roger Collingwood, *The Idea of History* (Oxford: Oxford University Press, 1946),
    p. 218.

William H. Dray, *History as Re-Enactment. R.G. Collingwood's Idea of History* (Oxford:
    Oxford University Press, 1985).

David Edgerton, *The Shock of the Old. Technology and Global History since 1900*
    (London: Profile Books, 2008).

John Ellis, 'TV and Cinema: What Forms of History Do We Need?', in *Cinema,
    Television & History: New Approaches*, ed. by Laura Mee and Johnny Walker
    (Newcastle-Upon-Tyne: Cambridge Scholars Publishing, 2014), pp. 12–25.

Jeffrey Ferguson (ed), *Designing Experimental Research in Archaeology: Examining
    Technology through Production and Use* (Boulder, CO: University of Colorado
    Press, 2010).

Andreas Fickers, 'Design als "mediating interface". Zur Zeugen- und Zeichen-
    haftigkeit des Radioapparats', in *Berichte zur Wissenschaftsgeschichte* 30, no. 3
    (2007), pp. 199–213.

Andreas Fickers, 'Hands-on. Plädoyer für eine experimentelle Medienarchäologie',
    in *Technikgeschichte* 82, no. 1 (2015), pp. 67–85.

Andreas Fickers and Annie van den Oever, 'Experimental Media Archaeology: A
    Plea for New Directions', in *Technē/Technology: Researching Cinema and Media
    Technologies – Their Development, Use, and Impact*, ed. by Annie van den Oever
    (Amsterdam: Amsterdam University Press 2014), pp. 272–278.

Patrice Flichy, *The Internet Imaginaire* (Cambridge, MA: MIT Press 2007).

Giovanna Fossati and Annie van den Oever, *Exposing the Film Apparatus. The Film
    Archive as a Research Lab* (Amsterdam: Amsterdam University Press, 2016).

André Gaudreault and Tom Gunning, 'Early Cinema as a Challenge to Film History',
    in Wanda Strauven (ed.), *The Cinema of Attractions Reloaded* (Amsterdam:
    Amsterdam University Press, 2007), pp. 365–380.

Doris Gerber, *Analytische Metaphysik der Geschichte. Handlungen, Geschichten
    und ihre Erklärung* (Frankfurt: Suhrkamp Verlag, 2012), pp. 39–48.

Rolf-Jürgen Gleitsmann, Rolf-Urich Kunze, and Günther Oetzel, 'Zwischen Insze-
    nierung und Zeitgeist – Technikmuseen', in *Technikgeschichte* (Konstanz: UVK
    Verlagsgesellschaft, 2009), pp. 92–110.

Tom Gunning, 'The Cinema of Attraction: Early Film, Its Spectator and the Avant-
    Garde', in *Early Cinema: Space Frame Narrative*, ed. by Thomas Elsaesser and
    Adam Barker (London: British Film Institute, 1990), pp. 56–62.

Tom Gunning, 'Re-newing Old Technologies: Astonishment, Second Nature and the
    Uncanny in Technology from the Previous Turn-of-the-Century', in *Rethinking
    Media Change: Aesthetics of Transition*, ed. by David Thourburn and Henry
    Jenkins (Cambridge, MA: MIT Press, 2003), pp 39–60, available at (Accessed
    8 September 2016): http://web.mit.edu/m-i-t/articles/index_gunning.html).

Hans Peter Hahn, 'Von der Ethnografie des Wohnzimmers', in *Die Sprache der Dinge: Kulturwissenschaftliche Perspektiven auf die materielle Kultur*, ed. by Elisabeth Tietmeyer *et al.* (Münster: Waxmann, 2010), pp. 13, 16.

Mikael Hård and Andrew Jamison (eds.), *The Intellectual Appropriation of Technology. Discourses on Modernity, 1900–1939* (Cambridge, MA: MIT Press 1998).

Peter Heering and Roland Witje (eds.), *Learning by Doing. Experiments and Instruments in the History of Science Teaching* (Stuttgart: Steiner Verlag, 2011).

Siehe Peter Heering, Michael Markert, and Heiko Weber (eds.), *Experimentelle Wissenschaftsgeschichte didaktisch nutzbar machen. Ideen, Überlegungen und Fallstudien* (Flensburg: Flensburg University Press, 2012).

Martina Heßler, *Kulturgeschichte der Technik* (Frankfurt: Campus Verlag, 2012).

Jochen Hörisch, *Der Sinn und die Sinne. Eine Geschichte der Medien* (Frankfurt: Eichborn Verlag, 2001).

Erkki Huhtamo, 'From Kaleidoscomaniac to Cybernerd. Towards an Archaeology of the Media', *Leonardo* 30, no 3 (1997), pp. 221–224.

Erkki Huhtamo, 'Elements of Screenology: Toward an Archaeology of the Screen', *ICONICS: International Studies of the Modern Image*. 7 (2004), pp. 31–82.

Erkki Huhtamo, 'Thinkering with Media: On the Art of Paul DeMarinis', in *Buried in Noise*, ed. by Paul DeMarinis (Heidelberg: Kehrer, 2011), pp. 33–39.

Erkki Huhtamo, *Illusions in Motion. Media Archaeology of the Moving Panorama and Related Spectacles* (Cambridge, MA: MIT Press, 2013).

Wolfgang König, *Technikgeschichte. Eine Einführung in ihre Konzepte und Forschungsergebnisse* (Stuttgart: Steiner Verlag, 2009).

Albert Kümmel-Schnur and Christian Kassung (eds.), *Bildtelegraphie. Eine Mediengeschichte in Patenten (1840–1930)* (Bielefeld: Transcript Verlag, 2012).

Colin Lawson and Robin Stowell, *The Historical Performance of Music. An Introduction* (Cambridge: Cambridge University Press, 1999).

Cécile Méadel, *Quantifier le public. Histoire des mesures d'audience à la radio et la télévision* (Paris: Economica, 2010).

Eggo Müller, 'Formatted Spaces of Participation: Interactive Television and the Reshaping of the Relationship between Production and Consumption', in *Digital Material*, ed. by Marianne van den Boomen *et al.* (Amsterdam: Amsterdam University Press, 2009), pp. 47–61.

Julia Noordegraaf, Vinzenz Hediger, Cosetta Saba, Barbara Le Maitre (eds.), *Preserving and Exhibiting Media Art. Challenges and Perspectives* (Amsterdam: Amsterdam University Press, 2013).

Annie van den Oever, 'The Medium-Sensitive Experience and the Paradigmatic Experience of the Grotesque, "Unnatural" or "Monstrous"', *Leonardo* 46, no. 1 (2013), pp. 88–89.

Nelly Oudshoorn and Trevor Pinch (eds.), *How Users Matter: The Co-Construction of Users and Technologies* (Cambridge, MA: MIT Press, 2003).

Jussi Parikka, 'Practising Media Archaeology: Creative Methodologies for Remediation', in *What Is Media Archaeology?*, ed. by Jussi Parikka (Cambridge: Polity Press, 2012), pp. 136–158.

Sibylle Peters, *Der Vortrag als Performance* (Bielefeld: Transcript Verlag, 2011), p. 187.

Mario Praz, *Histoire de la décoration d'intérieur: La philosophie de l'ameublement* (London: Thames & Hudson 1994), p. 19.

Hans-Jörg Rheinberger, 'Experiment: Präzision und Bastelei', in *Instrument – Experiment. Historische Studien*, ed. by Christoph Meinel (Berlin: GNT Verlag, 2000), pp. 52–60.

Stephen Riggins, 'Fieldwork in the Living Room. An Autoethnographic Essay', in *The Socialness of Things: Essays on the Socio-Semiotics of Objects*, ed. by Stephen Riggins (Berlin: De Gruyter, 1994), pp. 101–147.

Martina Roepke, *Privat-Vorstellung: Heimkino in Deutschland vor 1945* (Hildesheim: Olms, 2006).

Monika Röther, *The Sound of Distinction. Phonogeräte in der Bundesrepublik Deutschland. Eine Objektgeschichte (1957–1973)* (Marburg: Tectum Verlag, 2012,) pp. 34–62.

Stephen C. Saraydar, *Replicating the Past: The Art and Science of the Archaeological Experiment* (Long Grove: Waveland Press, 2008).

Michael B. Schiffer and James M. Skibo, 'Theory and Experiment in the Study of Technological Change', *Current Anthropology* 28 (1987), pp. 595–622.

Michael B. Schiffer and James M. Skibo, *The Archaeology of Science. Studying the Creation of Useful Knowledge* (Heidelberg: Springer, 2013).

Jeffrey Sconce, *Hounted Media. Electronic Presence from Telegraphy to Television* (Durham, NC: Duke University Press, 2000).

Michel Serres, *Die fünf Sinne. Eine Philosophie der Gemenge und Gemische* (Frankfurt: Suhrkamp Taschenbuch [Wissenschaft], 1993).

Clay Shirky, *Cognitive Surplus. How Technology Makes Consumers into Collaborators* (New York and London: Penguin Books, 2010), pp. 12–20, 161–183.

Roger Silverstone and Eric Hirsch (eds.), *Consuming Technologies: Media and Information in Domestic Spaces* (London: Routledge, 1994).

Gilbert Simondon, *Du monde d'existence des objets techniques* (Paris: Éditions Aubier, 1958).

Mark M. Smith, *Sensing the Past. Seeing, Hearing, Smelling, Tasting, and Touching in History* (Berkeley, CA: University of California Press, 2007).

Wanda Strauven (ed), *The Cinema of Attractions Reloaded* (Amsterdam: Amsterdam University Press, 2007).

Wanda Strauven, 'Media Archaology: Where Film History, Media Art, and New Media (Can) Meet', in *Preserving and Exhibiting Media Art. Challenges and Perspectives,* ed. by Julia Noordegraaf, Cosetta Saba, Barbara Le Maitre, and Vinzenz Hediger (Amsterdam: Amsterdam University Press, 2013), pp. 59–80.

Marita Sturken, Douglas Thomas, and Sandra J. Ball-Rokeach (eds.), *Technological Visions. The Hopes and Fears That Shape New Technologies* (Philadelphia, PA: Temple University Press, 2004).

Simone Venturini, 'Technological Platforms', in Julia Noordegraaf, Vinzenz Hediger, Cosetta Saba, Barbara Le Maitre (eds.), *Preserving and Exhibiting Media Art. Challenges and Perspectives* (Amsterdam: Amsterdam University Press, 2013), pp. 201–202.

Bernhard Waldenfels, *Phänomenologie der Aufmerksamkeit* (Frankfurt: Suhrkamp Verlag, 2004).

Geoffrey Winthrop-Young and Annie van den Oever, 'Rethinking the Materiality of Technical Media: Friedrich Kittler, *Enfant Terrible* with a Rejuvenating Effect on Parental discipline – A Dialogue', in *Technē/Technology: Researching Cinema and Media Technologies – Their Development, Use, and Impact*, ed. by Annie van den Oever (Amsterdam: Amsterdam University Press, 2014), pp. 219–239.

Ian Woodward, 'Material Culture, Narratives and Social Performance. Objects in Contexts' in *Understanding Material Culture*, ed. by Ian Woodward (London: Sage, 2007), pp. 151–168.

About the authors

Andreas Fickers is Professor for Contemporary and Digital History at the University of Luxembourg. His fields of specialization are European history of technology, transnational media history, and digital historiography. He is currently directing the Luxembourg Centre for Contemporary and Digital History (C2DH) and coordinator of a Doctoral Training Unit (DTU) on 'Digital History and Hermeneutics'. He is co-founder of the European Television History Network (ETHN), the Network of Experimental Media Archaeology (NEMA), and member of the Management Committee of the 'Tensions of Europe' Network.

Annie van den Oever is Head of the Film Archive and Associate Professor of Film at the University of Groningen, and Professor by special appointment to the chair in Film and Visual Media at the University of the Free State, South Africa. Since 2011, she is Associated Researcher and in 2017 Visiting Professor for Cinema and Audiovisual Studies of the Research Institute ACTE – UMRS

CNRS Université Paris I, Panthéon-Sorbonne. She is founding editor of the book series The Key Debates at Amsterdam University Press, and Editorial Board Member of NECSUS. She has published on cinema, aesthetics, technology, and experimental media archaeology (with Andreas Fickers). Recent publications: *Ostrannenie* (Amsterdam University Press, 2010); *Sensitizing the Viewer* (University of Groningen, 2011); *Techne/Technology* (Amsterdam University Press, 2014); *Exposing the Film Apparatus* (Amsterdam University Press, 2016, with Giovanna Fossati).

3. The Ghosts of Media Archaeology

Mark Goodall

Abstract

This chapter focuses on the experimental nature of media archaeology and the *avant-garde*. The chapter discusses some of the potential applications of *avant-garde* methodology to objects and material relating to the field of media archaeology. It extends the calls already made by media archaeology theorists (Cf. Fickers and van den Oever) into the domain of experimental techniques and practices and offers examples of where and how radical texts and methods may be applied to curatorial work and academic research. The text acknowledges the potential for current thinking on media archaeology to affect a wide range of creative endeavours including museum practice, artistic practice and research.

Keywords: experimental media, avant-garde, artistic practice, heuretics

'A spectre is always a *revenant*. One cannot control its comings and goings because it *begins by coming back*' (Derrida, 1994, p. 11)

'The writing of history is as personal an act as the writing of fiction' (Susman, 2003, p. xiii)

This chapter is concerned with the experimental nature of media archaeology, an aspect of the discipline that is receiving a growing amount of attention. Since its inception, the study of media archaeology has encouraged a diversity of approaches, practices, and voices. Erik Huhtamo and Jussi Parikka describe this variety of perspectives and range of debates as 'polylogues' (Huhtamo and Parikka, p. 2). Gilles Deleuze and Félix Guattari, seen as founders of media archaeological thinking, talked about the practice of 'nomadology'– the adoption of multiple narratives that are, in effect, the 'opposite of a history' (Deleuze and Guattari, p. 24). Meanwhile, Siegfried

Roberts, B. and M. Goodall (eds.), *New Media Archaeologies*, Amsterdam Universsity Press, 2019
DOI: 10.5117/9789462982161_CH03

Zielinski petitions for discovering 'fractures or turning points in historical master plans' (Zielinski, p. 7). His 'variantology' project (2007) is built on the urge to 'be different, to deviate, to change, to modify' (Huhtamo and Parikka, p. 12).

In 2013, Fickers and Van den Oever published an essay entitled 'Experimental Media Archaeology: A Plea for New Directions' (2013). The authors noted and praised the achievements made by the previous methodologies based on discourse, but at the same time stressed that 'the materiality of media technologies and the practices of use need more attention' (Fickers and Van den Oever, 2013). Reworking R. Collingwood's notions in *The Idea of History*, Fickers and Van den Oever propose that we view the 'idea of re-enactment as a heuristic concept of historical understanding'. This is an extension of Collingwood's idea of 'experiencing history' as doing historical re-enactments in practice, not just in theory – or, as *Gedankenexperimente*' (*Ibid.*, p. 273). The now somewhat unfashionable multi-stranded 'cultural studies' approach to the understanding of modernity, postmodernity, and media is never far away from the development of thinking on media archaeology. We can see, then, that current thinking in the field urges that we work on technologies and histories of media from a variety of diverse and experimental processes all the while keeping media technologies and materials close to hand.

While these proposals could work very well for the practice and method of media archaeology, it will be essential to also generate some new provocative thinking about how academics, writers, and critics write about and respond textually to the subject in an experimental manner. As Lev Manovich demonstrated in *The Language of New Media*, the development of new media technologies has actually always been linked to and developed out of various historical avant-gardes, and media archaeology also enjoys a similar potential to integrate (experimentally) science, technology, and the arts (Huhtamo and Parikka, p. 13). As Parikka points out, 'media archaeology is interested in the anomalous' (Parikka, p. 90) and in methods that 'use, pervert and modulate' (*Ibid.*, p. 161). Meanwhile, Elsaesser, in his work on the 'New Film History', has drawn attention to the connections between early cinema and the avant-garde tradition in defining the 'peculiar nature of the cinematic experience' (Huhtamo and Parikka, p. 12). This cinematic 'enchantment' was of particular interest to early surrealist, impressionist, and constructivist theorists and practitioners of the film arts. It is precisely this experimental approach that I wish to discuss here.

Avant-Garde Media Archaeology

The tradition in avant-garde movements is to proceed by way of the manifesto, a crystallization of thinking and method proposed to reinvent life and
art. Think of the famous revolutionary iconoclastic texts produced in the
early twentieth century by the Futurist, Dada, and Surrealist movements for
example (in 1909, 1916, and 1924/1929 respectively). In this essay, I obviously
want to stop well short of offering anything as presumptuous and grandiose
as a text of similar ambition, but I do wish to briefly discuss two possible
approaches to an experimental form of writing about media technologies
that may be useful for reinventing the field.

While Fickers and Van den Oever explain that 'Experimental Media
Archaeology' is 'inspired by the idea of historical re-enactment as a heuristic
methodology', I want to argue that it is possible to go a step further (or to the
side) and develop a strategy of *heuretic* methodology based largely on the
application of the ideas of the theories of American scholars Gregory Ulmer
and Robert B. Ray. It is not so much that their ideas can be incorporated
into media archaeology discourse, but more that they offer a set of open
and free approaches that are methodologically relevant and intellectually
stimulating.

In *Heuretics: The Logic of Invention*, Ulmer proposes that theory is assimi-
lated into the humanities by two methods: firstly, by 'critical interpretation'
and secondly by 'artistic experiment'– what he defines as 'heuretics' (Ulmer,
p. 3). This heuretic process belongs to the tradition of the 'discourse on
method' and can be represented mnemonically by the acronym *CATTt*. 'The
CATTt', explains Ulmer, includes the following 'operations':
  C = Contrast (opposition, inversion, differentiation)
  A = Analogy (figuration, displacement)
  T = Theory (repletion, literalization)
  T = Target (application, purpose)
  t = Tale (secondary elaboration, representability) (*Ibid.,* 8)

As a method for the proposal of inventing new ideas, I believe this 'CATTt'
could be relevant as an application for the study of media archaeology, or
at least the interpretation of media-archaeological objects.

At the very basic level, we can outline how this might work. We may
begin by firmly rejecting conventional thinking about archives and the
material and objects held within them ('Contrast'). The next stage is to find
an analogue ('Analogy') for our new method. Fickers and Van den Oever
suggest one method, that of 're-enactment'. While we may initially associate

this practice with the vaguely regressive form of historical reconstruction of important military battles, Fickers and Van den Oever believe re-enactment can 'make scholars of past media technologies 'experience' (rather than intellectually appropriate) the acts of making and screening film as social and cultural practices' (Fickers and Van den Oever, p. 275). Ulmer himself suggests a textual practice ('Theory') that may be of use to experimental media archaeologists when he discusses Derrida's book *Glas* – an experimental combination of considerations on the writings of the philosopher Georg Wilhelm Friedrich Hegel and the self-styled poet-thief Jean Genet. The texts in *Glas* are presented as two visually distinct but philosophically connected columns. It may be that this approach, simulating the way we experience electronic media, has a useful application for the study of media artefacts by offering a potential comparative method for a media object (for example, the electro-mechanical tape keyboard called the Mellotron) and its textual partner (the handbook manual), or to different media-archaeological texts, such as manuals and handbooks for the same piece of technology but from slightly different historical moments (or texts on the same piece of technology by different authors, etc.). The aim of an experimental heuretic approach would be to critique existing methods of media archaeology and indeed museum and curatorial practices/theories (which would be the 'Target') in order to reposition thinking on the subject. As to the form this new approach would take (what Ulmer calls the 'tale'), it would need to be a new and stimulating dialogue on the history of media and technology, surprising and challenging in its form and function, much as Benjamin's Arcades Project was. As Ulmer admits, such experiments are 'offered not as a proof or assertion of truth but as a trial or a test […] the value will be determined by those who choose to try it' (Ulmer, pp. 38–39). The forms of the CATTt can, of course, be altered by each user. Forms of current online interventions into media archaeology such as the cross-media Robin the Fog website (Accessed 2 June 2017: https://robinthefog.com) may offer guidance. Or, Piccini's radical work on a particular urban space (also in this volume), and the psychological, emotional, and spiritual evocation of a mediated technology environment could also be a method to be adapted and utilized.

While Ulmer has used the CATTt process to think about digital media, another academic, Robert B. Ray, has adopted the acronym as an exploration of analogue media, specifically film and music. Ray describes how developmental processes in general and academic practice in particular can become, like the technical processes of capitalist production, 'path dependent'. The field of media archaeology is no different in being vulnerable to this. So, for Ray, a heuretic methodology is a way of reinventing a discipline such as film studies (or, of course, media archaeology). In *How a Film Theory Got Lost*, Ray explains that '[a] heuretic film studies might begin where *photogénie*, third meanings and fetishism intersect; with the cinematic detail whose insistent appeal eludes precise explanation' (Ray, p. 13). This approach is part nomadic future-thinking and, as Ray takes a fresh look at early 'lost' film theory, part historical reinvention. It seems possible that within the study of media objects and their histories, we can locate and identify these small details that jump out and can lead to interesting and inventive investigative techniques. Ray, in another article on film theory, suggests adopting the psychogeographic techniques (where the film landscape can be traversed like a geographic space) evident in W.G Sebald's writings to uncover the meanings of a film text (Ray, 2000).

But, how could this work for media objects? An example from my own personal experience may be instructive here. Whilst investigating the history of the BBC Radiophonic Workshop in the collections of the National Science and Media Museum (part of the wider UK Science Museum group), I chanced upon a black-and-white press photograph of the Kentish home of Daphne Oram, one of the founders of the Workshop. As this image was intended for newspaper publication (it was part of an archive from the now defunct *Daily Herald*) it was marked on the reverse with various scribbles and pasted press cuttings. One particular phrase from a cutting caught my eye: 'Tower Folly – house of strange sounds'. Another image, a well-known portrait of Oram, also had pasted on the back an article leading with the sentence: 'The village constable here has been warned. Any shrieks coming from Miss Daphne Oram's house around 2 a.m. can be disregarded.' These seemingly trifling details are the kind of dialectical anecdotal fragments that so captivated Walter Benjamin in the production of his famous 'Arcades Project' and are drawn upon by Ray to discuss film culture. At one level, the words are just 'information'. Yet, the evocative presence and the imaginative power of these words on the back of the photographs led me to reflect on the almost supernatural nature of mid-twentieth-century electronic media; the (hidden) domestic sphere of experimental production; the often neglected role of women in this tale; the relationship between female avant-garde electronic composer and bewitchment. It is the aleatory element of Ray's writings that has perhaps the most to offer media archaeology. As Elsaesser (2008) has also suggested, these techniques can found in early film theory and follows a strong French tradition of wordplay and invention from André Breton to Georges Perec, Raymond Queneau, and the Oulipo Group of producing interpretations using chance, ludology, automatism, and improvisation.

In another essay, 'Tracking', Ray proposes to approach the study of popular music by writing an essay in the manner of the way in which popular music is produced. This means mimicking with words the mixing together of different sound elements found in the process of creating recorded music. Ray asks 'What if academics were to write essays the way that Paul Simon (or Public Enemy) write songs?' (Ray, p. 66). 'Tracking' proceeds by setting out six 'tracks' of thought on sound and theory, bringing them together for a final 'mix' at the end of the essay, if you like, a slightly more complex rework-ing of Derrida's *Glas*. This experimental process ends with an interesting reversal of what Ray started out with – the notion of recording as a form of writing. 'Writing, as the more advanced technology, has been the example for recording. What, after all, is sampling except quotation, which writers do all the time? [...] What are multi-tracks but columns?' (this also echoes Derrida's *Glas*). I can envisage this method working for both the experimental mixing together of found texts on media objects and/or the combining of different sound elements drawn from different audio-visual technologies to create a new work. The value of experimental techniques is therefore to open up the possibility of seeing media objects and archives another way round, from different, unforeseen perspectives, or to uncover some new thinking on what was thought to be a previously 'known' technology.

Ghosts In and Out of the Machine

Another way of resisting the academic tendency for repetition, stasis, or 'path dependency' is to search for what is to be found in the development of a phenomenon known as 'hauntology'. 'Hauntology' arises from Derrida's work on ghosts, history, and time in his book *Spectres of Marx*. Derrida's work in general is known for its utilization of avant-garde practice. For example, according to Ulmer (Ulmer, p. 5), Derrida's work is a 'renewal of the surrealist gesture' and it is this kind of gesture, of course, which has been problematic for analytic and rationalist schools of philosophical thinking (infamously resulting in Cambridge University casting him as an 'enemy of science and the Enlightenment' (*Ibid.*, p. 18). Derrida has regularly critiqued the linear notion of time and the determinist belief that ideas have their moment and then disappear on in to the historical past. According to Derrida, the peculiar state 'in-between' the living and the dead, applied to political thought, is also a space that has great potential for re-thinking and reinventing media artefacts. For Derrida, '[t]he logic of the spectre is that it regularly exceeds all the oppositions between visible and invisible, both phenomenal and nonphenomenal: a trace that marks the present with its absence in advance (Derrida and Stiegler, p. 117). Indeed, the appearance and re-appearance that occurs when we are arrested by media technologies is akin to a haunting: 'We are spectralized by the shot, captured or possessed by spectrality in advance' (*Ibid.*). Certainly, the more radical and playful interpretations of Derrida's concept of hauntology offer great potential for rethinking and reinventing our understanding of media technologies. Derrida's comments on the process of making the film *Ghost Dance* (which he 'stars' in) is also revealing in terms of how we interpret media. The strange experience he had when confronted with the image on screen years later of the actress (Pascale Ogier) in the film, who had since died, offers a reflection on the haunted nature of media and technology ('now yes, believe me, I believe in ghosts', Derrida says [*Ibid.*, p. 120]). At the same time, the more spectral dimensions of hauntology retain some of the more obvious aesthetic links between 'old' technologies and new methods of interpreting and examining film and media devices and artefacts. Friedrich Kittler, identified by Fickers and Van den Oever as the father of the material method, for example, found it instructive to combine technology with the supernatural in his texts, most startlingly in his analysis of Bram Stoker's *Dracula* novel and the media technologies deployed in the narrative by the protagonists (Kittler 1997). In this way, Kittler's work also becomes reminiscent of the aforementioned Sebald's 'novels' particularly *Austerlitz* (2001) and *Rings of Saturn* (1995), where history, myth, anecdote, and biography are freely combined. Derrida also reflects on the way in which film and photography as technologies of the image lack a 'tactile sensitivity' (Derrida and Stiegler, p. 115). However, it seems that the 'desire to touch, the tactile effect or affect' (*Ibid.*) could be realised and exploited by media archaeological practices, especially in the archive.

Derrida has also expressed a strong interest in what is known as 'Free Jazz' and musical improvisation. In his interview with the American composer and musician Ornette Coleman, Derrida explores the radical potential of repetition and improvisation stating that 'The very concept of improvisation verges upon reading, since what we understand by improvisation is the creation of something new, yet something which doesn't exclude the pre-written framework that makes it possible' (Murphy, p. 322). Derrida also repeats this theme in his reflections on the archive: 'There is no archive without a technique of repetition' (Derrida 1996, p. 11), the archive working against itself. This is perhaps something we can reflect on in thinking about media archives in order to resist stasis. Even seemingly random expressions grow out of some pre-existing structure. For his part, Coleman also reflects on the notion of the past being reborn in the present: 'In jazz you can take a very old piece and do another version of it. What's exciting about it is the memory that you bring to the present' (*Ibid.*). The creative impulse comes not out of nothing but draws on the internal psychological forces as the framework. It can also be akin to the aesthetics of 'outsider art', where the aim is to interpret and create outside of the conventional values of training and instruction – a truly free form of expression. This strikes me as being a potentially useful mode of analysing, understanding the framework, and using media technologies (especially audio technologies) from the past and reworking them into a new mode of experience and expression. 'Outsider' responses can be as valid and rewarding as those of the trained archivist. This despite the fact that the form that metamorphoses into another form is, Coleman admits, 'something healthy, but very rare' (*Ibid.*).

One of the intriguing ways in which hauntology could relate to media archaeologies is the way in which Derrida refers to the phenomena of the *no longer/not yet* and also the *not yet happened* (Fisher, p. 19). The *no longer* can be the original uses of the technology or some of the artefacts from that usage that are now lost, abandoned, or broken. The *not yet happened* encapsulates the possibility that these technologies can be brought back to life in interesting and creative new ways. The understandable error in compiling exhibitions and curatorial presentations of media archaeology is to ossify the technology and/or its users into 'dead' forms of culture (placing them in glass cases for an audience to 'gawp at' being the most obvious example). As Derrida notes (when speaking of video tape), media may serve as 'an archive, perhaps an exhibit, perhaps as evidence, but it does not replace testimony' (Derrida and Stiegler, p. 94). As he goes on to say, '[t]echnics will never produce a testimony' (*Ibid.*) and so we are left with the interpretation of the archivist.

It is fair to say that, more recently, thinking in the world of curatorial practice has begun to acknowledge this problem. A recent example is the 2011 Science Museum (UK) exhibition *Oramics to Electronica: Revealing Histories of Electronic Music*, which incorporated practices such as co-curation, nar-ratology, and the involvement of 'expert groups' to develop the exhibition. Despite these laudable and progressive aims, the exhibition, as at least one of the curators admitted, was flawed, as it did not develop the requisite level of creativity and deep encounter necessary to properly bring the specific audio technologies in the show 'back to life'. One of the authors of a report on the exhibition admits that '[if] audiences grab what they want from our displays, then it is arguable that the embodied narrative we impose becomes – in the purest case – chiefly a matter of convenience to us in deciding what we'd like to put where' (Boon *et al.* 2014). At the same time, they note that: 'It would be valuable to explore a more controversial theme using a public historical approach, where accounts would be likely to be contradictory' (*Ibid*). Thus, the need within archival and museum practice to encourage more experimental and radical, even contradictory approaches to an understanding of media archaeological phenomena and usages of that technology for new creative means, is clearly acknowledged. Derrida's hauntology project (and indeed much of his deconstruction work) set out to challenge existing certainties, notions of time and space, and to promote the rethinking of values and belief systems. As Fisher argues, 'hauntology concerns a crisis of space as well as time' (Fisher, p. 20). But this crisis can be turned to positive ends. From a creative, avant-garde perspective, a radical approach to both 'presence' and 'absence' in the cultural sphere is necessary and desirable. To repeat: it would therefore be intriguing if some of the more radical ideas about contemporary culture and academic practice could be brought to bear on media archaeology. Such radical ideas are, of course, concerned with avoiding stagnation of disciplines, a critical perspective on ideas and the goal to invent new approaches for the understanding of culture and media with potential further application or modification.

The link between material culture (media) and the occult (hidden) has been made before. As Winthrop-Young and Wutz acknowledge, the very idea of 'media' once 'conjured visions of spiritualism' (Winthrop-Young and Wutz, p. xii). Jeffrey Sconce has extended the discussion of media into the realm of the occult arguing that 'the electronically mediate worlds of telecommunication often evoke the supernatural' (Sconce, p. 4). The electronic presence inherent in such media has, from day one, been connected to paranormal or spiritual phenomena. More recently still, Simone Natale has connected spiritualism with modern media culture asking questions about the 'intersection of religious experience with popular culture and mass media' (Natale, p.15). Eric McLuhan's 'Fordham Experiment' also examined the sensual and perceptive responses to media. What is interesting about this study is that one of the media objects used in the experiment, the avant-garde 'hauntological' film *Le songe des chevaux sauvages* (1960), is both technological advanced and mystically evocative and surreal, leading to surprising and revealing (if scientifically inconclusive) results (McLuhan 2000). There is, therefore, nothing to fear from extending the interpretation or analysis of media archaeology into unknown of unfamiliar territories, moving away from the purely sociological or material.

One of the most interesting examples of an archaeological study combining media technologies, experimental methods, and occult hauntological dimensions is the project developed by the American cultural historian Michael Lesy. Lesy's book *Wisconsin Death Trip*, a text made up of photographs by Charles Van Schaick, news reports, advertisements, and hospital patient records from the years 1885-1900 in Black River Falls, Wisconsin, combines material objects, archaeological study and poetic interpretation with a clear hauntological dimension. The book is an attempt at recording a cultural history of a particular time and seemingly unremarkable place and the tragedies (murders, suicides, mental illness, infant mortality) that disproportionately seem to have emerged from that milieu. Lesy's work as an experimental interpretation of historical media has received its fair share of criticism. Gutman, for example, feels that Lesy 'ends up denying the existence of the people we see in the photographs' (Gutman 1973, p. 488) and undoes the belief systems the protagonists in the photographs are alleged to have held. Lesy's 'selection' process is also criticized, as is his tendency to combine 'historical account, the novel and psychological profile' with the language 'of a poet' (Smith, p. 48). Lesy himself describes *Wisconsin Death Trip* as 'an experiment of alchemy' (Lesy 1973) and his work in general as being akin to Freud's 'dream work' – 'multiple meanings, condensed, displaced, transformed and revised at the very moment, in the very act, of being remembered' (Lesy 2007, p. 143). The book's lack of page numbers is frequently remarked on as being problematic. Lesy's other open and experimental works have fared no better, one critic stating that his book *Bearing Witness* (1983) left a 'bad taste in my mouth' (Brown, p. 43). Yet, *Wisconsin Death Trip* now feels more like an exemplary instance of Walter Benjamin's methods as set out in the 'Arcades Project', a keystone text of media archaeology and the multiple meanings, etc. of a dream work offering exciting possibilities for interpretation of media objects. A student reviewer of Lesy's methodology hit the nail on the head when they remarked that 'I suspect that his book intends to call into question the accepted practices of historical scholarship and contemporary methods of preserving context and objectivity, as well as the over-estimated assumptions of photography's truthfulness' (Smith, p. 54). A film adaptation of the book made by James Marsh in 1999 similarly attempted to offer a 'self-contained world' (Dawson 2004), rather than a supposedly 'factual' historical document. Lesy's attitude to the accompanying text of the book echoes the experimental methods discussed above: 'The final text was composed of five types of people talking at once, sometimes about the same things, like witnesses to an accident, sometimes about different things, like the chroniclers of a court history' (Lesy 1973). In a sense, this is Lesy's version of Ray's 'Tracking'.

Fisher (2014) has identified the importance of analogue culture on our sense of the hauntological. In particular, he focuses on music culture and what he describes as the principle 'sonic signature of hauntology: the use of crackle, the surface noise made by vinyl' (*Ibid.*, p. 21). This sonic technical 'error' and failure has been turned into a virtue and a symbol of postmodern experience, a marker of the state we currently live in, where it is possible to challenge and subvert linear progressive thinking about technology and expectations of audio 'quality'. Our experience of listening to the 'crackle' of the past reminds us that we are self-consciously reconstructing something (both in terms of the object and its playback mechanism). This has exciting possibilities for media archaeologists where the 'faults' and 'errors' become part of the interpretive experience and the critical reading. It seems that as *Wisconsin Death Trip* captures the grain, degradation, and fade of Van Schaick's photographs, there is a possibility of re-enacting the historical past to better understand the future to come. Fisher goes on: 'Crackle makes us aware that we are listening to a time out of joint' (*Ibid*). So, why not embrace this kind of distortion and work with it, as the artists and musicians Fisher promotes – such as Leyland Kirby aka 'The Caretaker' – notably do? Kirby himself notes: 'More research will have to be done before I find the best pathway for future exploration' (*Ibid.*, p. 119). It is the very 'crackle' of past media that hold the greatest secrets, the 'refusal to give up on the desire for the future' (*Ibid.*). The nostalgia, even melancholia, for the materiality of the past, key to our understanding of the hauntological, can be harnessed by experimental archivists and curators. At the same time, the impact of internet technologies on the understanding of archives and archaeology is also relevant as this is the technology that has most radically altered space and time, or the 'tele-technology' (*Ibid.*, p. 20), of the contemporary world.

As Warren Susman lays out in the preface to *Wisconsin Death Trip*, Lesy has contributed to an experimental method in locating the 'underworld' (Susman 1973) of historical truth. He has produced the kind of 'surrealist montage' (Arendt, p. 47) that has been attributed to Benjamin's method, but in this instance and for our purposes is importantly about media (photographs, etc.) and so is concerned with a visual form of 'quotation' (Susman, p. 3). Above all, Lesy's work is about 'a willingness to see things anew' (*Ibid.*).

In 2012, Parikka, drawing on Michel Foucault's genealogical method, which avoids an obsession with the 'origins' of things, noted that the practice of media archaeology is 'looking for *alternative* presents and past- and futures' (Parikka, p. 12). Derrida argues that the archive was both '[r]evolutionary and traditional' (Derrida 1996, p. 7). It is perhaps the latter that has been foregrounded historically and we must celebrate somehow both the destruction and the preservation of media culture (a condition that Derrida calls 'archive fever' [*Ibid.*, p. 12]). Experimental media archaeology therefore must 'break the law' and offer new alternative visions on the technologies that have shaped our media world. It must somehow educate us about the significance of media in the modern world and, at the same time, capture the spirit of media artefacts, rising to the challenge of explaining the 'virtual space of spectrality' set by Derrida while answering his lament that '[t]here has never been a scholar who really, and as a scholar, deals with ghosts' (Derrida 1994, p. 11). Above all, it needs to achieve the power of radical imaginative retelling and interpretation, contentious but thrilling, that Lesy achieved with his study of a set of photographs from a small forgotten town in nineteenth-century America.

> [The book's] primary intention is to make you experience the pages now before you as a flexible mirror that if turned one way can reflect the odour of the air that surrounded me as I wrote this; if turned another, can project your anticipation of next Monday; if turned again can transmit the sound of breathing in the deep winter ait of a room of eighty years ago, and if tuned once again, this time backward onto itself, can fuse all three images, and so can focus who I was, what you might be, and what might have happened, all upon a single point of your imagination, and transform them like light focused by a lens on paper, from a lower form of energy to a higher. (Lesy, 1973)

Works Cited

Hanna Arendt, 'Introduction: Walter Benjamin 1892–1940' in Walter Benjamin, *Illuminations* (Glasgow: Fontana/Collins, 1973), pp. 1–55.

Tim Boon, Merel van der Vaart, Katy Price, 'Oramics to Electronica: Investigating Lay Understandings of the History of Technology through a Participatory Project' in *Science Museum Journal*, Autumn 2014, Issue 02 (2014). Available at: (Accessed 2 May 2017) http://journal.sciencemuseum.org.uk/browse/issue-02/oramics-to-electronica/.

Josh Brown, 'Bearing Witness: Michael Lesy and Photography as Historical Evidence' in *Film & History: An Interdisciplinary Journal of Film and Television Studies*, 13 (2) (1983), pp. 43–46.

T. Dawson, 'Wisconsin Death Trip' (notes) with James Marsh, (Dir.) (2004) *Wisconsin Death Trip* (DVD) (2004). Tartan Video.

Gilles Deleuze and Félix Guattari, *A Thousand Plateaus* (London: Bloomsbury, 2004).

Jacques Derrida, *Spectres of Marx: The Sate of the Debt, the Work of Mourning, and the New International* (New York: Routledge, 1994).

Jacques Derrida, *Archive Fever: A Freudian Impression* (Chicago, IL and London: University of Chicago Press, 1996).

Jacques Derrida and Bernard Stiegler, *Echographies of Television* (Cambridge: Polity, 2002).

Thomas Elsaesser, 'Afterword: Digital Cinema and the Apparatus: Archaeologies, Epistemologies, Ontologies' in *Cinema and Technology: Cultures, Theories, Practices*, B. Bennett, M. Furstenau, and A. Mackenzie (eds.) (Basingstoke: Palgrave Macmillan) (2008), pp. 226–40.

Andreas Fickers and Annie van den Oever, 'Experimental Media Archaeology: A Plea for New Directions' in Annie van den Oever (ed.), *Téchne/Technology. Researching Cinema and Media Technologies, their Development, Use and Impact.* (Amsterdam University Press, 2013), pp. 272–278.

Mark Fisher, *Ghosts of My Life: Writings on Depression, Hauntology and Lost Futures* (Alresford: Zero Books, 2014).

Judith Mara Gutman, 'Reading Pictures' in *Reviews in American History*, 1 (4) (1973), pp. 488–492.

Erkki Huhtamo and Jussi Parikka, *Media Archaeology: Approaches, Applications and Implications* (Berkeley, CA: University of California Press, 2011).

Friedrich Kittler, 'Dracula's Legacy' in *Literature, Media, Information.* (London and New York: Routledge, 1997), pp. 50–84.

Michael Lesy, *Wisconsin Death Trip* (Albuquerque, NM: University of New Mexico Press, 1973).

Michael Lesy, 'Visual Literacy' in *The Journal of American History*, 94 (1) (2007), pp.143–153.

Eric McLuhan, 'The Fordham Experiment', *Proceedings of the Media Ecology Association*, Volume 1, 2000, pp. 23–27.

Timothy S. Murphy, 'The Other's Language: Jacques Derrida Interviews Ornette Coleman, 23 June 1997' in *Genre* 37(2) (2004), pp. 319–329.

Simone Natale, *Supernatural Elements: Victorian Spiritualism and the Rise of Modern Media Culture* (University Park, PA: Pennsylvania State University Press, 2016).

Jussi Parikka, *What is Media Archaeology?* (Cambridge: Polity Press, 2012).

Robert B. Ray, 'Mystery Trains' in *Sight and Sound*, (November 2000), pp 12–13.

Robert B. Ray, *How a Film Theory Got Lost and Other Mysteries on Cultural Studies* (Bloomington, IN: Indiana University Press, 2001).

Jeffrey Sconce, *Haunted Media: Electronic Presence from Telegraphy to Television* (Durham, NC: Duke University Press, 2000).

C. Zoe Smith, 'The Questionable Uses of 19th-Century Photographs in Visual Research: Wisconsin Death Trip as Case Study' in *Journal of Visual Literacy*, Spring (1998), 18 (1), pp. 47–60.

Warren I. Susman, 'Preface' in M. Lesy, *Wisconsin Death Trip* (Albuquerque, NM: University of New Mexico Press, 1973).

Warrren I. Susman, *Culture as History: The Transformation of American Society in the Twentieth Century.* (Washington, DC: Smithsonian Institution Press, 2003).

Gregory Ulmer, *Heuretics: The Logic of Invention.* (Baltimore, MD: Johns Hopkins University Press, 1994).

Geoffrey Winthrop-Young and Michael Wutz, 'Introduction' in Kittler, F.A. *Gramophone, Film, Typewriter.* (Stanford, CA: Stanford University Press, 1999).

Siegfried Zielinski, *Deep Time of the Media: Towards an Archaeology of Hearing and Seeing by Technical Means.* (Cambridge, MA: The MIT Press, 2006).

About the author

Mark Goodall is Head of Film and Media at the University of Bradford. His research interests include cult, horror and experimental cinema, popular music and the avant-garde, and the mondo films of the 1960s and 1970s. His publications include *Sweet and Savage: The World through the Shockumentray Film Lens* (Headpress 2006, 2nd ed. 2017), *Crash Cinema: Representation in Film* (Cambridge Scholars, 2007) and *Gathering of the Tribe: Music and Heavy Conscious Creation* (Headpress, 2013). Forthcoming books are *Music and Fascism* (Routledge) and *The Beatles' White Album* (Headpress). He is the producer and director of the feature film *Holy Terrors* (2017) and plays in the indie chamber folk band Rudolf Rocker.

4.   (game)(code)

re-playing program listings from 1980s British computer magazines

Alison Gazzard

Abstract

Using examples from 1980s British computing magazines and emulators such as BeebEm and Spectaculator this chapter will trace example program listings only available in printed form in order to 'bring them back to life'. Recent emulation efforts, in order to preserve content provide a means for people to engage with the original platform in a modified form on a more contemporary machine. This chapter examines the role of emulation and the availability of the archive in a different light and will explore the spaces in between the combinations of code, object, and interaction (Lowood 2002) as magazine listings are 'bought back to life' through the emulation process. Discussions of both the archive and related emulation practices will allow for an "alternative history" of computer games to be exposed through the lens of media archaeology (see Parikka, 2012, Huhtamo, 2011).

Keywords: Media Archaeology, Videogames, Software Studies, Game History, Archives

Introduction

Conversations, articles and debates about how and why we should preserve computer game content have been developing over the last fifteen or so years, for nearly as long as the discipline of 'game studies' (Aarseth, 2001) has been interested in defining itself as a field for the study, design, and analysis of games. Situated within the category of born digital content, computer games have raised numerous issues and debates about how we can and might preserve these artefacts for years to come (Lowood, 2002; Newman, 2012).

Roberts, B. and M. Goodall (eds.), *New Media Archaeologies*, Amsterdam Universsity Press, 2019
DOI: 10.5117/9789462982161_CH04

In parallel to this, games have also been recognized as part of histories of software (Campbell-Kelly, 2004) or as ways of highlighting the affordances of particular platforms (Montfort and Bogost, 2009) as well as developing work on the history of games across various countries. Histories of digital games are discussed in terms of their materiality, instruction manuals, box art, walkthroughs, and design documents, amongst other factors. These histories provide us with recorded insights into game development, use, and play. However, given that bit rot and digital decay are inevitable, it is possible that some of the original storage media for game content, such as cassette tapes and floppy disks, may no longer exist. Although there are initiatives to preserve as much of this data as possible, related content such as magazine articles and books still remain, either in their original forms in public or private collection, or scanned by communities of users online. These '(para)texts' (Newman, 2011) allow for a searchable archive of preserved content related to the games scene at the time. The magazines provide not only a historical context for computer game research, but also a record of some of the source code for the platforms available at the time. While there have been discussions about game preservation and archives, as will be seen throughout this chapter, the history of software listings found in books and magazines are not always given as much thought within these multiple insights.

Despite their recognition as a component of how some people learnt about programming and computing (Lean, 2008; Swalwell, 2012), as well as how games could be made (Donovan, 2010; Wiltshire, 2015), a full study of game program listings found in magazines and books has yet to receive much attention. Whilst researching content for a journal article in 2013 about arcade game clones present in 1980s game software development on both the BBC Micro and the ZX Spectrum, I found that not only were arcade graphics and mechanics copied in games such as *Pi-Balled* for the ZX Spectrum and *Snapper* or *Hopper* for the BBC Micro, but they were also present in the magazine listings themselves (Gazzard, 2014) . One of the examples I found as a case study of an arcade clone listing had all the signs of being an arcade-type game in its title, and by the language used to describe the game, but I couldn't be 100 per cent certain what the game was really like until I actually played it. As a games scholar, I was interested to see what the game mechanics, graphics, and play style of the game were like and the text in the magazine did not offer me any insight into this. It was this intrigue, raised by recreating the listing in order to gain access to the playable experience, which was the starting point to this project.

In his research into computer game magazines in Britain from 1981 to 1995, Graeme Kirkpatrick (2012) notes that he found 25 per cent of early 1980s magazines were made up of listings for game programs. But beyond this statistic, the listings raise numerous questions for archival research; what was the relationship between the code and imagery displayed in the magazine and the recreated playable experience? And what can researchers, museums, and archives learn from bringing these games 'back to life'? Utilizing theoretical concerns and debates about emulation, game preservation, software studies, platform studies, and media archaeology, this chapter will attempt to answer some of these questions by examining one magazine listing for the BBC Micro and one for the ZX Spectrum in the archives of *The Micro User* and *Personal Computer Games* magazines, respectively, found in museum and personal archives.

Instead of using the archive as a means for telling timelines of narrative histories, we can use the archive as a means of recreating processes inherent in 1980s microcomputing practices. Examining archives in this way allows for a greater understanding of functions, uses, and experiences of code that media archaeology demands over more general timeline-driven, media historical narratives (Ernst, 2013, p. 55). Rather than only documenting the output of a particular text, we get to interpret the processes in-between, allowing us to not only understand the possibilities posed by the archive, but also the different ways in which it can be viewed, interpreted, and potentially played. To re-program and re-play this archive is to recognize not only the interplay of code, image, and process, but to also recognize the spatial-temporal nature of computer games as played forms. While the materiality of the magazine, the inscription of code, the fictions of related imagery tell one story, to emulate the process in order for the game to emerge and subsequently be played, tell another. As both Lev Manovich and Alexander Galloway suggest, to play a game is to try and understand its underlying 'algorithms' (Manovich, 2001) or, as Galloway (2006, p. 90) states, 'To play the game means to play the code of the game.' Therefore, to understand the code is to read, compile, and run it in order to see these algorithms at play beyond the printed page, in various layers, as the code becomes executed. And to be able to fully understand these layers, we must turn to the archive of texts and platforms used to create the games in the listings. Whereas writing code from scratch was often emphasized through initiatives to promote general computer literacy (Gazzard, 2016; Lean, 2008), there were multiple other examples found within print media at the time. These ranged from magazines such as *The Micro User, Acorn User, Crash,* and *Your Sinclair* to books such as the Usborne Computer Programs series.

An Archive of Paper and of Games

In his work outlining *What is Media Archaeology?*, Jussi Parikka notes, 'Media archaeology starts with the archive – the implicit starting point for so much historical research that in itself, as a place and a media form, has been neglected, become almost invisible' (Parikka, 2012, p. 113). Archives of games, both as playable artefacts and related material exist in a variety of places. In the UK, they can be found in museum settings, such as the National Media Museum in their Games Lounge, at the National Museum of Computing at Bletchley in their PC Gallery, and 1980s classroom spaces at the Centre for Computing History in Cambridge and at Nottingham's National Videogame Arcade. Some of these archives are publicly playable, such as in the spaces listed previously, as well as existing in additional spaces within the museums where researchers can gain additional access.

Along with public archives or playable museum spaces, games are also often preserved in private collections by those never disposing of their past hobbies, and/or those seeking to add to existing or growing collections as nostalgia or a change in interest takes hold. These collections are often documented in magazines such as *Retro Gamer*, where the archive becomes the centre piece of the article as the proud owner shows pictures and details how their interest started or continued from their own generation of game playing.

Both of these public and private archives, in some instances, appear to be ad hoc in their creation, and unlike national libraries, such as the British Library, there is not necessarily a publicly available catalogue to search when trying to access particular information. However, what all of these archives have in common is their connection to what can be termed the 'multimedia archive', one discussed by Wolfgang Ernst as existing as 'algorithmic dynamics instead of documentary stills' (Ernst, 2013, p. 97). Whereas Ernst points to the 'regeneration' of the archive being '(co-) produced by online users for their own needs' (*Ibid.*, p. 95), we can also see how this regeneration can occur through the materials found within the archive itself. This is summed up by Ernst in his discussion of how the multimedia archive (or *arché* from Kant) also allows for the possibility of performance. In the case of program listings, the memory related to this archive also exists within the magazines or books themselves, as the code remains embedded within printed form, ready to the performed again by the user once retrieved from the archive. By performing the archive through the related or emulated hardware, we are able to interpret it in multiple ways.

Recreating these listings allows for the performative act inherent in media-archaeological approaches, as pointed to by Ernst and the variety of labs that enable students and researchers to play with the materiality of hardware, but also what the hardware enables.[1] As Huhtamo and Parikka note, 'Media archaeology rummages textual, visual, and auditory archives as well as collections of artefacts, emphasizing both the discursive and the material manifestations of culture' (Huhtamo and Parikka, 2011, p. 3). It is this approach to the archive, as offered by a media-archaeological perspective, which enables us to start to understand the role of these program listings within not only computer game histories, but also preservation, interpretation of source material, and cultures of production.

For the purposes of this chapter, the listings chosen were done so by platform, in order to show some of the differences in methods used to re-program the listings. Each listing was also selected based on its belonging to a similar genre of games, highlighting not only how the labelling of games was already inherent at this time, but also to show how the type of game could be subsequently interpreted in a multitude of ways. It is for this reason that one listing for the BBC Microcomputer was chosen and one for the ZX Spectrum. In the first edition of *The Home Computer Course* magazine, along with articles about choosing a microcomputer, there was also an article about 'Games People Play' (1983, pp. 14–15). The article lists six genres of games that they thought summed up the type of experience offered by games software on the market, or found in magazines at the time including, 'Adventure, Board and Table, Learning through Play, Arcade-style, Grand Strategy, and High Flying.' Both of the games selected from magazines fit primarily into the 'arcade-style' category, although this is loosely defined in relation to the ZX Spectrum listing. The purpose of recreating the listings was not purely to show the differences in platforms, but also the differences in how various types of games were presented to the user. 'Arcade-style games' in *The Home Computer Course* were discussed as 'games for fast action and movement' (*Ibid.*, p. 15) in reference to the types of games found in the arcades before and during the life of home computers. The article about such games continues to discuss how 'with a home computer there is a wider choice of fast and thrilling arcade-style games, all ready to be played when you want, and with no hungry cash slot

---

1   Examples of such labs include the Media Archaeological Fundus in Berlin and the Media Archaeology Lab in Boulder, Colorado. For an interview with the founders see: (Accessed 2 June 2017) https://blogs.loc.gov/digitalpreservation/2013/02/archives-materiality-and-agency-of-the-machine-an-interview-with-wolfgang-ernst/.

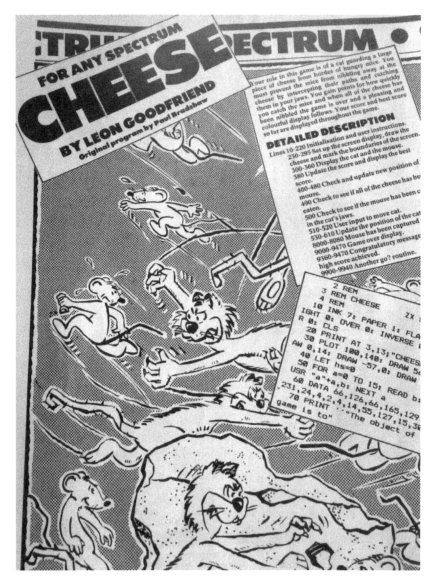

4.1: Section of the *Cheese* Spectrum listing, March 1984 issue of *Personal Computer Games* magazine (from personal collection)

gaping'. Although the re-programmed games within this chapter may not necessarily lend themselves to this description of 'fast action and movement', as will become apparent later on, each game does involve timed play and movement, as delivered by some of the arcade games on offer, and, as such, they lend themselves more to this category than any other. This is not to say that other categories of games were not discussed at the time, but the general discussions of game genres often used the arcade as a starting point for people recreating known or discussed experiences.

The games discussed in this chapter came from listings within magazines found within separate archives. The BBC Microcomputer listing was found in *The Micro User* magazine, a magazine centred on the BBC Microcomputer and other Acorn Computer machines running from March 1983 until September 1992. This listing is for a game called *Galactic Invaders*, printed in the September 1983 issue of *The Micro User* magazine. The ZX Spectrum listing was found in *Personal Computer Games* magazine, which covered a range of computing platforms, including the BBC Micro and had a short run from the early 1980s until February 1985. This listing, titled *Cheese*, was found in the March 1984 issue of the magazine (see Figure 4.1). These magazines were encountered in different ways, with *The Micro User* issue found within the archives at the National Museum of Computing, and *Personal Computer Games* existing in my personal collection. The physical archive was used in this instance due to the ability to flick through the pages of magazines, find articles, and situate them within the contents of the issue they were found in. Whereas this can also be achieved within online archives of content, such as those found at The Internet Archive, the serendipity of finding articles and sifting through the information amongst the pages is not always as immediate as those found on the physical page.

However, this materiality of the print archive poses further questions in relation to this work, to be explored at a later date. Although the print archive allowed for a materiality of the page, the process of re-creating the listing did not rely on the same materiality of the original hardware. Media archaeology has been discussed by Parikka as allowing us to think about the 'materialities of technologies' by 'digging into how technologies work' or even 'reverse-engineering' (Parikka, 2012, p. 164). The program listings presented in this chapter do not have to be reverse engineered to discover how they work, as the code is laid out on the page for us to understand. However, these listings do allow us to understand how the technologies they were written for work, in some sense, and how, perhaps, more importantly, could be experienced by others. Yet, for this research, the materiality of the machine lies not just in the hardware the listings were written for, but also in the emulators that have been developed in recent decades for others to re-interpret and re-use some of these functions on 'more modern day machines'.

Materiality and the Machine

As Henry Lowood discusses,

> Computer and video games are both dynamic and interactive. Dynamic, in the sense that no matter how linear, how narrative-driven the game, each instance of it being played results in a different set of experiences. The text is never the same. (Lowood, 2002, p. 7)

It is for this reason that reading the magazine listings was not enough and that this was only part of the game's state. To program the listing and play the game, whilst examining the code and imagery related to the playable game, provides a more well-rounded perspective of what these games could offer at the time, and also presents a method for being able to study these games again today. This is noted by Berry in his examination of the differences and relations between code and software, where he states that 'code and software are two sides of the same coin, code is the static textual form of software, and software is the processual operating form' (Berry, 2011, p. 32). Using this comparison, we can see how the listings exist as code on the page, whereas, by programming the listing, we are able to appreciate the computer game as a form of software. Although linked, these can be read in different ways, as will be discussed later on in this chapter.

However, the first challenge to overcome in examining this link was finding the means to program the listings themselves, raising issues about the materiality of hardware and possible research methods. Although both hardware platforms were available to me in their original forms (in my home collection as well as in working museum spaces), as a researcher I chose to use an emulator for the purposes of re-programming the listings. For me, this wasn't a project about the materiality of the platform, the way the keys felt to touch and the processes of saving the listings to tape, as much as this would have been possible. It was rather a project about recreating the listing in a playable state. For the purposes of this chapter, debates about emulation and the original platform will not be addressed in any length, as many of these have already been summarized by authors such as James Newman (see Newman, 2012, pp. 140–142). However, it is appropriate to note how some of these differences appear within the methods of recreating the listing and how programming game listings using emulators is not a one-size-fits-all approach.

What is interesting to note, beyond the materiality of the platform, is how aspects of the platform can still be revealed via the way the emulators work on mimicking past processes, as will be shown when discussing the listings in more detail. As Nick Montfort and Clara Fernadez-Vara note in their discussions of platforms and emulation for the study of computer games, 'emulators provide another way to see how games function' (Fernandez-Vara and Montfort, 2013, p. 5). In their article about using older hardware and software as a way of understanding creative practices and the study of games, the authors continue to discuss how 'in more technical terms, emulators allow significant access to and understanding of how games and other software make use of the hardware' (*Ibid.*) of each platform.

During this process, I used Beeb Em to recreate the BBC Micro listing, and Spectaculator to recreate the Spectrum listing. The Spectrum listing was also later run on the zxsp emulator for the MacOS as Spectaculator is a Windows-only emulator. Moving games across platforms also shows how researching across platforms from the past and present day must also be taken into consideration. The BBC Micro emulator BeebEm runs across Windows, Mac (ported by Jon Welch), UNIX/Linux (ported by David Eggleston), as well as the Playstation Portable and Pocket PC. As the corresponding website for the emulator reveals, 'BeebEm was first developed for UNIX systems in 1994 by Dave Gilbery and was then ported to Microsoft Windows' (Wyatt, n.d.). Opening up BeebEm reveals a windowed version of what looks like a BBC Micro display, along with a flashing cursor at the bottom prompting a 'please input somewhere here' response. The emulator offers the user various settings, such as the type of BBC Micro that they want to use, including having an additional processor, or what speed they want the emulator to run at. Although materially different processes, the emulator portrays as much of the same as possible, albeit through menu systems rather than physically attaching additional hardware in some instances. What is slightly different and, again, can be different depending on the emulator, is the keyboard mapping. Whereas the BBC Microcomputer had a full keyboard, the mapping of key presses from the original machine to a Windows or Mac keyboard is slightly offset or different in some instances. Therefore, the user either has to remember where the equivalent BBC Micro key presses are, or they have to create their own mapping for them. These initial processes can mean that programming the listings is slightly slower, but continued use, as with many things, means this process can speed up.

This keyboard mapping was of particular importance when it came to typing in the ZX Spectrum listings, as the Spectrum's rubber-key keyboard is not laid out in the same way as the BBC Microcomputer's keyboard. The Spectrum keyboard relies on inputting keywords (such as RUN, or INPUT) linked to the keys these keywords are found on. Unlike the BBC

Microcomputer, the Spectrum was designed so that its BASIC was very memory efficient. Rather than storing BASIC commands as a series of letters (e.g. P, R, I, N, T for PRINT) it instead stored a single byte value for each keyword. When entering a listing into a Spectrum, it was necessary to press the correct key to provide the correct command, for example, pressing P when the computer was expecting a keyword would produce the command PRINT. Therefore, mapping the keyboard relies on mapping the keywords to particular keys, rather than typing directly as per the BBC Micro emulator (and original hardware). The emulator correctly handles this, but the process of linking up keywords is initially slower when using the software to program the listing. The Spectrum listing was programmed using two different emulators, as I worked across different computing platforms (both Windows and Mac) depending on location and access to a machine. Whereas the free zxsp was used for MacOS, I used Spectaculator for Windows, which costs £9.99. Whereas Spectulator also has iOS and Android versions, there is no MacOS version, which is why zxsp was also used, due to there being limited Spectrum emulators for the Mac. Spectulator on Windows was also one of the most supported emulators available, and although it had to be paid for, it offered a stable environment and more functionality. However, zxsp offered enough functionality to be able to program a listing, save it, and play it back, which was more than adequate for the research.

In fact, the ability to save snapshots of my progress as I typed in the listings, as well as being able to save these snapshots in formats that could work across modern platforms was an important part of recreating the listings. Fernandez-Vara and Montfort (2013, p. 6) also state how the ability to save the state of a game on an emulator, even if the original hardware didn't have a save point, was a recognizable additional feature of using an emulator. In the case of programming the game listings, some of them can be quite large, and require subsequent debugging, either because of errors made in copying the listing from print to machine, or through printed errors in the book or magazine that only come to light once the listing is run. Whereas in the 1980s, when these listings were first typed in, the user had to painstakingly type in the listing in one sitting, or wait for their progress to be saved to a cassette tape or floppy drive (with risks of this failing), the modern equivalent of using an emulator means that the save process is not only faster but more reliable. The ability to save my progress when typing in the listing, or at the end when I had finished typing in (and debugging) the listing, meant that I was able to return to the game as code and software any time I needed to. Using an emulator also allowed for these listings to form an archive of software, no longer confined to the pages of the book or magazine, but on a modern hard-drive. In the past, turning off the microcomputer without saving often meant losing the data, therefore the ability to now save this data so quickly meant that this was no longer an issue. From a research perspective of wanting to examine the relationship between code, software, and related imagery (in the magazine and in the game), this meant that the emulator functioned as a vehicle in order to do this. This is not to say that this recreates the same experience, as it is also recognized that the reading of the images does not go down to a display level, where Cathode Ray Tube screens and monitors would provide different nuances to those found on the LCD monitor the re-created games are now viewed on. With these limitations noted and recognized, we can now start to see what emerges when these games are recreated, and how this helps our understanding of not only games history, but also methods of examining these games in more detail.

Text and Image

Starting with the *Galactic Invaders* listing from the September 1983 *The Micro User* magazine, we can see not only how emulating this listing starts to reveal more about the game, but how this contrasts to the description and imagery posted alongside the code. The opening paragraph to the article about the listing before the code is shown starts by stating, 'As its name suggests, *Galactic Invaders* is a cross between two well known arcade games. What the name doesn't reveal, however, is the amount of pleasure to be had from this hybrid' (*The Micro User*, 1983, p. 51). As much as *Galactic Invaders* as a name lends itself to a hybrid between *Galaxian* and *Space Invaders* (both released in the arcades in the late 1970s), the images drawn to accompany the game description and listing do not depict anything resembling either game. Instead, something akin to an elaborate space warrior is depicted, shooting a laser gun at an evil-looking humanoid alien-type character. The intertextual references between the evil alien character and Ming the Merciless from Flash Gordon show the crossover of pop cultural icons from around a similar decade, yet do nothing to depict any of the actual graphics that will be displayed when the listing is typed in and run. However, we can see these images as part of our interpretation of the game in addition to the playable game software and the written code on display.

These drawings are part of game history in their own right, something recognized by Raiford Guins, who writes about the related artwork, including box art and advertisements for videogames. In the same way that Guins details Chris Spohn's Atari VCS game box covers as 'evocative surfaces' (Guins, 2014, p. 198), we can see the magazine listing artwork in a similar context. Guins notes how the game box art allows us to 'retrieve a history of graphic design instrumental in helping to shape video game culture' and adds another dimension in the museum context, beyond the playable game as we 'need to cast a wider net for trawling the past' (*Ibid.*). In the case of the magazine listing, the artwork allows us to explore the interplay of other possible references to pop culture in amongst computer and arcade games. The images of fantasy worlds that the games might evoke in what Michael Nitsche terms the 'fictional spaces' of game, 'that live in the imagination, in other words, the space "imagined" by players from their comprehension of the available images' (Nitsche, 2008, p. 16), are also present in game advertising found within the same magazines. Commercially packaged software sold and advertised in the pages of the magazines were often presented with small screenshots of actual game imagery, alongside larger, more elaborate images of the fictional drawn spaces of the game that could not be realized through the graphical limitations of the platform. In much the same way, the type-in program listing also has a placeholder advert on page 53 of the issue of *The Micro User*, whereas the listing itself doesn't appear in full until page 102. These images invited the reader or programmer into the depicted world found in the spaces of the magazine, but also hopefully in the mind of the player once they started the game and imagined a space beyond the limited graphics on offer.

Comparing the illustrations of the 'fictional spaces' depicted in *Galactic Invaders* to the Spectrum listing of *Cheese* (Goodfriend, 1984, p. 146), we can see how, although the introductory text and image serve a similar purpose, they do so in a different way. Unlike the graphics from the BBC Micro listing, the images presented in the magazine represent a cat, a mouse, and some cheese, and although they are more detailed than the game graphics, they at least show the key characters to be expected upon typing in the listing. This is backed up by the introductory text before the listing that outlines the rules of the game stating, 'Your role in this game is of a cat guarding a large piece of cheese from hordes of hungry mice. You must prevent the mice from nibbling away at the cheese by intercepting their paths and catching them in your jaws.' Once again, before even running the game code, we can start to get a sense of the game and the platform through examining the listing. However, unlike *Galactic Invaders*, the reader/programmer does not have a sense of the influences of the game. Whereas *Galactic Invaders* draws on generational pop cultural references in the descriptive introductory text and the illustrations of a fantasy game,

Cheese is more basic in its offering, acting purely as an example of how to program a game. Although the game itself does not have any obvious arcade-style mentions within its title, descriptive text, or cat and mouse imagery, it is upon typing in the listing and playing the game that the mechanics and subsequent relations to similar genres of games start to be revealed. Therefore, taking the image and magazine text at face value, even with reading the code of the listing, cannot provide the whole picture. It is only upon emulating the listing that the larger picture can start to be revealed, and thus examined further.

Code, Software, and Play

Returning to Berry's (2011) differentiation between 'code' and 'software', we can see how reading the game can occur through both text as code and game as played experience. Reading the code of the *Galactic Invaders* type-in listing first reveals it is written in BBC BASIC by the iconic step numbering system that is recognizable as the user starts to 10, then 20, and mostly writes lines in similar increments until the end when the listing is run. However, this is a characteristic of many BASIC programs, not just for the BBC Micro, but as we continue to examine the code we can see the BBC version's qualities start to reveal themselves. One of the most obvious set of instructions we can read are located near the end of the program listing, where the start screen information is presented. The first part of this listing is as follows:

```
700 MODE 7:PRINT TAB(7);CHR$141;CHR$129;"GALACTIC INVADERS":PRINT
TAB(7);CHR$141;CHR$129;"GALACTIC INVADERS"
710 PRINT 'CHR$134;" This is a mixture of two well known"
720 PRINT CHR$134;"arcade games. The idea is to destroy"
730 PRINT CHR$134;"as many of the invaders as you can"
```
(*The Micro User* 1983, p. 104)

This, then, corresponds to the opening lines of the start screen when the whole listing is final typed in and run (see Figure 4.2). The 'PRINT' command displays the words on the screen along with the CHR$ command that in this instance embeds commands to change the colour of the text, or the display type.

As well as these commands, there are other ways that the code can be read to show how imagery is dealt with in the game. At line 30, VDU

> GALACTIC INVADERS
>
> This is a mixture of two well known
> arcade games. The idea is to destroy
> as many of the invaders as you can
> before you single proton base is
> obliterated. You move and fire faster
> than the invaders, but they have a
> kamikase ship to hit you with. Also on
> each of the following sheets there is
> less chance of killing an invader in a
> single shot
>
> You move using 'A' and 'S' for left
> and right and fire using 'RETURN'.
>
> You can only fire one shot at a time
> as your base must be recharged after
> each shot. you can fire again when the
> missile appears on the launcher of
> your ship.
>
> PRESS ANY KEY TO BEGIN YOUR DEFENCE

4.2: Start screen of *Galactic Invaders*

commands are stated, a unique function of BBC BASIC that allows for direct communication to the part of the system that dealt with the visual display. For example:

```
30 VDU 23,224,24,24,60,126,60,231,231,195,23,225,24,24,24,24,24,24,24,
24,23,226,219,60,90,126,165,60,102,204,23,227,90,60,90,255,36,60,102,5
1,23,228,41,0,136,18,8,34,16,133,23,229,16,68,16,2,72,0,33,8
```

Drawing out these commands, by translating the numbers presented to visuals, shows us how the characters within the game are defined and will be represented on screen. Before even running the game, we can see how the graphics will not be like those drawn within the magazine but are now becoming recognizable as arcade-type images that the title of the game originally hints at. The first part of the command VDU 23, 224 asks the video chip to redefine the character shape for character 224. Looking at the first eight numbers after the commands VDU 23, 224, we can see how they equate to the imagery found in Figure 4.3 by mapping the numbers to the equivalent make up of the byte on each line.

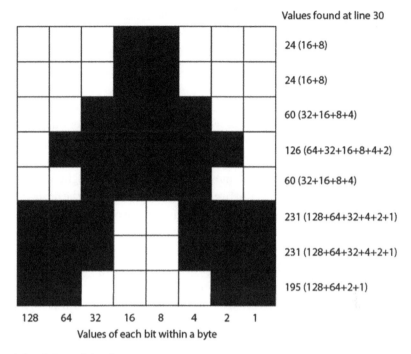

Values found at line 30

24 (16+8)

24 (16+8)

60 (32+16+8+4)

126 (64+32+16+8+4+2)

60 (32+16+8+4)

231 (128+64+32+4+2+1)

231 (128+64+32+4+2+1)

195 (128+64+2+1)

128   64   32   16   8   4   2   1
Values of each bit within a byte

4.3: Translating code into imagery

Similarly, line 61 reveals how the program will be presented in Mode 2, one of eight display modes possible on the BBC Micro, showing how the program will be presented within the limitations of 160 x 256 pixels allowing for eight colours. This choice of screen mode allows us to see how in this listing the role of the platform is shown through the code without it even being run. However, upon being run, the game shows these elements combined, how the listing images are unlike the playable graphics, and how the structure of the code comes together in order for the user to now have a playable game. Although not as detailed as *Space Invaders* in terms of the amount of characters on screen, the game play allows enough replayability for the player to continue enjoying the game not only from its basic arcade style mechanics but also seeing the results of their own typing.

As Montfort and Fernandez-Vara note in their discussion of ports,

ports, like translations, are certainly worthy of study as new works in and of themselves, but they can also be seen as editions of the game on which they are based. In the same way that a translation involves interpreting the original text and deciding what is essential to it to carry it over to the target language, ports involve making decisions about how to transfer the original program, from the user interface to the gameplay to the algorithms that determine the behaviour of game objects (Fernandez-Vara and Montfort, 2013, p.7).

It is in the act of running and playing the game that we can start to see the similarities or differences with games such as *Space Invaders* or *Galaxians*. Playing the game shows how the control commands have to be learnt in order to control the space ship at the bottom. In this version, A and S on the keyboard allow the player to move the spaceship left or right, with the Return key allowing the player to fire the spaceship to destroy the onslaught of aliens. By 'reading' the playable game in this way, we can see how there are fewer aliens on screen that in arcade versions of *Space Invaders* or *Galaxian*. Reading games, with reference to various forms of textual analysis has been examined in depth by scholars such as Carr (2009), Bizzocchi and Tanenbaum (2011) and Fernandez-Vara (2015). These approaches showcase how we can examine games through intertextual references (Carr, 2009) and close readings (Bizzocchi and Tanenbaum, 2011), as well as game genres, game mechanics, gameplay experiences, and historical analysis (Fernandez-Vara, 2015) amongst other approaches.

As such, the compiled program listing and resultant game and game play can be read in various ways. We can examine how *Galactic Invaders* runs slightly faster than either of the arcade versions, limiting play time and highscores for those unable to keep up. However, it is this same mechanism of speed, agility, and time that contributed to how the original arcade games function, and kept players inserting more coins to continue. In the absence of inserting coins, the end screen to *Galactic Invaders* states that, 'You have been destroyed by the Galactic Invaders', followed by listing your highscore and asking if you want 'Another Go?' at which the player can press the Y key to start their play cycle over again. Even with limited characters, colour schemes, and items such as turrets at the bottom of the screen missing from this version of the game, the likeness is enough that connections to previous arcade games are possible. Although such connections can be drawn from the program listing without typing it in, as the instructions and aims of the game can easily be read in their static form, it is not until we play the game that we are able to make these more definite links.

From these initial observations, it is now possible to use this same system of reading code, software, and playable game to discuss the *Cheese* listing for the ZX Spectrum.

The first part of the code that can be easily read is the REM comment of the listing, where the game title and platform are defined. Any comments written after the REM statement do not contribute to the running of the program itself, but are there to give the user notes about what particular parts of the code are. At line three of the listing the code reads:

```
3 REM CHEESE    ZX SPECTRUM
```

Here, we can see the basic facts that the game is called cheese and it is written for the ZX Spectrum. These hints at platform specificity continue by examining other REM comments, such as the one at line 285 that states,

```
285 REM S in lines 290 and 295 are the black squares you get by
pressing CAPS Shift 8 in graphics mode.
```

Here, the way the Spectrum user would type in a listing, differs in that they had to select the correct input 'mode' whilst typing in order for the correct character to be selected from the keys pressed. If they had simply typed 's' whilst not in this mode, the program would display a normal s on screen, rather than the defined graphic character they intended.

Upon running the game, we can see how the use of particular graphics characters are used to draw the cat and mouse characters on the screen. In the gameplay mode, they help the player recognize what they are controlling and what they are trying to overcome. Much like the *Galactic Invaders* game, the timing and speed of characters help to determine the gameplay, with the mouse moving more rapidly across the screen than the player is able to control the cat. The aim of the game is to capture the mouse by being in its path. Once captured, a short sound clip plays accompanying a rotation of the mouse on screen to show it was caught. The game continues as the play attempts to beat their previous high score, or ends if the mouse ends up removing all of the cheese on screen due to the player not capturing it in time. The core character images, as seen in the listing, are then repeated elsewhere in the game, such as at the end when the cat is used as a repeated pattern to give the player an end game animation (see Figure 4.4).

Being able to run the program on an emulated platform along with reading parts of the BASIC programming languages that are platform specific allows us to uncover other aspects of the listing that a packaged software product would not, i.e. instant access to its inner workings. It also shows us another example of an arcade game, one that is listed as such in the *World of Spectrum* archive (under 'Arcade: action in game genre'), and one that is

4.4: End part of *Cheese* game animation

different from the *Galactic Invaders* game with its more direct references to previous arcade games.

Conclusions: Re-Programming the Archive

As we try to preserve videogames, the discussion of code, artefact, platform, and so on raise questions as to what we are preserving, and how are we preserving it. Henry Lowood argues that, in the case of hypermedia works and computer games, 'these artefacts cannot be adequately interpreted without establishing contexts of design, creation, and technology, and for this we need documentation, texts, source code, artwork and so on' (Lowood, 2002, p. 12).

In the case of the magazine listing, it gives us as researchers, preservationists, and curators not only the documentation, source code, and some of the initial narrative linked to the game, but by emulating the code we can also start to see how the platform gives us some hints to the context of the game's design, creation, and associated technologies. Although some of these games could be found on cassette tapes that were sent away for or found on the front of magazines, it is by seeing the listing and typing it in that we can reveal another part of the archive not always found in the end software product.

However, bringing back the archive, and re-constructing the code into the playable form also allows for the performance of games that Lowood states as being an important part of preserving game content. Here, we can see that although the magazines themselves may fall into the category of what James Newman would term 'paratextual materials' (Newman, 2011, p. 109) of 1980s computer game culture, the listing within the magazine becomes a text in itself. Therefore, by re-programming and re-playing the game, we can start to create another text, open to further research, examination, and presentation.

As an extension of this work, we can see how emulating these experiences in the museum context, whether literally through emulation software, or on the original platforms themselves, allows for a model of engagement that links to the Strong Museum's triangular model of curation in terms of 'artefacts-interpretation-interactivity'. In an interview with Guins, as published in his book *Game After*, Dyson states how, 'most museums do two out of three [...] Our goal is to combine the three. Within this model and when doing an exhibit on video games, you need to have the games available. There is such a separation between the experience of playing the game and the game itself' (Guins, 2014, pp. 43–44). Subsequently, Guins connects the thoughts of Dyson to the work of Henry Lowood, who also acknowledges the distinctions between 'physical artefacts necessary for gameplay, the code underlying a game, and the "conceptual" object perceived by the player' (*Ibid.*, p. 44). However, these distinctions are discussed in reference to ready compiled games and not listings found in books or magazines. Therefore, further recognition is needed of practices that enable us to recreate games from listings, in order for them to be played and performed, recognizing Ernst's writings on the 'algorithmic dynamics' of the multimedia archive that becomes exposed in a multitude of forms. Whether this is through emulation or by using the original hardware, our ability to expose the archive in this way allows us to showcase further aspects of games culture, history, design, and play. Similarly, we can see how re-programming and re-playing the archive (in an act of re-winding to 1980s programming cultures) allows for audiences to engage with these principles of computer games through code, object, and interaction, drawing connections and possible conclusions between these elements. This is important not only for researchers, but also museums, exhibitors, and the public, especially in an age where computer literacy continues to dominate educational agendas and public policy (Livingstone and Hope, 2011).

Works Cited

Espen Aarseth, 'Computer Game Studies, Year One', *Game Studies*, 1,1 (2001), Accessed 3 June 2016, http://gamestudies.org/0101/editorial.html.

David M. Berry, *The Philosophy of Software: Code and Mediation in the Digital Age*. (New York: Palgrave Macmillan, 2011).

Jim Bizzocchi and Joshua Tanenbaum, 'Well Read: Applying Close Reading Techniques to Gameplay Experiences' in D.Davidson (ed.) *Well Played 3.0: Video Games, Value and Meaning*. (Pittsburgh: ETC Press, 2011), Accessed 3 June 2016, http://press.etc.cmu.edu/content/well-read-jim-bizzocchi-joshua-tanenbaum.

Martin Campbell-Kelly, *From Airline Reservations to Sonic the Hedgehog: A History of the Software Industry*. New Ed edition. (Cambridge, MA: MIT Press, 2004).

Diane Carr, 'Textual Analysis, Digital Games, Zombies'. In Proceedings of the 2009 International DiGRA Conference: *Breaking New Ground: Innovation in Games, Play, Practice and Theory*. (London: Brunel University, 2009).

Tristan Donovan, *Replay: The History of Video Games*. (Lewes: Yellow Ant, 2010).

Wolfgang Ernst, *Digital Memory and the Archive*. (Minneapolis, MN: University of Minnesota Press, 2013).

Clara Fernandez-Vara, *Introduction to Game Analysis*. (New York: Routledge, 2015).

Clara Fernandez-Vara and Nick Montfort, 'Videogame Editions for Play and Study.' TROPE-13-02. The Trope Tank. (Cambridge, MA: Massachusetts Institute of Technology, 2013).

Alexander R. Galloway, *Gaming: Essays on Algorithmic Culture*. (Minneapolis, MN: Minnesota Press, 2006).

Alison Gazzard, 'The Intertextual Arcade: Tracing Histories of Arcade Clones in 1980s Britain'. *Reconstruction* 14 (1), 2014, Accessed 3 June 2016, http://reconstruction.eserver.org/Issues/141/Gazzard.shtml.

Alison Gazzard, *Now the Chips Are Down: The BBC Micro*. (Cambridge, MA: MIT Press, 2016).

Leon Goodfriend, 'Cheese'. *Personal Computer Games*, March 1984, pp.146–147, 151.

Raiford Guins, *Game After: A Cultural History of Video Game Afterlife*. (Cambridge, MA: MIT Press, 2014).

Erkki Huhtamo and Jussi Parikka. 2011. 'Introduction: An Archaeology of Media Archaeology', in *Media Archaeology: Approaches, Applications, and Implications*, ed. by Erkki Huhtamo and Jussi Parikka (Berkeley, CA: University of California Press, 2011), pp.1–24.

Graeme Kirkpatrick, 'Constitutive Tensions of Gaming's Field: UK Gaming Magazines and the Formation of Gaming Culture 1981–1995'. *Game Studies* 12.1 (2012), Accessed 3 June 2016, http://gamestudies.org/1201/articles/kirkpatrick.

Thomas Lean, '"The Making of the Micro": Producers, Mediators, Users and the Development of Popular Microcomputing in Britain (1980–1989)'. PhD, (Manchester: University of Manchester, 2008).

Ian Livingstone and Alex Hope, *Next Gen*. (London: NESTA, 2011), Accessed 3 June 2016, http://www.nesta.org.uk/publications/next-gen.

Henry Lowood, 'Shall We Play a Game: Thoughts on the Computer Game Archive of the Future', Paper presented at BITS OF CULTURE: New Projects Linking the Preservation and Study of Interactive Media, Stanford University, 7 October 2002.

Lev Manovich, *The Language of New Media*. (Cambridge, MA: MIT Press, 2001).

Nick Montfort and Ian Bogost. *Racing the Beam: The Atari Video Computer System*. (Cambridge, MA: MIT Press, 2009).

James Newman, '(Not) Playing Games: Player-Produced Walkthrough as Archival Documents of Digital Gameplay'. *The International Journal of Digital Curation* 2.6 (2011), pp.109–27.

James Newman, *Best Before: Videogames, Supersession and Obsolescence*. (Abdingdon: Routledge, 2012).

Michael Nitsche, *Video Game Spaces*. (Cambridge, MA: MIT Press, 2008).

Jussi Parikka, *What Is Media Archaeology?* (Cambridge: Polity Press, 2012).

Melanie Swalwell. 'The Early Micro User: Games Writing, Hardware Hacking, and the Will to Mod', in *Proceedings of DiGRA Nordic 2012 Conference: Local and Global – Games in Culture and Society*. Tampere, Finland, (2012).

Alex Wiltshire, *Britsoft: An Oral History*. (London: Read-Only Memory, 2015)

Mike Wyatt, 'BeebEm – BBC Micro and Master 128 Emulator', Accessed 3 June 2016, http://www.mkw.me.uk/beebem/index.html.

'Galactic Invaders', *The Micro User*, September 1983. pp. 53, 102–103.

'Games People Play', *The Home Computer Course*, 1983, pp. 14–15.

About the author

Alison Gazzard is a Senior Lecturer in Digital Media Arts at the UCL Knowledge Lab, UCL Institute of Education, University College London. She has published widely on a range of ideas about game play, game design, interactive media technologies, and histories of games in journals such as *Game Studies, Convergence: The International Journal of Research into New Media Technologies* and *Games and Culture*. Her books include, *Mazes in Videogames: Meaning, Metaphor and Design* (McFarland, 2013), and *Now the Chips Are Down: The BBC Micro* (MIT Press, 2016 as part of the Platform Studies series).

Part 2

Media Archaeological Theory

5. Cinema, Motion, Energy, and Entropy

Thomas Elsaesser

Abstract

For nearly one hundred years, we have been discussing the cinema primarily from the perspective of photography, organizing our theories around iconic realism and the indexical-physical link to that which it represents: cinema as primarily an ocular dispositif, theorized either in terms of projection and transparency, or as a recording dispositif, to be understood in terms of imprint and trace. However, photography, as a photo-chemical process, involving the registration of light on a sensitive surface is an increasingly obsolete imaging technology, also for the cinema. What might be needed is a film history, conceived as a 'media archaeology', to enable a different future: one that includes thinking about cinema in terms of motion and energy, animation and agitation, agency and automatism.

Keywords: Media Archaeology, Cinema, Energy, Animation, Agency, Automatism

For nearly a century, we have been discussing cinema primarily from the perspective of photography. Organizing our questions and theories around iconic realism and the indexical-physical link that ties a photograph to that which it represents, we have debated cinema in terms of truth and illusion, image and representation, and we have considered cinema as a primarily ocular dispositif, theorized either in terms of projection and transparency or a recording dispositif, to be understood in terms of imprint and trace.

If the problem of a history of cinema is that it relies almost exclusively on photography as its founding genealogy, then what we might need is a different 'archaeology' to enable a different future: one that not only goes beyond the 'death of cinema', but also acknowledges the changing function of the moving image for our information society, our service industries, our memory cultures, and our 'creative industries' more generally.

Roberts, B. and M. Goodall (eds.), *New Media Archaeologies*, Amsterdam Universsity Press, 2019
DOI: 10.5117/9789462982161_CH05

A Different Media Archaeology of Cinema?

Until roughly the 1990s, the foundational genealogies of cinema would have been organized around the persistence of vision, photography, and the projection arts. From today's perspective, not only are these three lines of descent inaccurate and lacunary, perhaps more importantly, they are non-foundational and contingent.

To give one example from the so-called persistence of vision: the impression of movement in cinema is not based on a retinal afterimage, but on one of the many perceptual (rather than optical) illusions by which our brain tries to anticipate the future. When shown two images in quick succession, one of a dot on the left of a screen and one with the dot on the right (as on electronic noticeboards), the human brain sees motion from left to right, even though there was none. The human visual system apparently construes scenarios of continuity, reconciling jagged images by imputing motion. Because it takes the brain at least a tenth of a second to model visual information, it is working with old information to give meaning to new information. By modelling the future during movement, it is 'seeing' the present.

To give an example of contingency: the fact that we think of cinema as requiring projection has become a contingent fact ever since the arrival of television, and has become even more evident with the computer monitor, giant LED screens in open air spaces, and the tiny screens on mobile devices: in each case, we can still think of the experience as 'watching movies' without contradicting ourselves.

We can also see more clearly that several constituent factors we now consider integral to the media history of cinema have been left out or sidelined by highlighting merely projection, photography, and persistence of vision: think of the phonograph, the telegraph, telephony and wireless transmission, the photoelectric selenium cell and the cathode ray tube, but also Babbage's difference engine or Hollerith cards that take us from the mechanical looms and IBM calculating machines to the computer and digital images, just as the development of radar has given us monitors and touch screens – both of which now belong to the genealogy of the moving image, alongside the various projection devices and traditional cinema screens.

Although I have been involved in this kind of archaeological revisionism for several decades, looking at cinema from the perspective of 'energy' is a new departure for me, and thus what follows is a preliminary attempt to map an outline of such an approach. Given that watching movies is considered one of the less energy-consuming activities one can engage in, it is not at all evident how it connects with energy at all. Yet, what I try to sketch is a new archaeology of what was once referred to as 'living pictures', as opposed to moving pictures, thus hopefully also making a contribution to the ongoing discussion of what we mean precisely by 'living' and 'life' today. However, a disclaimer is in order:

- I will not be talking about films that 'represent' energy and sites of work. However, several of Harun Farocki's films and installations are devoted to precisely this topic.[1]
- I am not concerned with 'representations of', that is, with how a pre-existing physical reality is being processed, represented, or misrepresented by and through the medium of film. One of the reasons why this domain of cultural studies is not on the agenda is because the turn to energy as a topic is in some ways directly related to the origins of the paradigm of representation itself, which, if we follow Michel Foucault, began in the seventeenth century and, if we follow Bernhard Siegert in his monumental 'Passage of the Digital', is marked by the ascendancy of bookkeeping, bureaucracy, and mathematics during the first Age of Globalization, i.e. the time of the great sea empires of Spain, Portugal, Britain, and the Netherlands (Foucault, 1970; Siegert, 2003). To put it more positively: I am concerned with the inherent energy of moving images (and how they convert or transmit this energy), rather than with moving images as media of energy (and how they represent this energy).
- A more serious lacuna – because it touches on aspects that belong to my topic – is the absence of the following questions: first, how does contemporary mainstream cinema, whose images mostly have the movements of the human body as their norm, meet the challenge of visibility and visualization when more and more phenomena that govern our lives are not visible to the human eye, because they are either too big or too small, too fast or too slow, or deal in magnitudes and quantities we cannot comprehend other than in visual metaphors? This issue is, of course, intimately linked to what I have just called the 'crisis in representation', and I have tried to address some of these issues in my various essays on what I have called 'the mind-game film' (Elsaesser, 2009b).

---

1   Farocki contributed to this debate with films like *Workers Leaving the Factory*, his *Eye Machine* series, and his installation on brickmaking (*By Comparison*). The project *Labour in A Single Shot* assembled images of labour and sites of work from different countries and involving sixteen urban sites of production.

The other issue, only touched on briefly, is how to think the transition from mechanical energy and electricity to quantum physics and the cybernetic age, that is: how to think about the relation of energy to information? In what universe are they versions of each other? Perhaps we can only speak about energy in connection with moving images because energy as a topic in physics is now viewed primarily from the side of information. It makes an approach such as mine focused on its mechanical history already obsolete and nostalgic, but as so often: a new theory is also the funeral of a practice. Media archaeology, as I understand it, is intended to bridge this gap, by showing how each relates to the other self-referentially and retroactively.

Cinema and Energy: A Multiple Agenda

Given these caveats and disclaimers, my working definition of energy is very simple: 'Energy is the capacity of a physical system to perform work. Energy exists in several forms such as thermal, kinetic or mechanical energy, light, potential energy, electrical, etc'.[2] Evidently, when talking about cinema, we are only partly concerned with physical systems, although one could argue that the photographic process is based on a physical system where energy is put to work: the photographic image is an energy system in the sense that the image produced is the result of an optico-chemical reaction, where light interacts with a silver emulsion to perform 'work': in this case, to produce degrees of combustion in sensitive particles that register on a transparent surface.

But, as indicated, I do not want to rely solely on photography. Instead, I would like to concentrate more on other kinds of performativity of cinema, that is, on types of kinetic and thermodynamic energy, their constraints, their discharges, their transfers. In what ways can we consider, for instance, the 'system cinema' to be about the conservation of energy, the exchange of energy, its conversion, waste, and entropy, and with what other systems does cinema interact?[3] Before I go into these questions in more detail, let me offer a few remarks about cinema as a nineteenth-century invention, as part of the epoch when people were pre-occupied, indeed obsessed, with issues of energy.

---

2   This is the definition given at, among others, at http://physics.about.com/od/glossary/g/ energy.htm. Accessed 1 July 2016.
3   'Reibungsverlust' , i.e. loss of friction, is a term used by Alexander Kluge when speaking about cinema. See Eder and Kluge (1980).

Cinema arose surprisingly late in the nineteenth century, but at a time when energy capture, conversion, and convection were instrumental in bringing about the industrial revolution. Cinema, as it were, is located between two types of devices that successfully harnessed thermal energy and turned it into motion: the steam engine and the internal combustion engine. Cinema also emerged in close temporal proximity to the electrical motor and urban electrification. With the first type of machine, cinema shares the problem of how to contain and harness – and thus turn into 'work' – not the thermal energies of combustion or the kinetic energy of motion, but affect energy: the new bodily sensations, the optical data, and the acoustic stimuli that the cinematograph was able to capture. With the second source of energy, which exploits the conversion of magnetic fields into electricity and electric energy into mechanical energy, cinema shared the fact that mechanically generated movement could be converted into nervous or physiological energy, i.e. perceptions in the brain and sensations in the body of the spectators.

The fact that, within less than ten years of its existence, cinema became a predominantly storytelling medium might in this light be given a different kind of explanation: cinema's turn to sequential narrative can be seen as a way of harnessing the sensory stimuli and optical data into 'linear' forms of progression, articulation, and propulsion: the optical situations on the screen – together with sensory, affective, and motoric input by the spectator – are engaged in semantic 'work'. Narrative would be the name for this work, i.e. for the energy expended in organizing these situations and data streams into units of information that are discrete but continuous, sequentially storable but recallable, causally connected but associative.

In the second half of this chapter, I shall return to the cognitive and affective labour of which cinema is a crucial dispositif. Cinema – if one accepts serial photography as a precursor – emerged in part from the nineteenth-century preoccupation with how to represent motion; or rather, it was part of two complexes: how to represent (i.e. break down, analyse, and reconstitute) movement and motion, and also how to convert energy into motion via different forms of transmission and transduction, always in a tension between linearity and circularity. The linear strip of film, transported by different kinds of mechanisms and picked up by a circular reel, suggests all manner of analogies with other nineteenth-century transport and motion devices, for instance, the railway – an often invoked parallel with which it shares the framed view, but also the simultaneous experience of stasis and motion, real in one case, imaginary in the other, but exploited in countless film scenarios and movie attractions such as Hale's Tours and phantom rides.

Similarly, if we take a look at the cinematic apparatus (notably the film projector), we see a typical piece of nineteenth-century technology. In its very dispositif – made up of mechanisms that are reverse-engineered or adapted from the magic lantern, the sewing machine, and even the machine gun – the film projector (as indeed the cinematograph) is a bricolage assemblage of very different, but nonetheless distinct and related technologies. Apart from focusing light, they are concerned with transmission and transport, with conversion and interaction: grips and sprockets, eccentric discs like the Maltese cross, springs, and pick-up mechanisms. In its outer appearance and inner workings, the film projector has retained an identical shape and construction for more than 100 years, long after the technologies to which it owed its existence had been modified or altogether replaced. Cinema is thus not a purpose-built, fully designed, and engineered object, but a hybrid that has always relied on the interaction between several heterogeneous systems. Conceiving these interactions as energy exchanges may be unusual and even counterintuitive, but, as we shall see, they fit into an 'archaeology of movement' as I am proposing.

For instance, the basic definition of energy just given also stipulates that any form of energy can be transformed into another form. When energy is in a form other than thermal energy, it may be transformed with good or even perfect efficiency to any other type of energy (*the first law of thermodynamics*). Thermal energy, on the other hand, is also subject to *the second law of thermodynamics*, which implies that there are often limits to the efficiency of the conversion to other forms of energy, usually called 'entropy'.

Film needs energy to be made, which is transferred to the product. If we accept that, in order to come into being as an event and an experience, cinema requires the active cooperation of an audience, and if the spectators' total perceptual responses can be considered forms of energy transfer, then we can venture a further hypothesis, namely that the first law of thermodynamics applies to cinema. Energy, being the common denominator of any mass – prior, that is, to any distinction between the multiple manifestations of mass (electromagnetic, material, organic, inorganic, technical, and so on) – necessarily underpins the interaction of all systems. The cinema system would, in this perspective, not only be made up of the many different mechanical forms of mass (the apparatus), but also combine and pool physical and psychological energy, which interact with each other. The focus on cinema as networked energy, where an exchange between physical, technological, physiological, and neural forms of energy takes place, would thereby constitute something like a contemporary equivalent of 'nature'; it might even prepare a new definition of 'life' in the digital environment.

Movement: Analytic and Synthetic

A quick look at some of the origins of moving images reminds us that the second half of the nineteenth century saw the invention of all manner of devices, instruments, and types of measurement designed to capture, record, and adequately 'represent' not only movement and motion, but also other transitory sense data and sensory information. The two outstanding names in this endeavour were Eadweard Muybridge and Étienne-Jules Marey.

Their use of the photographic and cinematic apparatus was intended to record the different phases of movement. Almost as a by-product and afterthought, however, chronophotography also *produced a seemingly self-generated movement*: with the result that the cinematic apparatus is both an analytical (breaking down) and synthetic (reconstituting) instrument, both active and passive, both projective and receptive. This *dual nature* is crucial for the history of cinema: it can be (and has been) read as *either complementary, or contrary*.

Usually, Muybridge and Marey are named together, since they are credited with developing chronophotography into workable scientific instruments and useful tools for the measurement of moving phenomena. But if we look at their respective projects from an *ideological* point of view, it would seem that rather than belonging together, each falls on a different side of a divide that later opens up between America and Europe, between *optimizing* and *maximizing* the uses that can be made of studying motion. Marey's experiments would be in the 'European' tradition insofar as he set out to record, analyse, and classify by means of chronophotography the movement and exertion of energy in human bodies, animals, insects, and birds. By contrast, Muybridge belongs to the American tradition because, after the worldwide success of his book *Animal Locomotion*, he became a major proponent of using chronophotography for maximizing the transmission and transformation of specifically bodily energy, notably at the industrial workplace, synchronizing human and machine energy and thus becoming a pioneer of the time-and-motion studies that subsequently came to be identified with Taylorism (Hendricks, 1975).

What is striking about Marey is that his efforts were concentrated on ways of tracking, tracing, and recording movement of all kind and emanating from all living phenomena: he was as interested in the possibility of recording the shapes of smoke as he was in the movement of humans; as interested in the vibrations of bees' wings as he was in recording blood pressure, heartbeat, pulse, breath, or any other vitalist manifestations (Braun, 1992). His was an ideology of letting nature *self-write* herself by tracing its processes and emanations as closely as possible with technologies (e.g. the camera) that could also generate a symbolic code (a graph, a diagram, numbers, relations).

While not forgetting what he owed to Muybridge's *Animal Locomotion*, it is important to stress that Marey's use of different recording instruments such as the cinematograph, the oscillograph, x-rays, and other evolving technologies were aimed at phenomena that previously could not be recorded, stored, or imaged. In other words, he pursued and explored new forms of visualizing natural, sentient phenomena. In this respect, one might say that he continued the promise of photography, that of being 'the pencil of nature' (in W.H. Fox Talbot's poetic phrase), working without the intervention of human agency.[4] Thanks to the moving image in particular, apparently contingent phenomena could now be visualized, and hopefully this visualization would reveal hitherto undiscovered patterns, regularities, and 'laws'. For Marey, machine vision captured traces of movement and the inscription of time rather than an image and a representation as we normally understand it. Indeed, his work could be called the first natural history of the agency of matter and the body at the level of 'embodied mind' and 'distributive action' rather than individual volition and human consciousness.

Still/Moving

Regarding the analytic-deconstructive versus the synthetic-reconstitutive treatment of movement and motion, the first years of cinema reflected the complex picture of complementariness and contrariness: on the one hand, there is the conservation/containment of motion in single images, arrested to the point of stillness, while their re-activation through mechanical movement produces also a sudden, gradual, or violent release of energy. On the other hand, montage and special effects rely on the interplay of the analytical and the synthetic.

An example of the former would be the Lumière Brothers' first presentations of their cinematograph, which initially revolved around the energy activated by sudden motion. Although cinema's most essential feature and primary public attraction was that the images moved, the Lumières surprised their audiences by seemingly 'animating' photographic slides. In their shows, a 'living picture', a moment in time, fixed and preserved,

---

4   Marey seemed little concerned with the paradox that has preoccupied film theory ever since: how can such a non-human gaze as that of a camera convey so much affect, emotion, and embodied vision?

suddenly came to life, re-animated by mechanical action as if reviving the dead (Gunning, 1989).[5]

As an interplay of analysis and synthesis of movement, cinema soon became the site par excellence of kinetic energy: thermic-kinetic energy in its most centrifugal, explosive forms (energy as unleashed by nature in its most unbound forms: earthquakes, storms, waterfalls, as well as the *mise-en-scène* of the destruction of the planet now transferred to, stored, and released by moving images); kinetic energy in its technical forms (what would Hollywood movies be without explosions, destructive machinery of all kind, car chases, and smash-ups?); and kinetic energy in human forms (boxing fights were some of the first movies that convinced Thomas A. Edison that his kinetoscope had a commercial future). In short: action films, i.e. the staging and display of kinetic energy of all kinds, has been since the beginning and still is what most people consider and expect from cinema.

Cinema around 1900, especially the work of British film pioneers James Williamson and Cecil Hepworth, was imbued with kinetic energy effects, seemingly preoccupied with rendering visible these new kinds of motion and manifestations of energy, along with their often violent impact on the human body. Films with titles such as 'How it Feels to be Run Over', 'Explosion of a Motor Car', and 'Mary Jane's Mishap' are typical examples and tell their own story about the public's fears and anxieties sparked by these new forms of energy as well as the thrills derived from them.[6]

Five Types of Energy

More generally, one can speak of five types of energy manifesting itself in cinema: agitation, animation, agency of things, assemblages of automatisms, and attention as work.
- agitation (how movement, motion, and motivated sequence came into the image);
- animation (how we attribute to motion and sequence the quality of outer and inner life, project onto lines in movement an external body and an inner soul), i.e. energy exchange of the systems cinema-physiology (see reference to Walter Benjamin, below);

5   Tom Gunning, 'An Aesthetic of Astonishment: Early Film and the (In)credulous Spectator', *Art & Text* 34 (1989): 31-44.
6   On early cinema, see Charles Musser (1994) and Thomas Elsaesser (1990).

–   agency of things (and following on from this, how we distribute agency
    and intentionality in moving pictures while also making room for
    unconscious motivation), i.e. energy exchange of the cinema system
    and the psyche system (e.g. Freudian or psychoanalytic film theory);
–   automation (i.e. on the one hand, the energy exchange between the
    cinema system and the 'work/factory' system – think of Muybridge
    and the use of the cine-camera for time and motion studies – but
    also in a more philosophical sense if we think of the importance of
    cinema's automatism for the film theories of André Bazin and Stanley
    Cavell).

The fifth follows on from both Benjamin and Cavell and has special relevance
for our understanding of cinema today:
–   attention as work (monitoring and observation, listening and empathy,
    i.e. the kind of 'attention economy' for which cinema – and television
    soap opera – trains us. This would be attention considered as reaction to
    a stimulus or an interpellation, but also attention as a suspended state
    of work, paraphrasing it as 'waiting as working/working as waiting'.
    It may well be one of the strongest legacies of cinema, when we think
    about the shift from a cinematic episteme of voyeurism/disavowal to
    the contemporary episteme of surveillance and control.

Agitation: natural motion, as the manifestation of invisible forces (of
nature). Audiences had seen mechanical motion prior to the invention of
the cinematograph in their magic lantern shows (one of the most popular
slides was *The Swallower of Rats*), so that they were not that surprised by
seeing motion in human beings. However, accurately capturing the waves
lapping around a jetty seemed unfathomable and endlessly fascinating. For
instance, in Louis Lumière's *Boat Leaving Harbor* (1895) there is no action,
no narrative, no particular telos or motive, but you see the effects and
the energy of waves in motion: the tides. The 54-second film – a favourite
among audiences for years to come – is reminiscent of the Roman poet-
philosopher Lucretius, who in *De Rerum Natura* talks about nature not as
solid but in constant motion, not uniform but 'agitated'.[7] Interestingly, he
illustrates this agitation by two examples, both of which are relevant for
cinema. One is the example of the agitated sea seen from the shore, with a
hapless boat tossing and turning in the storm, accompanied by the guilty
pleasure derived from watching it all from a safe distance. The popularity

7   On Lucretius' *De Rerum Natura*, see also Stephen Greenblatt (2011).

and attraction of *Boat Leaving Harbor* might be incomprehensible to us today if we do not contextualize it within the nineteenth-century motion and energy discourse briefly outlined above or see it as an illustration of *De Rerum Natura*.

The second example of Lucretius' agitation are the motes or dust specs in a sunbeam when suddenly visible in an otherwise darkened room:

> Just look when sunbeams shine in a darkened room,
> you will see many tiny objects twisting and turning
> and moving here and there where the sunlight shows.
> It is as though there were an unending conflict
> With squadrons coming and going in ceaseless battle,
> Now forming groups, now scattering, of nothing lasting.

We can now recognize Lucretius as describing the effects of a *camera obscura* before the light shapes itself into an image as representation. Following his lead, what if we were to see the cinematic image not as solid picture, analogous to paint on canvas, but as precisely such a constantly agitated surface whose elements – specs of dust, which is what the silver grain particles also amount to – are in suspended animation or suspended agitation? From this photographic suspension, subsequent technologies of visible/invisible motion, such as the scanning light beam of the cathode ray tube of television and the pixels of the digital image, are once more 'liberating' the dust specs and particles, returning to them the kind of motion – Lucretius' ceaseless battle – that keeps them in an aggregate state of permanent potentiality. Think of the Danish painter Vilhelm Hammershoi's *Dust Motes Dancing in the Sunbeams,* or more recently, Anthony McCall's now immensely popular installation *Line Describing a Cone* (1972) as inspired by Lucretius' observations.

The other point of interest is that Lucretius recognized agitation as movement that moves and at the same time is moved, with the visible forces only part of the energy that is in play. The philosopher might have been describing Brownian motion and thus been one of the first to reflect on what we now call 'stochastic' motion, whose mathematics are as crucial for modern physics as they are for electronic movement, such as the instant relay of packets of information on the internet.

Animation: here, we can think of Georges Méliès' substitution tricks and metamorphoses (*The Magician*, 1898) or Emile Cohl's *Fantasmagorie* (1908). Dividing an action into discrete phases and depicting them successively was a technique known to the Egyptians as well as to Greek vase painters and

Leonardo da Vinci. Perhaps we can only speak of animation when there is a device to join these phases into a continuous movement (with a vase, the 'device' would have been human hands turning the vessel so that the eye could perceive movement). However, the effect of joining is such that, owing to the fundamental discontinuity of cinema (i.e. that a film strip is made up of individual frames), any succession or sequence not only affords the representation of continuous motion, but also allows the objects or persons represented to change shape and form in a seemingly fluid and apparently self-generated process. Energy, when manifest as motion, is constantly being transformed or mutates into another aggregate state. But animation applies to cinema also in the sense that its ability to represent movement endows the world it depicts with intentionality and volition: animation creates situations and contexts where cinema 'animates' things and has the capacity of spirit and breath, that is, of giving 'life'. It would be the point where 'animation' goes beyond representation and becomes a manifestation of 'agency'.

The names initially proposed for the motion picture device (e.g. cinematographe, theatrograph, animatograph, kinetoscope, bioscope) reflect its dual or triple nature: always between life (Greek: bios, zoon), vision (scopein) and writing (graphein): vision-writing-life. Motion and animation imply or presuppose energy and agency – whether attributed to humans, to vegetal and mineral life, whether to spiritual sources, natural resources, or mechanical processes. Animation also establishes a relationship between image and writing, materiality and sign, as well as between matter, energy, and information.

If these intuitions of the pioneers were correct, then cinema – in its widest sense, i.e. including its digital forms – ought to be seen not as an image system only but as a 'life system', once we accept the idea that cells, organisms, groups, corporations, nations, networks, and other assemblage-ensembles all process matter, energy, and information – an idea proposed, for instance, in James G. Miller's *Living Systems Theory* (1978) and not unfamiliar to Niklas Luhmann (1990) or Humberto Maturana (1974). However, the reverse is also true and explains one of the darker sides of this 'invention of the devil', as it was once also called. If cinema animates things to make them appear endowed with 'life', by the same token, human beings in cinema are closer to automatons: animated from the outside, manipulated by invisible hands. Humans become ghosts or 'ventriloquists of themselves', as Jacques Derrida once described himself, when interviewed, in a film tellingly called *Ghost Dance* (1984).

The Agency of Things

From its very beginnings, cinema wanted to demonstrate that motion is something that not only human beings are capable of, but things, too, maybe even especially things.[8]

The slapstick films of Buster Keaton, Max Linder, or Charles Chaplin, while emphasizing the mechanical side of the human body just mentioned, also play on the recalcitrance of things and the wilfulness of matter. Keaton's *It's Late* (from *Seven Chances*, 1925) is an example of the different aggregate states of matter in motion, as nature – trees, rocks, hills, ravines – and mankind – machines, fences, doors – both mimic and impede the human motor that is the Keaton character, in his headlong rush to meet a deadline: his own wedding.

Phrased more generally, one of the great philosophical challenges of cinema for film theorists from André Bazin to Jean-Luc Nancy is that it does not (have to) distinguish between the motion of humans and the motion of things. Cinema is indifferent to crucial ontological distinctions we normally make between animate and inanimate, the living and the dead, the visible and the invisible: as a consequence, cinema presupposes a notion of energy that combines the mechanical with the psychological, while also fusing motion with motivation. Such a 'cinematic' perspective might be said to inform, consciously or not, more general theories such as Bruno Latour's actor-network theory, where such non-human entities as things, institutions, sites, and places can have agency, especially in the performative mode. Likewise, if we follow Gilles Deleuze, cinema endows thoughts with motion.[9] Uncanny agency, on the other hand, is at the core of horror films, where the dead and the undead, zombies, vampires, ghosts, and apparitions all have agency, irrespective of their degree of materiality or mortality, because they embody what Freud called the 'death-drive': the very principle of life, when considered in terms of impersonal, biological energy, i.e. untrammelled by human volition, desire, or self-preservation.

Assemblages (of Man-Machine-Metropolis)

Although I began by excluding the representation of energy or work from my considerations, a reminder may still be relevant of how cinema, in its constructivist phase during the 1920s, was fascinated by the interaction

8   On the agency of things, see Bruno Latour (1996),
9   On the concept of energy in Gilles Deleuze, see Manuel DeLanda (1998).

between different social agents – human and non-human, abstract and material. The very principle of montage can be understood as an energy-transfer process in that sets of relations, layers, and networks are linked by virtue of their discontinuity, each element energizing the other through rupture and collision. While a more complex interplay of material and semiotic relations can be found in the films of Eisenstein and Vertov, it is Fritz Lang (*Metropolis*, 1927) and Walter Ruttmann (*Berlin – Symphony of a Big City*, 1927), who foreground the machinic, serial, and repetitive aspects of their metropolitan ensembles, where energy relays appear to make no distinction between 'man' and 'machine'. Examples of cinematic montage and motion and machine interaction and people can be found in:

– *Metropolis*' opening scenes: the pistons, the clock, the regimentation, the human assembly line, but then also the compensation and collusion: bodybuilding (care of the self) and dance/mating, until confronted with the social contrasts;

– *Berlin – Symphony of a Big City*: we see water (natural energy, agitation, tides), thrusting motion (train and pistons, wheels and tracks), machine parts interacting (the workers' mighty hand is shown in close up, illustrating the trade union slogan: 'alle Räder stehen still, wenn dein starker Arm es will'), automation (when a bottling plant for milk comes into view), the city itself as a machine, traversed and mobilized by different kinds of energy: a street brawl, erotic energy (man and woman eying each other across shop window), traffic flows and switching energy, bureaucratic machineries, administration, ledgers, communication: typewriters and telephones, etc.: Ruttmann's city symphony is most consistently readable not as free association and not even as musical form but as a machinic ensemble of energy transfer and energy conversion at different levels and in different degrees of density and intensity.

Energy Exchange: Physical, Physiological, Psychological?

One of the key questions our topic raises with regards to cinema is how one can connect these representations of physical energy depicted on the screen with the physiological energies set free by the screen. In other words, we need to distinguish between physical energy (transmitted to images, resulting in movement) and physiological energy (the human body/labour), as well as the transfer from physiology (body) to psychology (psyche). Among the names of those who have engaged with these modes of energy transfer and exchange are Hermann Helmholtz, Alfred North Whitehead, Henri Bergson, and Sigmund Freud.

As a preliminary deduction of what has been said so far, one might be tempted to posit for cinema something like the first law of thermodynamics: energy can be neither created, nor destroyed; it can only change forms. At the same time, if we think about one of the classic distinctions of cinema between 'documentary' and 'fiction', there is a case to be made to reformulate this divide, by saying that cinema, from a media-archaeological perspective, can be situated between energy as matter in motion and energy as vital force. The first form of energy would refer us to the physical side of the world, where cinema is able to organize matter as mass, potentially capable of releasing energy into motion. The second case, energy as a vital force, highlights the degree to which anything cinema presents seems animated by a force coming from within and without, pervading every phenomenon –be it human, animal, mineral, vegetable, or mechanical – with the breath of life, the vital spark that ignites the spirit and the imagination but can also transmit itself to the body and the senses.

The concept of energy that seems relevant in a consideration of cinema would have to take account of very different kinds of energy, all of which stand in a relation of exchange or transfer with each other. How 'integrated' are the circuits between physical modes of energy and physiological sources, between physiology and the psyche? Sigmund Freud, although no particular friend of cinema, did have, besides an archaeological model of layers and sediments, several energy models for the psyche: hydraulic (repression) but also electro-magnetic (cathexis, charge, condensation, discharge). While in film theory, his writings have been immensely influential for its narratological uses (e.g. the Oedipus complex) and for his emphasis on vision, when coupled with disavowal as a way of explaining sexual difference (castration anxiety, fetishism, voyeurism, the uncanny), there has yet to be a close examination of his energetic vocabulary, in the light of the extended agenda of finding models that allow for an energy transfer from body to mind, across the theoretical construction he called the psyche.[10]

Towards a Holistic Theory of Energy: Humans and Things

If one is looking for a more philosophical elaboration of a notion of energy that encompasses the physical as well as the physiological, matter as well as

---

10   On Freud's energy model of the psyche in relation to media, see Thomas Elsaesser (2009a).

the vital spirit, then next to Freud a closer look at Henry Bergson might be in order, but similar ideas can also be found in the later writings of Alfred North Whitehead.

Already in *The Concept of Nature* (1920), Whitehead had taken issue with the idea that nature can be understood as the sum of objects and their relations (conceived in terms of force and power). It is, however, in *Process and Reality* (1929), and *Nature and Life* (1934) that he outlines the notion of nature and matter as a set of 'events' that are in constant Heraclitean flux. In *Process and Reality* Whitehead specifies what he understands by 'event' in terms of 'quantum expressions of energy', while a few years later, in *Nature and Life*, he proposes that 'the deficiencies in our concept of physical nature should be supplied by its fusion with life' (Whitehead, 1934, p. 58) – in other words, Whitehead wants the physical concept of energy supplemented by the physiological concept of life.[11] Deeply influenced by the reformulations of the laws of physics by Einstein, Planck, and Heisenberg, Whitehead even suggests that the physical transformation of energy into quanta is related to 'its analogues in recent neurology', without however specifying on what basis these analogies might be valid or validated.

Whitehead's line of thinking might take us to the philosophy of one of the most influential thinkers on cinema in recent decades, Gilles Deleuze, who redefines it, precisely, around certain complex and philosophically sophisticated, if also highly contested, notions of energy, information, and life. In his two cinema books, *The Movement Image* and *The Time Image*, Deleuze proposes nothing less than abandoning the idea of cinema as a vision machine and to see it primarily as an aggregate of all possible modes of matter and forms of energy (1996a, 1996b). It is not my intention here to add to the already very voluminous literature on Deleuze and his concept of cinema as a type of thought and a form of life, except to acknowledge that the presuppositions I am exploring are similar to those that Manuel DeLanda (1998) has traced, even if I come to them via a different route.

Cinema and Entropy: The Human Motor and Fatigue

Initially inspired by Michel Foucault's (1972) *Archaeology of Knowledge* in my re-examination of early cinema, I am now taking my cue from another philosopher, i.e. Howard Caygill, when asking whether by not retaining a strict division between a physical definition of energy and a physiological

11   In this section and the following, I am indebted to Howard Caygill (2007).

one, first insisted upon by Helmholtz and generally maintained by all physicists, we might not be able to open up another, quite different line of inquiry, one that would highlight the much more ambiguous, perhaps even duplicitous, role that cinema has played in the twentieth century. This we need to confront and accommodate if, as indicated at the outset, one tries to rethink the fundamentals of cinema for the twenty-first century, but also if one wants to confront cinema's critics, of which there have been many, both on moral as well as philosophical and political grounds. Such a line of thinking starts by first making a distinction between energy as the capacity of a physical system to perform work, i.e. work in a thermodynamic sense and work as the labour power that human beings are able to perform within different systems of exchange. In a second move, one then has to make connections between the two kinds of energy.

It was Helmholtz, discoverer of the law of the conservation of energy, who promoted conservation of energy as the universal principle that applies equally to nature, machines, and humans. Helmholtz 'portrayed the movements of the planets, the forces of nature, the productive force of machines, and of course, human labour power as examples of the principle of conservation of energy' (Rabinbach, 1992, p. 3). All work was understood as the expenditure of energy, with a crucial consequence of redefining human labour as labour power, the expenditure of the energy of a body. Thus, a worker was redefined as a 'human motor', and it was life itself that came to be redefined as the capacity to perform work. Helmholtz bridged the gap between the physical and the physiological by more or less subsuming the physiological under the physical, whereas Whitehead, as indicated, was to do the opposite: infuse into the physical some of the associations that go with élan vital, with 'process' and 'life', as forces that cannot be reduced to the energy they exchange with other systems in the form of 'work'.

During the Industrial Revolution, the question of *how to harness, contain, transform, and transmit* the natural sources of energy into energy that is useful to human beings and can be turned into work – becoming the forces of production, as is the case under capitalism, which treats humans as resources – exercised the best of the scientists and engineers. But it also preoccupied many a philosophical mind, not least that of Karl Marx. As Anson Rabinbach has argued very persuasively, by the mid- and late nineteenth century, the 'possibilities and limits of conserving, deploying, and expanding physical energy into productive power had become the obsession of several generations of thinkers'. Studying a wide variety of literary sources and technical manuals, Rabinbach noted that a metaphor that rapidly gained prominence was that of the working body, both individually and collectively, as a 'motor': capable of transforming the diverse sources of energy to be found in nature – from food and carbon-based fuel to sunlight, wind, and water – into the productive work that make up the lifeblood of industrial society. The name for this version of pragmatic utilitarianism underpinning industrialization in the late nineteenth and early twentieth century is, of course, Taylorism.

Interestingly, Rabinbach in *The Human Motor: Energy, Fatigue, and the Origins of Modernity* takes up the distinction I already made with respect to Muybridge and Marey, between American profit-maximizing efficiency thinking and European forms of social engineering, when it comes to turning human energy into work, thereby also highlighting aspects about the way we have been thinking about cinema along a Europe-Hollywood divide. To quote Lev Manovich, who paraphrases Rabinbach:

> Taylorism [in the USA] aimed for maximum productivity, and had no concern for the exhaustion and deterioration of the human motor. In contrast, European scientists aimed for optimum productivity, and therefore were concerned not only with the rationalization of the workplace, but also with the workers' health, nutrition, safety, and the optimal length of a workday. In short, Taylorism had no reservations about replacing one exhausted human motor with another – the philosophy which in the U.S. seems to go hand in hand with the emerging ethics of the consumer society and with immigration policies which assured the constant supply of a cheap labour force. Europeans, on the other hand, were committed to caring for and servicing the human motor. The two paradigms converged after World War I, when European industrialists partly adopted the more brutal, but ultimately more effective Taylorist methods, while U.S. management experts became more sensitive to workers' physiology and psychology (Manovich, p. 5).

This passage allows me to extrapolate a further hypothesis about cinema's critical and, in many ways, paradoxical relation to movement and energy in general, and to chronophotography (especially its uses in time-and-motion studies) in particular. Cinema, from this perspective, must be seen as the direct result of three major socio-historical factors. First, cinema is unthinkable without urbanization, i.e. the large-scale migration of the workforce from the country into the cities. Second, cinema is unthinkable without electricity and electrification. And third, cinema is unthinkable without the new work-disciplinary regimes in the factory and in offices, which, besides piece work on the assembly line, created leisure time as a distinct category and then required this leisure time to be filled with mass forms of labour power regeneration, commonly called 'entertainment' but actually a very complex set of practices and processes that mimic (and reproduce) aspects of working life, while also compensating for (the stress of) working life.

Extending Foucault's thinking about social institutions, 'going to the cinema' would be a socially sanctioned activity precisely to the degree that it functions as a disciplinary *dispositif*. It 'disciplines through pleasure', that is, it invests with libido or laughter the hardships and humiliations of being a time slave and a workhorse. Put differently, one way of understanding the social uses of cinema is to grasp it as a discourse engaged in training the body and the senses in such a way that we experience as entertaining what our society requires from us as a necessity, in order for its particular form of energy transformation – in this case, capitalist production methods – to function.

One of the first thinkers to appreciate cinema within this complex of the body in motion, of capitalism as a mode of energy conversion, and the modern city as the site of 'disciplinary distraction' was, of course, Walter Benjamin. 'In a film', he wrote, 'perception in the form of shocks was established as a formal principle. That which determines the rhythm of production on a conveyer belt is the basis of the rhythm of reception in the film' (Benjamin, 1968, p. 175). While it is not clear which film(s) Benjamin has in mind (other than Chaplin's), he detects a mimetic doubling of the work-discipline in the emerging forms of mass entertainment. He is elaborating a delicately articulated theory of how the body's regimentation at the factory when reproduced on the screen, in the form of slapstick comedy, is both terrifying and deeply gratifying. By extension, Benjamin's model can also apply to a city symphony such as Ruttmann's, which seems to empower the working class (the close up of the worker's hand on the machine), while reinforcing its exploitation.

Yet, following Rabinbach and Caygill, we can perhaps clarify further the roots of this duality, i.e. that the intensified self-experience of the working classes also increases their self-exploitation by pointing once more to the potentially contradictory implications of the second law of thermodynamics: *the entropy of an isolated system never decreases, because isolated systems spontaneously evolve towards thermodynamic equilibrium, which is the state of maximum entropy.* Cinema, considered as a psychosocial system and tied into industrial society as its necessary environment, would invariably tend towards disorder, or rather: it would constitute an *unstable equilibrium*. It would be both disruptive and supportive of the environment within which it functions, posing a challenge to ideological critiques because too much (psychic, affective, kinetic) energy in the film experience remains unaccounted for. Even if one considers cinema as a self-regulating, regenerative relation of work to leisure, which the compensatory model posits, it has to draw its energy from somewhere outside. While in the context of social systems, we may prefer to think of disorder in terms of chaos theory and complexity rather than thermodynamics, once cinema is considered as an energy exchange system – physiologically, economically, and aesthetically – the language of entropy and maximum disorder may not be out of place.

Much of the above is speculative and may be valid only metaphorically. Yet, 'entropic' could also be another name for a type of cinema encountered in the digital age, when classical – linear – narratives compete with hybrid, open-ended, or stochastic narratives. Variously referred to as video game-enabled and multiple-choice narratives, as modular narratives and network narratives, as forking path stories or fractal narratives, as database or hyper-link narratives, as puzzle films or mind game films, examples like *Donnie Darko, Inland Empire, Through a Scanner Darkly,* and *Inception* stage the interchange between a dystopic social system and the psycho-pathological of the protagonist. While several of the names given to these films gesture in the direction of digital media, their very proliferation would indicate that the actual logic underlying them has not yet been fully understood, so that metaphoric analogies have to make do instead. What is notable, however, is that many of these films not only present correlations between deviant psychologies and 'worlds out of joint', but also play with the coordinates of time and space and suspend linear causality through repetition and recursiveness, retroaction and loops, as if to introduce a different physics into popular culture, for which cinema turns out to be an apt vehicle.

After what has been said about the function of linear narrative, namely that classical film narrative serves the ergonomically efficient processing of mechanically produced sensorial, affective, and motoric impulses and stimuli and thus constitutes a specific type of energy transfer (mitigating an otherwise inevitable sensory overload), it would seem that the forms of narrative that I provisionally call 'entropic' point towards the emergence of a new kind of equilibrium. This new *equilibrium of disorder* is perhaps best characterized by aligning it with 'positive feedback', which here signifies complex fields of reactive, interactive, and looped mechanism and effects. One of the most prominent – and for the future of cinema, especially notable – fields of positive feedback is surveillance. Put more positively, entropic narratives are aesthetic (i.e. sensory-cognitive) *responses* to the control societies and the security state, and thus are harbingers of a paradigm shift, with 'cinema as surveillance' representing the successor to two other paradigms: 'cinema as window on the world' (realist paradigm) and cinema as mirror of the self (modernist paradigm). But they also remind us that the moving image has always been a *tracking device* and a *monitoring tool* and thereby confirm that surveillance has always been one of the (not-so) hidden regimes of cinema, which an archaeological approach can help to *un*cover and *re*cover.

'Cinema as surveillance' functions more explicitly as monitor and self-monitor in today's control society, but it corresponds, across a gap of a hundred years, also quite closely to the Muybridge version of chronophotography as the analysis of time and motion for the purposes of testing and tracking, with 'animal locomotion' being the name for maximizing the efficiency and naturalizing the self-monitoring of the human body – except for one difference, namely that the observer is no longer under the illusion that he stands outside that which he observes, so that the cinema of surveillance is doubled by 'cinema as positive feedback loop'.

Once we bracket off Renaissance perspective, photography, and modernist media specificity from our genealogy of cinema, we can see that its invention and history have been implicated in the monitoring and the analysis of movement right from the start. According to the compensation theory, by breaking 'work' down into the component parts of time and motion and newly arranging or reconstituting it mechanically, cinema has helped productivity not only at the place of work – the factory or office – in the form of maximizing the amount of labour that could be extracted from the combined energy of worker and machine, but also at the sites of leisure and distraction, in the form of regenerating human labour power while at the same time training the body and disciplining the senses.

Workers Leaving the Factory: Cinema, the Disease of which it Pretends to be the Cure?

So far, so well known, but perhaps no longer quite sufficient. What I am proposing, by introducing entropic narratives, is to modify and extend the usual lessons drawn from Benjamin's shock theory of cinema. In particular, I want to add to it Rabinbach's analysis of the concept of (and concern with) fatigue: 'Central to the quest for the efficiency of the human motor was the struggle against fatigue, understood as the equivalent of entropy' (Rabinach, 1992, p. 8). In this struggle to eliminate fatigue, the utilization of leisure time became an important part of social engineering, which in most European countries, from around 1912 onwards, focused on the use (or abuse) that the working classes were making of the cinema, attracting armies of reformers and commentators. In this respect, one can view one of the very first films ever made, Workers Leaving the Factory (1895), as emblematic for a whole subsequent part not only of film history, but indeed as the site of one of the most crucial struggles of the twentieth century: that between the 'worker/factory' system and the 'cinema/entertainment' system. For what the Lumière film says, in effect, is 'as these workers are leaving the factory, the cinema (in which they see themselves) is already waiting for them'. This would be cinema's allegorical truth for the first half of the twentieth century: moving pictures envisaged as the necessary compensation for the rigors of the industrial labour process, but also as a machine for self-display and self-representation. In terms of the intermediate phases, one can point to the fact that, throughout the second half of the twentieth century, ever more workers are indeed leaving the factory for good, in the process of being replaced not just by robots, but by screens and monitors, of which the first screen was the retrospectively ambivalent antecedent. Conversely, the computer terminals can be seen as techno-mutants of the cinematograph, now firmly installed both at the workplace and inside the workers' homes.

Benjamin's argument on behalf of cinema now appears as a sophisticated counterargument to the concerns of the *Kino-Reformer*, seeing their panic motivated not by the needs of the working class, but by the requirement of the social engineers trying to optimize the smooth functioning of the human motor in the productive process. By claiming that cinema became socially relevant and historically significant because of the unconstrained 'free' time it buys for the spectator, Benjamin can make the case for its emancipatory potential. For it puts at the disposal of the masses a privilege hitherto reserved for the aristocratic class, namely *otium*, leisure, which is to say the privilege of ostentatiously 'wasting time' and thus expending energy without doing useful work. In the context of labour and working class existence, the need to waste time, on the other hand, is itself a function of our specific Western modernity. This modernity, via the factory's assembly line and railways' fixed timetable (i.e. the technologies of industrial production and the technologies of mass transport) has standardized, regimented, and synchronized time to a point where leisure becomes synonymous with simply escaping these time constraints of clocked and measured time. The social uses of cinema as a 'waste of time' and its technical origins in chronophotography (literally, the 'writing of time with light', but, in practice, the breaking down of the movements of bodies into segmented and measurable units of time) would therefore seem to stand in conceptual conflict and irresolvable tension to each other. Put even more sharply, cinema is based on a technology (chronophotography), whose social uses (in the workplace) function as the causes of a problem (alienation from one's own productive capacities in Marx's sense, fatigue of the body in Rabinbach's analysis), for which cinema's artistic uses (telling stories, providing views) appeared to be the solution. But, at the same, by being implicated in the dual process of taking away that which it gives, cinema is indeed in more ways than one the disease of which it promises to be the cure (to modify Karl Kraus' dictum about psychoanalysis). But perhaps it also works the other way around: might cinema be the cure that allows us to better understand the disease, i.e. the bodily regimes of energy expenditure; the relation of leisure to work; the obsession with sports, workouts, and bodily directed 'care of the self' as has become the norm in contemporary society?

If we posit a close relationship between the classical origins and conceptions of cinema and the specific regimes of the body in the social and industrial processes of energy conversion, then it follows that changes in these societal processes will also affect our view of cinema, or at least of those aspects and practices of distraction, time management, and sensory experience we habitually associate with cinema in its widest sense. Indeed, changes have de facto occurred in these societal processes of energy conversion, and they can be briefly listed, by way of a provisional conclusion.

From Energy to Information: Attention, Affective, and Perceptual Labour

Since the 1950s, and increasingly so in the last decades of the twentieth century, cognitive psychology has been displacing the dominant forms of behaviourism in psychology that concerned themselves with the human motor. What has caught the attention also in the social sciences are mental functions: perception, attention, problem solving, and social skills of affective comprehension, empathy, as well as individual memory, information retention, and general information processing.

These developments are widely considered one of the hallmarks of the transition from an industrial and manufacturing society to a post-industrial information and service society. But by way of a footnote, it is important to remember that the result is not that physical labour has been substituted by mental labour, even in our Western societies – it has not. What is significant is that the preoccupation of social scientists as well as intellectuals in the humanities has shifted to the measurement and rationalization of the movements of the mind and the emotions, rather than of the body and the muscles in the form of cognitive psychology, artificial intelligence, and the neurosciences. Whether this endeavour also splits into an 'American' version of output maximization and a more socially aware, holistic 'European' optimization of the movement of the mind and of bodies remains to be seen. Often, the issue does not even arise, as researchers are trying to extract 'useful' information from the ever-increasing magnitudes of measurable data, which today means *methods* derived from biology and genetics or validated by an MRI scan, and *uses* that can be monetized.

If we briefly recapitulate the typical form of energy conversion in cinema as it prevailed in the industrial phase, it would be in terms of the dynamic but uneven exchanges between work and leisure as just outlined, in which the latter has to compensate for the former, on the former's terms. To paraphrase Benjamin, cinema would be exploiting the mimetic impulse in order to establish a relay of compensatory regeneration, which also acts as a protective shield against the overload of sensory stimuli, generated by the technological environment or urban living. Referring himself to Benjamin and leaving behind the compensatory model but addressing the problem of protection against sensory overload, Manovich takes the argument into the information society, identifying two kinds of work, as they typify so-called post-industrial societies: a) perceptual shocks and overload as work, and b) work as waiting for something to happen:

> A radar operator waiting for a tiny dot to appear on the screen; a technician monitoring an automated plant, power station, or nuclear reactor, knowing that a software bug will eventually manifest itself – these are contemporary forms of work, where it is not a matter of exertion of the body, but an expenditure of attention. [...] With Taylor[ism], it was the question of the speed of muscular movements; now, it becomes the question of reaction time: the minimum time in milliseconds required for an operator to detect a signal, to identify it, to press a control. (Manovich, 2017, pp. 3, 10)

Manovich's argument is that to the extent that factory labour in the West is increasingly supplemented by work in the service and surveillance industries, the primary energy humans give to the system is time and attention. As part of this process, attention has become one of the most critical/crucial of energy (re)sources. It is within this attention economy that the different definitions of work redefine much more than work: if, according to Manovich, watching a screen is work, then this applies not only to the workplace but also to the home when we surf the web, monitor our incoming e-mails, update our Facebook page, upgrade our operating system, service our bank account online, or pay for water, gas, and electricity bills.

At one end of the spectrum, capitalism needs our attention time for consumption (which is why advertising pays for our free access to – portions of – the internet), and at the other end, attention time models our labour processes (whether supervising machines or servicing human beings). In this configuration, however, cinema and television (as 'leisure') would no longer be in a compensatory relationship to 'work', but would also stand for an extension of the workplace, which is to say that worker/factory, cinematic city/distracted subjectivity, office/consultancy, social system/pathological personality no longer form relationships of antagonistic co-option but are different modalities of the self-same process within which all images (even in feature films) consist of operational or technical images, i.e. images whose meaning lies in the action commands and self-monitoring controls they imply (euphemistically called 'interactivity'). Rather than inviting a dialogical exchange with the spectator or demanding a relation of alterity (as in avant-garde theories of cinema), the cinema of surveillance, of entropy, and of feedback loops more likely emulates the logic of the control societies, where previously Hollywood musicals or comedies had (in Benjamin's terms) mirrored and mimicked assembly line work.

In this context, then, *waiting, too, is work*. Earlier, I called waiting a suspended state of work, not only because in cinema suspense is the anticipation of an action or event, but because active waiting requires patience and receptivity, both of which are forms of harnessing and managing the energy of expectation and anticipation. The reverse, however, is possibly even more significant: in the service industries, in retail, and in the wellness business, *working means waiting*, but also in the many occupations where people have to be on standby, not just in such traditional standby jobs as the fire brigade or the police. Security guards, people manning monitors of surveillance cameras, vendors in luxury boutiques at airports – all of them spend most of their lives 'waiting, until something happens'. If, for Manovich, this applied above all to information processing as work (in the military or energy generation), we should not forget that empathy is work, listening to others is work: a whole range of states of body and mind that used to be seen as passive are now activities and classified (even if poorly remunerated) as 'work'. This reversibility of active and passive, of moving and being moved, of agitating and being agitated we have already noted, both in relation to movement, from Lucretius to the Lumière Brothers and from Deleuze's film philosophy to entropy in closed systems.

It suggests that a new hermeneutics – searching for clues, looking for patterns, scanning the image for unusual signs and objects – is now also an integral part of the attention economy, for which the aforementioned puzzle narratives and mind game films are meant to train us: as do, of course, computer games and the physiological interaction of attention, action, and reaction they require. The vision/voyeurism paradigm that underpinned so much of film theory until now has given way to the monitoring/surveillance paradigm, where we are 'watched' as we watch, even if no specific instance is indicated (the logic of the Panopticon, in other words). It extends across the whole spectrum, with the double bind of commercial television, namely that 'television does not deliver programmes to audiences, but audiences to advertisers', now extending to the Web, and advertisers extending to include the State. We, as spectators, are no longer in a mode of energy exchange but in an information feedback loop, where all activity on the side of the attention worker (whether spectator, user or service provider) necessarily feeds more affective and biographical information into the system, than s/he can draw in terms of attention, waiting, and interacting. Watching has become a zero-sum game, including watching movies …

Such a negative conclusion notwithstanding, I hope to have mapped the outlines of a media archaeology for cinema, which, based on the energy models I have been discussing, brings together the nineteenth century with the twenty-first century. It tries to make visible (and comprehensible) some of the networks that link the period of early cinema and pre-cinema to contemporary cinema and the post-cinema of the internet age. The former's typical kinds of attractions – now understood as moments and modes of *energy exchange* within a dynamic of the body and the senses – can now be aligned with the types of *information exchange* known as data mining and as the feedback loops of 'preferences', 'likes', and 'sharing'. In a kind of retroactive self-movement, such media archaeology could ensure that the history of cinema, far from consigning it and its pre-history to obsolescence, remains one of the indispensable conditions for understanding its present manifestations.

Works Cited

Walter Benjamin, 'The Work of Art in the Age of Mechanical Reproduction', in H. Arendt (ed.) *Illuminations* (New York: Harcourt, Brace & World, 1968).

Marta Braun, *Picturing Time: The Work of Étienne-Jules Marey (1830–1904)* (Chicago, IL: University of Chicago Press, 1992).

Howard Caygill, 'Life and Energy', *Theory, Culture & Society* 24 (6) (2007), pp. 19–27.

Manuel Delanda, 'Deleuze and the Genesis of Form', *Art Orbit* 1 (1998), pp. 1–6.

Gilles Deleuze, (1996a) *Das Bewegungs-Bild: Kino 1*. Frankfurt: Suhrkamp.

Gilles Deleuze, (1996b) *Das Bewegungs-Bild: Kino 2*. Frankfurt: Suhrkamp.

Klaus Eder & Alexander Kluge (eds.) *Ulmer Dramaturgien. Reibungsverluste.* (Munich: Hanser, 1980).

Thomas Elsaesser, *Early Cinema: Space, Frame, Narrative.* (London: British Film Institute, 1990).

Thomas Elsaesser, 'Freud as Media Theorist: Mystic Writing-Pads and the Matter of Memory', *Screen* 50 (1) (2009a), pp. 100–113.

Thomas Elsaesser, 'The Mind-Game Film', in W. Buckland (ed.) *Puzzle Films: Complex Storytelling in Contemporary Cinema.* (Malden, MA: Wiley-Blackwell, 2009b), pp. 13–41.

Michel Foucault, *Archaeology of Knowledge.* Trans. A. Sheridan. (London: Pantheon Books, 1972).

Michel Foucault, *The Order of Things: An Archaeology of the Human Sciences.* (New York: Pantheon Books, 1970).

Stephen Greenblatt, *The Swerve: How the World became Modern* (New York: Norton, 2011).

Tom Gunning, 'An Aesthetics of Astonishment: Early Film and the (In)credulous Spectator', *Art & Text* 34 (1989), pp. 31–44.

Gordon Hendricks, *Eadweard Muybridge: The Father of the Motion Picture.* (New York: Dover, 1975).

Bruno Latour, *Aramis, or Love of Technology.* (Cambridge, MA: Harvard University Press, 1996).

Niklas Luhmann, *Essays on Self-Reference.* (New York: Columbia University Press, 1990).

Lev Manovich, 'The Labour of Perception', 1995, Accessed 2 June 2017, http://manovich.net/content/04-projects/007-the-labour-of-perception/05_article_1995.pdf.

Ken McMullen, *Ghost Dance* (film) (1984). [online]. Available from: http://www.imdb.com/title/tt0085589/ (Accessed 10 July 2017).

James Grier Miller, *Living Systems.* (New York: MacGraw Hill, 1978).

Charles Musser, *The Emergence of Cinema: The American screen to 1907.* (Berkeley, CA: University of California Press, 1994).

Anson Rabinbach, *The Human Motor: Energy, Fatigue, and the Origins of Modernity.* (Berkeley, CA: University of California Press, 1992).

Bernhard Siegert, *Passage des Digitalen: Zeichenpraktiken der neuzeitlichen Wissenschaften 1500–1900.* (Berlin: Brinkmann & Bose, 2003).

F.G. Varela *et al.*, 'Autopoiesis: The Organization of Living Systems, Its Characterization and a Model', *Biosystems* 5 (4) (1974), pp. 187–196.

Alfred North Whitehead, *Nature and Life*. (Cambridge: Cambridge University Press, 1934).

Alfred North Whitehead, *Process and Reality: An Essay in Cosmology*. (Cambridge: Cambridge University Press, 1929).

Alfred North Whitehead, *The Concept of Nature*. (Cambridge: Cambridge University Press, 1920).

About the author

Thomas Elsaesser is Emeritus Professor in the Department of Media & Culture at the University of Amsterdam. From 2006 to 2012, he was Visiting Professor at Yale University, and now teaches part-time at Columbia University, New York. He has published widely on Film History, Film Theory, New Media and Installation Art. Among his most recent books are: *German Cinema Terror & Trauma: Cultural Memory since 1945* (Routledge, 2013), *Film Theory – An Introduction through the Senses* (Routledge, 2nd edition, 2015), *Film History as Media Archaeology - Tracking Digital Cinema* (Amsterdam University Press, 2016) and *European Cinema and Continental Philosophy - Film as Thought Experiment* (Bloomsbury, 2018). He is currently completing a book on European Cinema and Continental Thought (Bloomsbury, 2018).

6. Collector, Hoarder, Media Archaeologist

Walter Benjamin with Vivian Maier

Peter Buse

Abstract

In this chapter, I will take up the question of media archaeology as a mode of collecting, and the collection as a media archaeological object. I will ask whether media archaeology, in its materialist attitude, emancipates the object, as Ernst and Benjamin suggest, or whether it verges towards a mere connoisseurship in its fetishisation of outmoded processes and technologies. I will do this by examining the case of the recently rediscovered Chicago street photographer, Vivian Maier. I will interrogate the media archaelogical habits of Maier (a hoarder of newspapers as well as film, and many other objects), as well as those of the guardian of the largest part of her archive, John Maloof, whose own media archaeological passions are much in evidence in his film *Finding Vivian Maier* (2013).

Keywords: Collecting, Walter Benjamin, Vivian Maier, Hoarders

'I never counted actually. I don't have a full catalogue, but it's a few, some thousands of items. I think the sad part would be, you know, one day to have to sell it all in an auction because that would mean that all these pieces would travel in different ways and you would lose track of many of them. If you let these things pass by, there's a risk that they disappear from the history, if they are unique documents and things that tell this part of the story. So that's why I've been trying my best to [...] store these things and store them properly.'
Erkki Huhtamo, 2013[1]

'the person who collects is taking up the struggle against dispersion'
Walter Benjamin, *The Arcades Project*, 1999, p.211

---

1   'Artefacts of Media Archaeology: Inside Professor Erkki Huhtamo's Office'.

Roberts, B. and M. Goodall (eds.), *New Media Archaeologies*, Amsterdam Universsity Press, 2019
DOI: 10.5117/9789462982161_CH06

A Media Archaeologist in his Collection

Even before he properly starts *Illusions in Motion: Media Archaeology of the Moving Panorama and Related Spectacles*, Erkki Huhtamo gives the reader of his exemplary media-archaeological text some vital clues about the materials and modes of its composition. His acknowledgements pages contain the usual recognition of public archives and collections, but prior to that he gives thanks to numerous *private* collectors of visual-mechanical artefacts whose 'treasure troves', he says, 'I have excavated'. (Huhtamo, 2012, p.xiii) The metaphor stands out, but it is the matter that raises the bigger question about the identity of media archaeology as a practice. Is it simply the case that the media archaeologist's search for lost technical artefacts and 'lacunas in shared knowledge' (*Ibid.*, p.xviii) led him to obscure spots on paths far from conventional archives? Or is there something about the private treasure trove that is already media archaeological? Is the passion of the private collector, in contrast to the 'elite filter' (Belk, 1995, p. 153) of the museum, closer to the media archaeological spirit? Near the end of his acknowledgements, Huhtamo gives a special mention to David Hildebrand Wilson and his most singular Museum of Jurassic Technology in Los Angeles, implying that this eccentric assemblage performs the same sort of work that Huhtamo is seeking to carry out in his own scholarship.

As Jussi Parikka has pointed out, Huhtamo is himself a dedicated collector and regular curator of his own collection of media-objects. It is an activity in which he is not alone: many media archaeologists have 'an enthusiasm for objects, and [...] many are miniarchivists themselves, frequent visitors of flea markets, antiquariums, and old electronic shops'. (Parikka, 2013, p. 12) Huhtamo's own testimony to his collecting and its importance can be found on a UCLA YouTube channel in a video with the intimate-sounding title 'Artefacts of Media Archaeology: Inside Professor Erkki Huhtamo's Office'. Surrounded by shelves lined with proto-cinematic optical devices, the media archaeologist handles and demonstrates in turn a zoetrope, a mutoscope, a kinetoscope. This collection of technologies of the moving image has, above all, a pedagogical value, Huhtamo says. Students exposed to it will learn of alternate histories, and be able to question their relation to their own 'devices'. And yet, in spite of this optimistic orientation towards a future in which lost technical devices will be redeemed, there is a melancholic strain to Huhtamo's presentation. Even as he displays his objects, all stored together safely in one place, he cannot help but anticipate their dispersion: he imagines one day having to sell them at an auction, after which they would 'travel in different ways', separate and far from each other. In the very midst of the lovingly gathered objects, then, he issues a *memento mori* to the entire project, a warning note against the media-archaeological aspiration to uncover, recover, and classify the unique items that might one day make the collection complete ...

Antiquarian, Media Archaeologist

This chapter addresses the question of media archaeology as a mode of collecting, and the collection as a media-archaeological object. It asks whether media archaeology, in its materialist attitude, emancipates the object from a narrow textualist regime, as Wolfgang Ernst and Walter Benjamin suggest, or whether it verges towards a mere connoisseurship in its fetishization of outmoded processes and technologies. It will take as its main example the case of the recently discovered Chicago street photographer, Vivian Maier, who left behind her an enormous cache of negatives and rolls of undeveloped film, as well as storerooms packed with other objects, some of them media-technical, others not. Maier's example opens up the problem of the borderline between collecting and hoarding, just as the guardian of the largest part of her archive, John Maloof, presents a compelling instance of a media-archaeological tension between preservation and reanimation.

The first modern media archaeological statement on collecting begins not with cinematic memorabilia, but with books. Collecting, Benjamin admits at the end of 'Unpacking my Library' (1931) is a 'passion' that is 'behind the times'. Because of this, he says to his reader, he will not attempt to dispel 'your distrust of the collector type'. (Benjamin, 1969, p. 66) Benjamin was a collector himself, and he knew perfectly well that collectors are widely seen as acquisitive cranks or eccentric obsessives. It was against this background that the figure of the collector, along with the *flâneur*, became one of the major characters of *The Arcades Project*, a text that remains to the end ambivalent about collecting and collectors. On the one hand, the collector, by removing an object from circulation, breaks the spell of the commodity, but, on the other hand, through collecting things 'bestows on them only a connoisseur value, rather than use value'. (Benjamin, 1999, p. 9)

This ambivalence persists amongst the major theorists of media archaeology, some of whom, like Huhtamo, are enthusiasts, while others are distrustful, even while they accept the centrality of collecting to their field. So, for example, Siegfried Zielinski invokes positively a sixteenth-century model of collecting when he says that an 'anarchaeology of the media is a collection of curiosities':

By curiosities, I mean finds from the rich history of seeing, hearing, and combining using technical means: things in which something sparks or glitters – their bioluminescence. (Zielinski, 2006, p. 34)

Here, virtually undiluted, is an appropriation of the idea of the marvels or wonders that made up the *naturalia* and *artificialia* of Renaissance cabinets of curiosity. In fact, with the one word, 'bioluminescence', his technical discoveries become simultaneously *naturalia* and *artificialia*. Not only is Zielinski himself a scholarly collector of such technical wonders, but he collects such collectors, such as Giambattista della Porta and the Brothers Quay (first film: *Nocturna Artificialia*, 1979). And yet, in the foreword to the very same book, Timothy Druckery starkly warns against media archaeology descending into mere 'oddball paleontologies' and becoming a sort of 'connoisseurship, or worse, antiquarianism'. (Druckery, 2006, p. ix) It is only one small step, Druckery implies, from the media archaeologist detecting ruptures and discontinuities in media history to the basement filled with early model Ataris.

In one of the central texts of media archaeological theory, Ernst proposes a 'media-critical antiquarianism', suggesting that the apparently quaint and parochial pursuits of the antiquarian have many parallels with the work of media archaeology. This is because

Antiquarians have tried to bridge the gap [between physical presence and discursive absence of the past] by touching and tasting the immediate, material object. For antiquarians, history is not just text, but the materialist emancipation of the object from an exclusive subjection to textual analysis. Antiquarianism acknowledges the past as artefactual hardware. (Ernst, 2013, p. 43)

The antiquarian gives the physical object its due, and does not attempt immediately to reduce it to the discursive level of written history, and so provides a vital lesson to the media archaeologist, who needs to get the piece of hardware in his or her hands, and become 'an amateur engineer who opens, checks physically, tests, and experiments' with the thing. (Parikka, 2013, pp. 12–13). As Benjamin writes in *The Arcades Project*, 'Collectors are beings with tactile instincts' (Benjamin, 1999, p. 206). But Ernst also distances himself from the oddball connotations of collecting, preferring instead the metaphor and actuality of the archive. According to Ernst,

An archive is not an arbitrary quantity, not just any collection of things can be an archive. The archival regime of memory is [...] a rule-governed, administratively programmed operation of inclusions and exclusions. (Ernst, 2013, p. 129)

Like Druckery, Ernst wants to avoid the degrading of media archaeological work into 'a nostalgic collection of "dead media" of the past, assembled in a curiosity cabinet.' (*Ibid.*, p. 240) Less fascinated by curiosities than Zielinski, and more interested in the analytic value of rigorous storage regimes, Ernst also underestimates the 'rule-governed' nature of the serious collection, with its strict protocols for the admission of new items, and its carefully worked out logic of arrangement and display. It is also possible that he wants to distance himself from Benjamin, who finds in the collection some of the same critical values that Ernst discovers in the archive. The following section outlines in more detail some of the key theories of collectors and collecting in order to prepare the ground for a discussion of Vivian Maier's reputed hoarding of media objects.

Collectors and Collecting

The origins of the modern Western collection are usually traced to the mediaeval practice of collecting relics, which were stored in church treasuries. The singularity of these objects and their sacred value found secular equivalents in the Renaissance collector's appetite for rare objects, and in the sanctity of any collection's principles of organization. At the same time, the Renaissance collection also had a rational foundation. As Russell W. Belk explains, the cabinet of curiosity, or *Wunderkammer*, operated on the basis of a tension between two principles. On the one hand, it was driven by eclecticism, turning it into a storehouse of marvels and wonders, as its German name indicates. On the other hand, it served to order and classify, bringing such heterogeneous objects under the rule of positive knowledge. (Belk, 1995, p. 32) According to Patrick Mauriès, by the 1560s there was already a 'republic of collectors, who shared the single aim of pinning down the universe in order to obtain rapidly, easily and safely a true and unique understanding of the world'. (Mauriès, 2002, p. 23) The cabinet of curiosities, he goes on, 'was nothing more nor less than a sequence of containers holding within them yet more containers in diminishing order of size, in the ceaseless quest for the allusive essence of a particular realm of knowledge' (*Ibid.*, p. 35). Jean de Berry, the fourteenth-century collector of illuminated manuscripts and other artworks, is often taken to be a transitional figure, the first to collect objects for their own sake. (Belk, 1995, p. 28) Collecting reached its apotheosis in the Baroque period, with the Kunstkammer of Rudolf II and the cabinet of Athanasius Kircher, among others.

As both storage devices and modes of transmission, cabinets were clearly media forms. Indeed, Jay Bolter and Richard Grusin count cabinets of curiosity alongside illuminated manuscripts, Dutch painting, and modernist collage as instances of hypermediacy (Bolter and Grusin, 1999, p. 34); and Barbara Stafford has noted the parallels between the Wunderkammer and digital media. (Stafford, 1996, pp. 74–75) These parallels no doubt contribute to a revival of the cabinet, as well as the concept of curiosity, among artists in the digital age.[2] Between the first baroque period and the contemporary repurposing of the cabinet of curiosity in the second baroque of hypertext, collecting of course continued, but Enlightenment values ensured that the collector, as Benjamin noted, became a figure of suspicion or satire.

What, then, does a collection do? According to one standard thesis, a collection preserves or rescues things that would otherwise decay or disappear. This thesis paints the collector in a heroic light as one who redeems lost objects, saving them from oblivion, or as Mauriès puts it, 'the aim of any collection is to halt the passage of time, to freeze the ineluctable progress of life or history'. (Mauriès, 2002, p. 119) A more nuanced perspective emphasizes instead how the collected object is not preserved, but in fact *transformed,* first through removal from its original context, and second by being put into a new set of relations with other objects in a collection. All 'collected pieces […] are wrenched out of their own true contexts', notes Susan M. Pearce (1995, p. 24), and the collector's 'impulse', says Susan Stewart, is 'to remove objects from their contexts of origin and production and to replace those contexts with the context of the collection' (1984, p. 156). The collected corkscrew, removed from the kitchen, or bar, or restaurant, finds its place and meaning alongside other corkscrews (and also, why not, bottle openers?) in a series or sequence determined by relations between objects in the collection. We could debate whether or not the corkscrew has some original or true context, but one thing is certain: once in the collection, it will never again be used to open bottles. For this reason, Stewart claims, 'all collected objects are […] *objets de lux*, objects abstracted from use value and materiality within a magic cycle of self-referential exchange'. (*Ibid.*, p. 165)

In his essays and fragments on the subject, Benjamin came to the same conclusion as Pearce and Stewart, while adding a political turn to his analysis. In 'Unpacking my Library' he states that a collection sets up 'a

---

2   See, for example, *Curiosity: Art and the Pleasures of Knowing*, Turner Contemporary, Margate, 2013, and *Magnificent Obsessions: The Artist as Collector*, Barbican Art Gallery, 2015.

relationship to objects that does not emphasize their functional, utilitarian value – that is, their usefulness – but studies and loves them as the scene, the stage, of their fate'. (Benjamin, 1969, p. 60) In Convolute H of *The Arcades Project*, 'The Collector' (effectively a notebook on which 'Unpacking my Library' draws), he puts it like this:

> What is decisive in collecting is that the object is detached from all its original functions in order to enter into the closest conceivable relation to things of the same kind. This relation is the diametric opposite of any utility, and falls into the peculiar category of completeness. (Benjamin, 1999, p. 204)

Benjamin is writing within the context of a surging commodity culture, and a modernity in which the commodity, everywhere on display, takes centre stage in a phantasmagoric theatre of distraction and secular magic. The collector, who is, as we know, behind the times, not only divests the collected object of its utility, of its use-value, but, by removing it from the marketplace, drains it as well of its exchange-value. As modes of resistance to capitalism go, it is hardly the most deliberate or direct, but this does not prevent Benjamin from suggesting that in a collection 'We construct [...] an alarm clock that rouses the kitsch of the previous century to "assembly"' (*Ibid.*, p. 205). And here perhaps is where Benjamin, or at least Benjamin's collector, differs from the media archaeologist in Parikka's or Ernst's formulation. While the former takes the collected item out of circulation, emptying it of use-value, the media archaeologist wants to once again make use of the obsolete media-object, put it to the test, if not put it back in circulation.

Benjamin was not so naïve as to think that the items in a collection, emptied of one sort of exchange-value, could not be endowed with another, to be redeemed at auction or amongst traders in rare objects. The question of value, in fact, is never far away in the practice of collecting. Not only is any collection judged on the basis of the rarity of its constituent elements, but the collector's success depends on taste and discrimination, on an expertise that can distinguish the ordinary from the extraordinary. Equally, just as Ernst seeks to discriminate between what he takes to be the randomness of a collection, and the more orderly and rigorous structures of an archive, so theorists of collecting will generally attempt to separate the collector from someone who 'merely accumulates objects by failing to dispose of them', and who 'may also regard the objects as usable'. (Belk, 1995, p. 67) This person, or pathology, is the hoarder, who represents an absolute failure to differentiate, in contrast to the collector who brings selection, ordering, and arrangement to the world of things. However, as Pearce points out, the distinction between hoard and collection is not hard and fast, since the former is simply awaiting the right moment, or owner, to become the latter (Pearce, 1995, p. 21). What were the conditions that turned Andy Warhol's notoriously crammed apartment from hoard into famous collection if not his name combined with his death? In this case, it was the rarity of the owner, and not the rarity of the objects, that gave Warhol's accumulation of Americana its precise value.

A collection's value is determined by rarity, but among modern collectors there is the added complication that many, even most, collected items, are mass-produced, as was the case with Warhol's cookie jars and other ephemera. Benjamin captures this complication in the briefest of notes in *The Arcades Project*: 'Fundamentally, a very odd fact – that collectors' items were produced industrially' (Benjamin, 1999, p. 206). In such circumstances, it is still possible for the collector to acquire cultural capital and display connoisseurship, as John Davis has shown in relation to vinylphiles, and Kate Egan in relation to the collectors of video nasties. Both of these collector-types pride themselves on their specialist knowledge and can be seen as proto-media archaeologists in their fondness for supposedly 'dead media'. Mass production also ushered in the era of the 'collectible', whereby the parameters of any collection are established in advance by the manufacturer, who determines for the collector exactly what constitutes the 'set' and when it is complete. It is such developments that lead Belk to differentiate between the 'taxonomic' collector and the 'aesthetic' collector. Where the first might accumulate baseball cards or Panini stickers according to strictly defined boundaries, the second shows greater autonomy in choice of object and limits of the collection.

Is it any wonder that psychoanalysts, when they have addressed this issue, have concluded almost uniformly that collecting is a manifestation of the anal drive? Karl Abraham (1927, p. 67), Ernest Jones (1950, p. 430) and Otto Fenichel (1945, p. 383) have all had their say on the matter, but it is Jacques Lacan, intervening later on, who brings the question of the collector's passion back to the question of media, since he emphasizes collecting as a matter of *storage*. In his *Seminar VI: Desire and its Interpretation*, Lacan cites a scene in Renoir's *La Règle du jeu* (1939) in which the Marquis unveils the crowning piece in his collection of mechanical toys. For Lacan, the collector's passion is highly ambivalent, marked by pride, but also by shame at his proximity, as well as his audience's, to his obscure object of desire. (Lacan, 2013, p. 109) As Mauriès says, a collection is 'a sequence of containers holding within them yet more containers', and it is this aspect that Lacan focuses on in his seminar the following year, *The Ethics of Psychoanalysis*. There, he tells a story of his friend the poet Jacques Prévert, who collected matchboxes during the war, and with them created a snaking sculpture that threaded its way around his walls, each matchbox containing the emptiness of the previous one by pulling out its little drawer slightly to accommodate the next (Lacan, 1992, pp. 113–114). The emptiness of the boxes is critical – not only do they no longer fulfil their destiny to hold matches, but their vacancy allows them to store something entirely different. Lacan is not yet using this vocabulary in 1959–60, but we could say that the collected matchbox contains in its very emptiness the lost object, the *objet a*. Here is the treasure trove of every collection that a collector aims at, if only not to reach it. And here perhaps is why no institutional collection can match the purity of a private one. As Benjamin says, 'the phenomenon of collecting loses its meaning as it loses its personal owner. Even though public collections may be less objectionable socially and more useful academically than private collections, the objects get their due only in the latter' (Benjamin, 1969, p. 67). If so many private collections are of objects that themselves once stored things, perhaps it is because the concept of storage is precisely what they are storing: for Huhtamo, after all, the main purpose of his media-archaeological collection is to 'store these things and store them properly' ('Artefacts of Media Archaeology: Inside Professor Erkki Huhtamo's Office').

Vivian Maier's Storage Lockers

'The internet is no archive indeed, but rather a collection', writes Ernst. An archive, he goes on, 'is a given, well-defined lot; the Internet, on the contrary, is a collection not just of unforeseen texts, but of sound and images as well, an an archive of sensory data' (Ernst, 2013, pp. 138–139) It matters not so much that for Ernst the collection is always the slightly unruly and disorganized cousin of the archive, but that the internet brings the collection urgently back into sight as a critical media concept. Beyond the platitude that Web 2.0 makes everyone a curator, there is the fact that, on the web, the work of collecting, of pulling things from one context and juxtaposing them with others in a new arrangement is always and already at work, for, as Zielinski says, 'In the Internet, all earlier media exist side by side.' (Zielinski, 2006, p. 31) This is certainly true of the street photographer Vivian Maier, whose life and photographic work was entirely pre-digital, but whose current existence would not have been possible without the storing and collecting affordances of the internet.

Ever since her story first came to light around 2009, Vivian Maier – 'an extreme instance of posthumous discovery' – has been treated as a curiosity (Dyer, 2011, p. 8). Jim Dempsey, the first interviewee in Jill Nicholls's BBC documentary *Vivian Maier: Who Took Nanny's Pictures?* (2013), sets the tone, calling her 'an odd bird'. Every film, book, or newspaper article about Maier emphasizes the incongruity of her profession – as a nanny to wealthy families in Chicago – and her passion: taking photographs, thousands and thousands of them from the 1950s to the 1990s. To this incongruity is usually added the oddity that so many of Maier's photographs were never printed, or even developed, although Maier safely kept the rolls of undeveloped negatives. Around these basic facts is then woven a tale of a mysterious woman who spoke with a peculiar accent, went by many different names, erased or fabricated elements of her own past, and took great risks in wandering bad neighbourhoods of Chicago and New York, Rolleiflex hanging from her neck. A Mary Poppins with a camera to some of her former child charges, she was a cruel and unpredictable figure to others. This, at least, is the story told by Maloof and other dealers in her pictures who have a strong investment in Maier as one-off, as *naturalia*, or odd bird.[3] Alternately, as the scholar Pamela Bannos claims, it is not particularly remarkable that Maier was a nanny, since the profession ran in her family. And the profession itself was entirely quotidian in mid-century America, which is not to say that her photographs are not a valuable record of this world of domestic work.[4]

An inheritance in the late 1950s appears to have allowed Maier to go on an extensive trip round Europe and Asia, a trip on which she took many photographs, but most of her pictures were from the places she worked and lived in the United States, especially Chicago. Many of her photographs featured the children in her care, and she thoroughly recorded the middle-class milieu of the families in which she acted as a nanny. She also took numerous highly self-conscious self-portraits, using her own shadow in much of her composition. However, what has attracted the most attention since her discovery has been the candid photography of people in the streets of Chicago. Often taken from three to four feet distance, sometimes with the subject's apparent acquiescence, but generally fleetingly, these mainly black-and-white photographs have established Maier's reputation some thirty to fifty years after they were taken. The narrator of Nicholls' film, Alan Yentob, says that Maier was doing street photography before

---

3   See Kevin Coffee, 2014, p. 99, for a critique of the 'contrived narrative' of Maier's life put about by the marketers of her prints.

4   Bannos is interviewed in Nicholls, *Vivian Maier: Who Took Nanny's Pictures?*

the term was really invented, and one of the great proponents of the form, Joel Meyerowitz, is called upon in both Nicholls' film and in Maloof and Charlie Siskel's *Finding Vivian Maier* (2014) to praise Maier's achievements as a street photographer.

Meyerowitz makes much of the risks of street photography, of the inevitable intrusion into a subject's space that is required to effect a successful street photo. He speculates about the great courage, the *sang froid* that Maier must have possessed to get so close, so frequently, to the people that she photographed in the streets of Chicago. Some of those streets were affluent and her subjects were as well, but much of the time she was drawn to derelicts, oddballs, and men who were down and out, an unseen underside of urban America. In *Finding Vivian Maier*, Mary Ellen Mark compares her to Diane Arbus, and similarities have also been noted with the photography of Robert Frank (Sekula cited in Cahan and Williams, 2012, pp. 40–41) and Weegee (Meyers, 2012). Working their way backwards to reconstruct the scene of these photos, Meyerowitz and many others seize on the specific camera that Maier used most of her photographing life, the Rolleiflex. In most other amateur and professional cameras of the era, the viewfinder pointed in the same direction as the camera lens, so a photographer would conspicuously hold a camera up to his or her eye when focusing and taking a photo. With the rectangular box of the Rolleiflex, the viewfinder is perpendicular to the lens. This means that the photographer usually holds the camera at waist height and looks down into the viewfinder to prepare a shot.

The Rolleiflex, then, has a distinct set of 'affordances', and even if they do not use this term from technology studies, commentators like Meyerowitz draw on the concept to understand how Maier came to take the pictures she did. There appear to be two major consequences from Maier's choice of camera. First, her street portraits of people who are standing are almost always taken from a low angle, because Maier has shot them with the camera at her midriff. As a result, the figures tend to have a looming presence – an effect of low angle shots – and rarely look into the viewfinder, their gaze straying instead above it, and so giving them a detachment, a separation, from the photo (for reasons of proportion, Maier's images of children tend to be an exception to this rule). Secondly, with the Rolleiflex Maier could be relatively unobtrusive in situations where she was photographing strangers who might not want their photograph to be taken, because she did not need to hold the camera up to her eye to take a picture. Meyerowitz calls it 'a great disguise camera' in *Finding Vivian Maier*. Many of her subjects may not even have realized that she was taking their picture. So, any understanding of

Maier's photography inevitably involves a little basic media archaeological detective work, which is why the narrators of the films on Maier, or their expert interviewees, make sure to get their hands on a Rolleiflex, and demonstrate its quirks and workings.[5]

Entirely unknown until just before the photographer's death, Maier's work is a major media archaeological find. Its first discovery in 2007 was down to the laws governing long-term self-storage facilities in the United States. Maier, described by more than one person as a 'pack-rat' who 'couldn't bear to throw anything away', when retired as a nanny, stowed in storage lockers the belongings she could no longer carry with her from employment to employment (Matthews, 2015, pp. 38-39). It was in these lockers that Maier kept tens of thousands of negatives, thousands of rolls of undeveloped films, a much smaller number of prints, and multiple miscellaneous other articles, including sound recordings and 8mm and 16mm films. A medium-sized storage unit (10' x 10' x 8' with capacity of 800 cubic feet) in Chicago in 2016 cost between $70 to $150 dollars a month, so it was no small investment on Maier's part, since she had several of them (see 'Cubesmart', n.d.). Maier kept up her payments on her various storage lockers until she was quite elderly, but in 2007 fell behind, and so the contents of her lockers were put up for auction. The website for CubeSmart in Illinois explains slightly euphemistically how the system works:

> Self storage auctions are common in the storage industry and are typically open to the general public. A storage unit auction can be a great way to locate antiques and other unique items of interest for just a fraction of their cost. Storage auctions are held only as needed, which can make it difficult to find one in advance. CubeSmart will provide as much advanced notice as possible of storage unit auctions across all facilities throughout the country so you can find auctions in your area as they occur.

Owners of self-storage locker firms hold a 'lien' on the contents of lockers, which means that they can auction them off to recoup unpaid rent once they have given the owners of the contents sufficient warning and have widely advertised the auction. Maier was in hospital at the time of the 2007 auction, and so was unlikely even to have received the notices from the storage companies.

---

5   Kevin Coffee adds that the twin-lens format of the Rollei 'imposes the tripartite discipline of square frame, fixed focal length, and parallax effect on the viewing screen, all of which she mastered' (Coffee, 2014, p. 93).

In *Vivian Maier: Who Took Nanny's Pictures?*, it is noted that Maier regularly visited Chicago flea markets and photographed the modern-day rag pickers who frequented those sites, as buyers and sellers. The film then remarks that it was these same frequenters of flea markets who were responsible for the discovery of Maier's work. In *Finding Vivian Maier*, Maloof confirms that his youth was spent trawling such venues with his brother and father and learning to detect the valuable items concealed amongst the trash, and that auctions of storage lockers are another regular stop on the itinerary of those who bring the collector's eye to what for most are mere accumulations of stuff. It was into this subterranean economy that Maier's possessions entered when her storage lockers began to be auctioned, and then once auctioned, to be sold on again to connoisseurs of old photos, with Maloof tracking down the lion's share. Drawing on a familiar language, Yentob almost inevitably refers to the contents of the lockers as a 'treasure trove', but the trove was not immediately recognized as such. Initial postings of images on the internet by Ron Slattery, who held a smaller number of Maier's prints, did not generate much interest, and the images did not attract wider attention until Maloof posted some of his collection on a photo-blog via Flickr and received the advice and support of photo-critic Allan Sekula.[6]

The storage capacities of the internet are so immense that the treasure in the trove can become increasingly elusive; a problem that search engines purport to solve.[7] Maier's story depended in the first instance on these digital storage capacities to reach a wider audience, but the virtual dissemination of her work can also be seen through a reverse optic: might it not be the case that her story attracts attention precisely because the question of storage in the digital age has become so ubiquitous, and her modes of storage throw digital storage into sharp relief? It is certainly the case that many of the interviewees in *Finding Vivian Maier* dwell at length on the question of the storage of 'Vivian's stuff'. Former employers explain that her boxes filled a third of their garage, or half their veranda, that Maier came, literally, with a lot of baggage. This emphasis may, of course, be partly the work of the film's editors: Maloof emphasizes how 'she had stuff, wedged and hidden, in everything she had', and frequent shots of Maier's battered suitcases, hatboxes, and chests are inserted into the narrative.

6   This is reported in *Vivian Maier: Who Took Nanny's Pictures?* Bannos has subsequently published a book-length study of Maier, *Vivian Maier: A Photographer's Life and Afterlife*.
7   For a comparison between search engine protocols and the methods of Renaissance antiquarianism, see Preston, 2000, p. 170.

When storage increasingly becomes miniaturized, when the 1.44MB 3½ inch floppy disk has been displaced by the 8GB USB stick, storage methods that hungrily take up space, that have a stubborn physical presence, hold all the fascination of historical difference and disjuncture. The success of American reality television programmes such as *Storage Wars* (2010–) and *Auction Hunters* (2010–2015), suggests a wider appetite for manufactured drama about such spaces, for what we might call anachronic spectacle, so far as storage systems go. It was surely programmes like these that made the discovery of Maier's cache immediately intelligible, and the films about Maier fit comfortably within this popular genre, even if they have more highbrow ambitions. It would be too easy to reduce the appeal of such shows to the promise they offer of quick financial return from no real labour, although that clearly plays its part. The focus of both TV programmes and Maier films alike is on unearthing valuable artefacts of the past that are concealed among the belongings of ordinary people, and so it is no exaggeration to characterize them as a kind of populist media archaeology. 'Archaeology', Ernst says, 'refers to what is actually there: what has remained from the past in the present like archaeological layers, operatively embedded in technologies […] material objects that undo historical distance simply by being present' (Ernst, 2011, p. 241). Both the storage lockers and their contents are artefactual from this perspective.

We might also note in this context David Edgerton's warning words about the innovation-centrism of most histories of technology, that too often give priority to technological novelty. 'Technology-in-use', Edgerton argues, is a much better way of understanding the overlapping of old technology with new, the continued presence of old technology in daily life; and technology studies, he suggests, should pay attention to mundane matters such as maintenance as much as invention (Edgerton, 2006, pp. ix–xviii).[8] At a very practical level, the circulation of Vivian Maier's photography online and in books and films depended on technical equipment and skills that are fast approaching obsolescence: the chemical development of negative-based film. With approximately 150,000 of Maier's negatives in existence, not to mention the 2,700 rolls of previously undeveloped black-and-white and colour film, the old medium of film remained very much 'in-use'. The added complication, of course, is that the retro vogue for analogue film means that chemically based photography is paradoxically once again 'new' media.[9]

---

8   See also Edgerton, 2010.
9   For a discussion of this phenomenon see Buse, 2016, pp. 214–221.

The Thrilling Hoard

Early on in *Finding Vivian Maier*, Maloof enters an empty room, installs a camera in the ceiling, and proceeds to drag out boxes of Maier's belongings, which he arranges carefully on the floor below. The process is repeated throughout the first half of the film, with Maloof neatly displaying 'the stuff that she collected': bus tickets, train cards, buttons and badges, hats, uncashed income tax cheques, receipts, audio tapes, and, of course, film negatives. 'She was obsessed with saving bits of memories, of moments in time', reflects Maloof, who brings order and some of the collector's penchant for display to decades of accumulated possessions. Was Vivian Maier a collector? Or is it only Maloof and other curators who bring that level of arrangement to her work?

Most of those who encountered Maier's habits called her a hoarder. One of her employers, Linda Matthews, reports that Maier returned from daily excursions with miscellaneous objects – 'broken umbrellas, strangely shaped bits of wood or metal, old toys' – perched on a child's stroller (Matthews, 2015, pp. 38-39). In *Finding Vivian Maier*, Matthews quotes Maier saying of her alleyway finds, 'Is this art, is this not art? What is this? Oh, this could be useful, this could come in handy some time.' Most remarked upon was her hoarding of a specific media form: the *New York Times* and other newspapers. Among the material in Maier's storage lockers were albums of cuttings from these newspapers, but she also amassed complete issues. In her rooms at more than one employer, she had newspapers stacked from floor to ceiling, leaving only a tiny space to walk through to reach bed and desk, the weight of the papers leaving a permanent dent in the floor. In Matthews's house, the newspaper hoard spilled over into hallway and basement. In addition, among Maier's photographs are many of newspaper headlines, newspapers in garbage cans, children holding up newspapers.

In *The Hoarders: Material Deviance in Modern American Culture*, Scott Herring usefully explains that the compulsive saving and storing of newspapers is one of the most typical manifestations of Diogenes syndrome (Herring, 2014, p. 117). Masses and masses of newspapers were found in 1947 in the Harlem mansion of the Collyer Brothers, two of the most notorious twentieth-century hoarders. Herring is sceptical about Diogenes syndrome and all the other pseudo-medical concepts that have been devised to diagnose hoarding along pathological lines. Instead, he situates the discourse on hoarding in relation to practices such as hygiene reform and scientific housekeeping, but especially mid-century collectibles culture. It is the latter that has been set up as a normal against the supposedly deviant relation to objects at work in hoarding. Through a system of cataloguing and classification, collectibles have a recognized value within a structure of exchange. Hoarders, in contrast, Herring writes, 'appear to disregard both affective and socioeconomic worth as they gather about themselves things that do not [...] usually count as collectible goods' (*Ibid.*, p. 81) It follows from this that the hoarder challenges existing regimes of value in commodity culture, collecting and keeping items that one day 'might come in handy' but that have no immediate use.

Benjamin wrote that 'the person who collects is taking up the struggle against dispersion'. Who is to say that Huhtamo's orderly media-archaeological collection takes part in this noble cause, but Vivian Maier's disorderly Chicago hoard does not? One main difference is that Huhtamo's collection has an institutional context, a context that brings legitimacy to a set of objects that might be viewed in another light if encountered outside the institution. The same might be said for Maier's worldly possessions, which may only have taken on the connotations of a hoard because she was a peripatetic and property-less domestic servant without any permanent space in which to distribute her belongings. Spread those articles out through an average bourgeois interior, and would they still retain the connotations of a hoard? In any case, Maier's hoard now does have legitimacy, sustained by among other institutions, the 'Maloof Collection'. As Pearce says, every hoard is just waiting for the moment that, pupae-like, it is turned into a collection by the right owner or set of circumstances.

Another difference between Huhtamo and Maier is, of course, their gender. Media archaeology is not without its eminent female exponents, but amongst its leading masculine lights, how often are questions of gender brought to the fore? It is a division that is mirrored in the modes of collecting most typically found among men and women. Pearce drily tells us that most common among male collectors 'are those who collect machine parts of various kinds, including complete machines. These are the oily handed collectors who spend most of their free time working on their material in sheds and garages' (Pearce, 1995, p. 213). As Meyerowitz's emphasis on courage and danger in street photography shows, Maier was practicing a photographic form typically gendered masculine. And yet, in spite of her masculine penchants, or perhaps because of them, critics have worked hard to paint her back into one recognizable feminine corner or other. But as Terry Castle observes, 'None of the [...] stereotypes projected onto her – Mary Poppins with a Rolleiflex; frail spinster-genius à la Emily Dickinson; frumpy victim-beyond-the-grave of grifters – match up with the brisk, eagle-eyed, no-nonsense, and frequently intransigent figure' (2015, p. 82).

Perhaps Maier's accumulations are so consistently downgraded to 'hoarding' because they fail to conform to the gender norms of collecting. Castle also invokes the received view of Maier as a hoarder, but gives the familiar metaphor another meaning:

> She was waiting for us to find her, perhaps, to get *her* in focus. Now that we have – Tut's secret chamber stands open, revealing the heaps of gold – it's intoxicating. Like joyful marauders, we take our selfies, mug for the camera, and proceed to ransack the nanny's thrilling hoard. (Castle, 2015, p.83)

A hoard has come to mean a vast collection of trash, but it once referred to an accumulation of wealth, and it is this meaning that Castle confers on Maier's storage lockers with the image of a 'thrilling hoard' to be ransacked. Rather than claim for Maier the legitimacy of collector, Castle, in her feminist rereading, revalues the hoard.

No longer a pathology, but instead a regal and archaic site, Maier's hoard comes into its own, Castle implies, at the moment when everyone has become a street photographer, a self-portraitist. It is a vital media archaeological observation. If media archaeology, as Ernst argues, must pay attention to the continuing physical presence of old and abandoned media, it must also take into account the ways in which the abandoned takes on its significance in juxtaposition with contemporary, active media. Putting it another way, Thomas Elsaesser suggests that 'the insistence on the relevance of the old and obsolete may well be the necessary double of the celebration of the new we have been living' (Elsaesser, 2016, p. 206).

Maier's storage of her great wealth, her removal from circulation of her goods by immobilizing them in containers within containers within containers stands in stark contrast to the revolution in the movement of goods brought about by another storage mode developed in the same epoch that Maier was making photographs: the humble shipping container. It is easy to forget this revolutionary storage medium when by far the most attention is directed towards the proliferation of mobile 'black boxes' with inbuilt obsolescence whose inputs and outputs have been mastered by millions, but whose insides are understood by few and accessible to even fewer (see Parikka, 2015, pp. 146–150). From this perspective, perhaps the most important text of media studies in the past decade is Marc Levinson's *The Box: How the Shipping Container Made the World Smaller and the World Economy Bigger*. These containers, eighteen million of them and counting, circulate silently round the world's oceans, reducing the cost of transport, increasing the speed of movement, and ensuring the uninterrupted flow of the commodities that will make up the hoards of the future.

Works Cited

Karl Abraham, *Selected Papers on Psychoanalysis* (London: Hogarth Press, 1927).

'Artefacts of Media Archaeology: Inside Professor Erkki Huhtamo's Office' *UCLA Daily Bruin*, Youtube. https://www.youtube.com/watch?v=Ks9tyaft7Gs. Published 19 March 2013. Accessed 21 March 2016.

Pamela Bannos, *Vivian Maier: A Photographer's Life and Afterlife* (Chicago, IL: University of Chicago Press, 2017).

Russell W. Belk, *Collecting in a Consumer Society* (London: Routledge, 1995).

Walter Benjamin, 'Unpacking my Library: A Talk about Book Collecting,' in *Illuminations*, trans. Harry Zohn (New York: Schocken Books, 1969), pp. 59–67.

Walter Benjamin, *The Arcades Project*, trans. Howard Eiland and Kevin McLaughlin (Cambridge, MA.: Belknap Press of Harvard University Press, 1999).

Jay Bolter and Richard Grusin, *Remediation: Understanding New Media* (Cambridge, MA: MIT Press, 1999).

Peter Buse, *The Camera Does the Rest: How Polaroid Changed Photography* (Chicago, IL: University of Chicago Press, 2016).

Richard Cahan and Michael Williams (eds.), *Vivian Maier: Out of the Shadows* (Chicago, IL: CityFiles, 2012).

Terry Castle, 'New Art', *Harpers*, Feb 2015, pp.79-83. http://harpers.org/archive/2015/02/new-art/2/. Accessed 31 March 2016.

Kevin Coffee, 'Misplaced: Ethics and the Photographs of Vivian Maier', *Museum Management and Curatorship* 29: 2 (2014), pp. 93–101.

'CubeSmart', https://www.cubesmart.com/illinois-self-storage/chicago-self-storage/long-term/ Accessed 30 March 2016.

John Davis, 'Going Analog: Vinylphiles and the Consumption of the "Obsolete" Vinyl Record', in *Residual Media*, ed. by Charles R. Acland (Minneapolis, MN: University of Minnesota Press, 2007), pp. 222–236.

Timothy Druckery, 'Foreword', in Siegfried Zielinski, *Deep Time of Media: Toward an Archaeology of Hearing and Seeing by Technical Means*, trans. Gloria Custance (Cambridge, MA: MIT Press, 2006), pp. vii–xi.

Geoff Dyer, 'Foreword', in *Vivian Maier: Street Photographer*, ed. John Maloof (New York: PowerHouse Books, 2011), pp. 8–9.

David Edgerton, *The Shock of the Old: Technology and Global History since 1900* (London: Profile, 2006).

David Edgerton, 'Innovation, Technology, or History: What is the Historiography of Technology About?', *Technology and Culture* 51, no. 3 (2010), pp. 680–697.

Kate Egan, 'The Celebration of a "Proper Product": Exploring the Residual Collectible through the "Video Nasty"', in *Residual Media*, ed. by Charles R. Acland (Minneapolis, MN: University of Minnesota Press, 2007), pp.200–221.

Thomas Elsaesser, 'Media Archaeology as Symptom', *New Review of Film and Television Studies* 14:2 (2016), pp. 181–215.

Wolfgang Ernst, 'Media Archaeology: Method and Machine versus History and Narrative of Media', in Erkki Huhtamo and Jussi Parikka (eds.), *Media Archaeology: Approaches, Applications, and Implications* (Berkeley, CA: University of California University Press, 2011), pp. 239–255.

Wolfgang Ernst, *Digital Memory and the Archive* (Minneapolis, MN: Minnesota University Press, 2013).

Otto Fenichel, *The Psychoanalytic Theory of the Neurosis* (New York: Norton, 1945).

Scott Herring, *The Hoarders: Material Deviance in Modern American Culture* (Chicago, IL: University of Chicago Press, 2014).

Erkki Huhtamo, *Illusions in Motion: Media Archaeology of the Moving Panorama and Related Spectacles* (Cambridge, MA: MIT Press, 2012).

Ernest Jones, 'Anal-Erotic Character Traits' in *Papers on Psycho-Analysis* (London: Baillière, Tindall and Cox, 1950).

Jacques Lacan, *The Ethics of Psychoanalysis*, ed. Jacques-Alain Miller, trans. Dennis Porter (London: Routledge, 1992).

Jacques Lacan, *Le Séminaire livre VI, Le désir et son interprétation 1958–1959*, ed. Jacques-Alain Miller (Paris: Éditions de La Martinière, 2013).

Marc Levinson, *The Box: How the Shipping Container Made the World Smaller and the World Economy Bigger* (Princeton, NJ: Princeton University Press, 2006).

Patrick Mauriès, *Cabinets of Curiosities* (London: Thames and Hudson, 2002).

Linda Matthews, 'Diary', *London Review of Books*, 22 October 2015, pp. 38–39.

William Meyers, 'The Nanny's Secret', *The Wall Street Journal*, 3 January 2012.

Jill Nicholls, dir. *Vivian Maier: Who Took Nanny's Pictures?* (BBC, 2013).

Jussi Parikka, 'Introduction: Archival Media Theory' in Wolfgang Ernst, *Digital Memory and the Archive* (Minneapolis, MN: Minnesota University Press, 2013), pp. 1–23.

Jussi Parikka, *A Geology of Media* (Minneapolis, MN: Minnesota University Press, 2015).

Susan M. Pearce, *On Collecting: An Investigation into Collecting in the European Tradition* (London: Routledge, 1995).

Claire Preston, 'In the Wilderness of Forms: Ideas and Things in Thomas Browne's Cabinets of Curiosity', in Neil Rhodes and Jonathan Sawday (eds.), *The Renaissance*

Computer: Knowledge Technology in the First Age of Print (New York: Routledge, 2000), pp. 167–180.

Barbara Stafford, *Good Looking* (Cambridge, MA: MIT Press, 1996).

Susan Stewart, *On Longing: Narratives of the Miniature, the Gigantic, the Souvenir, the Collection* (Baltimore, MD: Johns Hopkins University Press, 1984).

Siegfried Zielinski, *Deep Time of Media: Toward an Archaeology of Hearing and Seeing by Technical Means*, trans. Gloria Custance (Cambridge, MA: MIT Press, 2006).

About the author

Peter Buse is Dean of the School of the Arts at the University of Liverpool, England. He has published widely on visual culture and cultural theory in journals such as *Parallax, Journal of Visual Culture*, *New Formations*, *Genre*, *History of Photography*, *Angelaki*, and *Continuum*. He is author, most recently, of *The Camera Does the Rest: How Polaroid Changed Photography* (University of Chicago Press, 2016), a media archaeology of instant photography.

7. Media Archaeology and Critical Theory of Technology

Ben Roberts

Abstract

This chapter examines the ways in which media archaeology addresses technological change. The term media archaeology encompasses a range of different approaches and attitudes to technology, from those that seem to embrace a certain kind of technological determinism to others that use archaeological perspectives to critique the idea of progress and produce nonlinear accounts of technical history. The aim here is to place these accounts in the wider context of critical theory of technology. The chapter pursues this argument through a close reading of the work of Walter Benjamin, Wolfgang Ernst and Bernard Stiegler.

Keywords: Benjamin, Ernst, Stiegler, Media Archaeology, Critical Theory

This chapter examines the ways in which media archaeology addresses technological change. The term media archaeology encompasses a range of different approaches and attitudes to technology, from those that seem to embrace a certain kind of technological determinism to others that use archaeological perspectives to critique the idea of progress and produce nonlinear accounts of technical history. The aim here is to place these accounts in the wider context of critical theory and philosophy of technology.

It is crucial to understand that media archaeology is both a new way of studying media and also a new way of thinking about technology. In this sense, it can also be seen as a return to the concerns of what has become known as medium theory (Meyrowitz, 1985, p. 16). Media archaeology focuses more on the apparatus itself as a mode of recording and organizing experience, as well as the cultural practices surrounding its use. As Wolfgang Ernst puts it, '[it] concentrates on the non-discursive elements in dealing with the past: not on speakers, but rather on the agency of the machine' (Ernst,

Roberts, B. and M. Goodall (eds.), *New Media Archaeologies*, Amsterdam Universsity Press, 2019
DOI: 10.5117/9789462982161_CH07

2005, p. 591). However, at the same time as embracing the technological constitution of media, media archaeology also questions existing *doxa* surrounding media-technological developments. That is, it interrogates traditional narratives about technical development or teleological accounts of progress, emphasizing instead discontinuities or the cyclical nature of change (Parikka, 2012). Media archaeology highlights the material form of media apparatus and devices at the same time as questioning the way we think about technological transformation.

As such, and as will be argued here, one might well see media archaeology as a form of philosophy of technology and one that has a particular relationship with what one might call 'critical theory of technology'. In order to develop this argument, I will examine the relationship here between media archaeology and the work of Walter Benjamin, Wolfgang Ernst, and Bernard Stiegler.

Walter Benjamin and Media Archaeology

Given the preoccupations of contemporary media archaeology just described, it is perhaps no surprise that it has drawn inspiration from the work of Walter Benjamin. The connections between media archaeology and the work of Walter Benjamin's *Arcades Project* are, in some ways, rather obvious. In *What is Media Archaeology?*, Jussi Parikka highlights Benjamin's 'cultural historical method which itself takes waste, rubble and ruins as its starting point for a multi-layered excavation of the slow emergence of modernity' (Parikka, 2012, p. 90). Media archaeologists often undertake, as Parikka puts it here, a 'multi-layered excavation' of apparatus such as Sony Walkman portable cassette players, 16mm film projectors, early home computers, children's stereoscopic viewers, and old video game consoles that would frequently, in a contemporary world of planned obsolescence, be considered rubbish. Their seeming obsession with recently obsolete forms of media mirrors Benjamin's own interest in the disappearing world of the nineteenth-century Parisian arcade. However, as I will argue here, the dialogue between Benjamin and media archaeology is more than simply superficial and points to the continuing influence of Frankfurt School critical theory on the way in which contemporary media technology is understood.

The Parisian arcades that interested Benjamin were largely built in the 1820s and the 1830s. By the time Benjamin was writing, the arcades were already in decline, having been supplanted by new forms of mass consumption such as the department store. As Susan Buck-Morss points out, the arcades of Benjamin's time had been transformed from 'consumer dream worlds' to 'commodity graveyards' (Buck-Morss, 1991, pp. 37–38). Their shops were full of bric-a-brac that had 'lost even the logic of their original place on the market' such as 'types of collar studs for which we no longer know the corresponding collars and shirts' and their hairdressers advertised out of date coiffure (Buse *et al.*, 2006, pp. 31–32; Benjamin, 2002, p. 872). And yet, in these decaying arcades Benjamin saw the potential for a remarkable kind of historical study, one which could clear the 'terrain of the nineteenth century' of the 'undergrowth of delusion and myth' (Benjamin 2002, pp. 456–457). As with the media archaeologist's interest in forms of media that represented a dead end, for example, like Sony Betamax, or the cinema of attractions as a forms of cinema that *could have been*, it was precisely the obsolescence of the arcades that was of interest to Benjamin. Retrieving the debris of the past provided a way to challenge historicism understood as the history of the victors (Benjamin 2003, p. 391). In this way, it allowed the historical materialist to interrogate victors' history as also the ideology of the dominant class. As Benjamin puts it in 'On the Concept of History', 'empathizing with the victor invariably benefits the current rulers' (*Ibid.*). Focusing on the 'losers' of media history is a way for media archaeology to challenge dominant narratives of succession and development (for example, the idea that magic lantern projection was merely a precursor to the moving image film, or that the cinema of attractions must be seen as a nascent form of classical cinematic narrative) (Elsaesser, 2004). Equally, both Benjamin and media archaeology wrestle with the question of how things could have evolved differently. As Howard Caygill argues, Benjamin's historical account is 'qualified continually by counterfactual imaginations of other possible outcomes, a method exemplified by his treatment of the arcade' (Caygill, 1998, p. 144).

At stake in this interest in the obsolete and counterfactual is the question of progress. In Convolute N of the *Arcades Project*, Benjamin outlines as one of its methodological objectives, 'a historical materialism which has annihilated within itself the idea of progress' (Benjamin, 2002, p. 460). As Buck-Morss suggests:

The *Passagen-Werk* is fundamentally concerned with debunking mythic theories of history whatever form their scenarios may take – inevitable catastrophe no less than continuous improvement. But Benjamin was most persistent in his attack against the myth of automatic historical progress. In his lifetime, at the very brink of the nuclear age and the twilight of technological innocence, the myth was still largely unshaken, and Benjamin considered it to be the greatest political danger. (Buck-Morss, 1991, p. 79)

Benjamin underlines the danger in 'On the Concept of History', where he argues that the German working class has been corrupted by the illusion that 'factory work ostensibly furthering technological progress constituted a political achievement' (Benjamin, 2003, p. 393). This illusory nature of the 'progress' has an historical dimension; Benjamin observes that during the nineteenth century the concept of progress no longer functioned as a form of critique (Benjamin, 2002, p. 476 [N11a,1]). By the latter half of the nineteenth century a powerful mythic form had evolved, where historical progress was simply equated with technological change. Benjamin sees the World Expositions as examples of this mythic form. Beginning with the Great Exhibition of 1851 in London and its famous Crystal Palace there was an almost 'viral proliferation' of these Exhibitions and World's Fairs in the period from then onwards; ostensibly, they were concerned with 'peace, education, progress' but, in reality, celebrated industry, commodity culture, and national production (Buse *et al.*, 2006, pp. 122–123). Benjamin was suspicious of the idea that technological improvement in itself could improve quality of life for the working class. Technological innovation offered a seductive alternative to real social change. As Buck-Morss argues, '[the] message of the world exhibitions as fairylands was the promise of social progress without revolution' (Buck-Morss, 1991, p. 86).

An attack on linear accounts of progress shapes much media-archaeo-logical endeavour. As Wanda Strauven (Strauven, p. 72) points out, Thomas Elsaesser's influential (2004) account of new film history *as* media archaeol-ogy exemplifies an approach that emphasizes discontinuities and ruptures within the development of media and media technology. Elsaesser histori-cizes and radicalizes new film history's argument that early cinema needed to be seen as a 'cinema of attractions' rather than a precursor of narrative cinema. His account therefore emphasizes the importance of interrogating all teleological accounts of media history. Elsasesser argues that the new film history valorized early cinema partly out of a desire to challenge the hegemony of classical cinema. Scholars of film history in the 1970s and 1980s linked the pre-1917 cinema of attractions to contemporary developments in post-classical film in order to reverse the relation between 'norm' and 'deviance': 'early cinema appears – flanked by the powerful, event-driven and spectacle-oriented blockbuster cinema – as the norm, making the classical Hollywood cinema seem the exception' (Elsaesser, 2004, p. 84). Elsaesser calls for a radicalization that not only displaces classical cinema, as the dominant model for understanding film history, but also critiques all teleological accounts of media history, including the contemporary one enshrining digital 'convergence'. For as well as questioning the idea that everything leads to cinema, one must now also query a logical progression between media developments:

> Causal models, problem-solving routines or even evolutionary explana-tions are of little help. Cinema did not relate to the magic lantern in strictly causal terms nor did it 'respond' to it by solving problems that had arisen in the practice of magic lantern shows. It re-purposed aspects of magic lantern technology and parasitically occupied part of its public sphere. Television has not 'evolved' out of cinema nor did it replace cinema. Digital images were not something the film industry was waiting for, in order to overcome any felt 'deficiencies' in its production of special effects. (*Ibid.*, p. 88)

In other words, this radicalized version of New Film History goes from un-dermining one particular 'story' about the evolution of narrative in classical cinema to interrogating stories of progress and development in general. Pulling at the thread of 'early cinema' turns out to unravel a whole web of assump-tions about media history. This unravelling takes place in the context of an all-encompassing digital convergence that seems to eliminate different media forms and their histories. Elsaesser calls our digital era 'a "now" for which there is no clear "before" or "after"' (*Ibid.*, p. 98). Our political imperative is no longer provided – as it was in the 1970s and 1980s – by Hollywood's hegemonic dominance of narrative form but by the even more pervasive dominance of cognitive capitalism and its conquest of networked mobility and attention.

This digital 'now' requires an 'archaeological perspective', but not in order to understand the origin and development of media technologies 'correctly'. Instead, this perspective is needed to hold media history open as a 'determined plurality' and 'permanent virtuality'; one must think not in terms of the 'past, present and future' of media technology, but rather the 'archaeology of possible futures and of the perpetual presence of several pasts' (*Ibid.*, pp. 99, 113). New Film History, with its emphasis on the 'other-ness' of early cinema, provides a model of practice for media archaeology. This model emphasizes the discontinuities in media history in order to disrupt the idea of continuous technological development and progress.

The imperative to challenge the concept of progress in media history is therefore both scholarly and political. Benjamin's materialist history is of interest to media archaeology for methodological reasons as well as critical ones. It is worth reflecting here on his historical method and particularly his concept of the dialectical image and what it offers to media-archaeological theory.

Benjamin's concept of the dialectical image aims to retrieve an object from the past by putting it in a new 'constellation' with the present (Buse *et al.*, 2006, p. 31). For example, he wanted the arcades to be understood as harbingers of the consumer culture of his own time. Yet, he wanted them to appear without any sense of continuity or progress between their heyday and the era in which he was writing. Buck-Morss suggests that Benjamin frees the historical object from 'history's continuum' in order to make visible both its fore-history, its 'possibility' or 'utopian potential', and its after-history, 'the conditions of its decay and the manner of its cultural transmission' (Buck-Morss, 1991, pp. 218–219). In a similar fashion, and noting its inspiration in Benjamin's work, Elsaesser argues that media archaeology occupies itself with historical apparatus and practices in order to draw on 'the resisting reminder of unfulfilled potential and the reservoir of utopian promise' (Elsaesser, 2016, p. 206). For Benjamin, this new configuration of past and present in the dialectical image then enables 'the unperceived significance of the past to appear as a force in the present' (Ferris, 2008, p.120). As Darrow Schecter suggests, through the dialectical image Benjamin is advancing a materialist approach to the 'history of what has not yet happened'. Although this articulation might seem contradictory, the argument is in fact dialectical: 'there is no history of the "already has been" without a history of the "not yet": if the past has simply occurred and is irredeemably gone, then so too must the future be already written, and this linear determinism, [Benjamin] insists, is falsified by experience' (Schecter, 2013, p. 83).

The dialectical image aims not to give us history 'as it was', but rather, through being brought into a constellation with our own time, to act as a form of historical truth that is also a form of revolutionary experience (Ross, 2015, p. 116). This experience is often presented by Benjamin terminologically in terms of political awakening; in *The Arcades Project*, as Bolz and Van Reijen put it, 'it is as though capitalism's dream sleep were waiting to wake up from its prehistory' (Bolz and Van Reijen, 1996, p. 46). Media archaeology's interest in the past stems equally from using it to confront the present. As Geert Lovink suggests, '[m]edia archaeology is first and foremost a methodology, a hermeneutic reading of the "new" against the grain of the past, rather than a telling of the history of technologies from past to present' (Lovink, 2012, p. 8; Huhtamo and Parikka, 2011, p. 3). Lovink's interest in this methodology stems directly from a concern with developments in contemporary digital culture and the need to write a 'critical history of the present'. As he suggests, we are already a long way from the utopian-libertarian days when John Perry Barlow could declare the independence from world governments of 'a civilization of the Mind in Cyberspace' (Perry Barlow, 1996). Indeed, as Edward Snowden's revelations have demonstrated, the internet age has greatly extended the power of government in terms of an unprecedented level of electronic surveillance which would have seemed barely conceivable a generation ago (Harding, 2014). These transformations have important implications for the critical project of understanding digital culture. As Lovink puts it,

> Streams of messages about corporate collapses and cyberterrorism have replaced popular cyberculture. There is a rising awareness of backlash. A part of this new consciousness could be translated as Internet culture's need to write its own history. It has to leave its heroic, mythological stage behind. (Lovink, 2012, p. 7)

Here, Lovink invokes history as a way to challenge the mythological foundations of the internet. Media archaeology, he goes on to suggest, provides a methodology with which digital criticism can confront this digital present with its past, motivated by the very specific political configuration provided by network culture. The physical (mechanical, optical, chemical) forms of 'old media' are also attractive in the digital age. Ernst argues that archaeological approaches are motivated by an apparent need to confront 'virtual, immaterial realities' with the 'insistence and resistance of material worlds' (Ernst, 2005, p. 589). Elsaesser interprets this project of confronting new media with old media, in a fashion highly reminiscent of Benjamin's *Arcades Project*, as a call for 'making a last stand against the tyranny of the new, for digging into the past, in order to discover there an as yet unrealized future' (Elsaesser, 2016, p. 206). Media archaeology, from this perspective, lies as much in the need to rethink the present and future as it does on reinterpreting the past. It draws inspiration from Benjamin's concept of the dialectical image as revolutionary experience, bringing the past into a new constellation with the present.

From Media Apparatus to Sonic Time Machines

Media archaeology also shares with Benjamin's approach an emphasis on the discontinuous in history. Ernst articulates this very clearly in an article on the work of the art historian Stephen Bann entitled 'Let There Be Irony: Cultural History And Media Archaeology In Parallel Lines' (2005). He argues that whereas cultural (and art) history values 'evolutionary continuities and soft transformations' the archaeological approach focuses more on ruptures within technological media. Ernst highlights here Bann's arguments about photography, especially as articulated in the latter's *Parallel Lines: Printmakers, Painters, and Photographers in Nineteenth-Century France* (2001). In this book, Bann argues against the case made by Benjamin, for example, that photography makes a break with existing forms of artistic production. Instead, he claims that photography emerged alongside, and competed with, other artistic practices such as engraving and lithography. For Bann, photography operated in an aesthetic and discursive continuum with these other forms of reproduction. He therefore disputes Benjamin's claim that photography is a 'unique harbinger of a crisis in the relation between the original and the reproduction' (Lang and Bann, 2013, p. 551). Here, Bann's position compares interestingly with Jacques Rancière's broader argument about photography in relation to Roland Barthes's *Camera Lucida* (1993). The *punctum* that Barthes finds in the photograph, contends Rancière, is not the product of a technical ontology of the photograph as the 'direct emanation of the referent' (Barthes, 1993, p. 26). It is instead the mechanical reworking of an aesthetic of indifference that can also be found, among other places, in paintings of beggars by Murillo and Flaubert's *Madame Bovary* (Rancière, 2009, pp. 13–14). This problem around the 'rupture' of photographic reproduction can then be seen as dividing Benjamin and Barthes on one side from Bann and Rancière on the other. Ernst puts the question as follows: 'was there a smooth evolutionary progression from etching to lithography to photography, or rather, was there a dramatic break as a result of the difference between genuinely *technological media*, such as photography, and earlier *cultural technologies*?' (Ernst, 2005, pp. 587–588, his emphasis). For Ernst, how we resolve this question depends on the way in which we interrogate and work with the past. In particular, it depends on whether we adopt the discursive, aesthetic, and narrative-driven approach of cultural history, or instead media archaeology's focus on the *non-discursive*:

> Photomechanical reproduction as a technology on the non-discursive level was a rupture in the fabric of pre-existing image-making ('because it is an indexical as well as iconic form; because it stops time, because it is machine-made'); on the level of discursive interface, it represented a continuation of older traditions in the reproduction of existing works of art and their circulation. (Ernst, 2005, p. 584; citing Solomon-Godeau, 2002, p. 220)

Rupture and discontinuity are essential for a media archaeological approach that emphasizes the technical and non-discursive aspects of media.

From this perspective, the shift from engraving to photography makes all the difference precisely because the human hand and interpretation has been replaced by a photo-mechanical process: Ernst insists that 'the photograph is an assemblage of optical signals' (Ernst, 2005, p. 593). This media-technical understanding does not in any way take away from Bann's 'discourse-oriented' contention that photographic representation was not absolutely new but actually a continuation of existing cultural forms. Ernst believes that cultural history and media archaeology are instead operating on 'parallel lines', that 'the two methods will continue to supplement each other without effacing their differences' (*Ibid.*, p. 601). Media archaeology, on this reading, does not supplant media history but operates instead on another analytic level.

Media archaeology, from Ernst's perspective, implicitly involves a different relationship between technology and time from cultural history. It does this because it invokes the centrality of technology to the constitution of temporality. We are no longer in the domain of simply challenging narratives of technological progress which could be seen, after all, as a cultural historical activity. Rather we need to 'listen' to technology in a new way. In *Sonic Time Machines* (2016) Ernst argues,

> Just as musical culture tries to save sound itself from ephemeral temporality (favouring invariance), signal recording media for the first time in cultural history mastered the time axis, thus enabling arbitrary manipulation and repeatability. Phonographic recording is not historiography but *signal storage.* Any such graphic trace of an acoustic event cannot be considered sound. The implicit *sonicity* of an acoustic event depends on a temporalizing medium like the record player to make it explicit through time-sequential unfolding, just like cinema needs the projector to restore movement to otherwise discrete chrono-photographical film frames. *Recording does not take place in or as historical time, but is a time operation itself.* This makes it a privileged form of investigating tempor(e)alities. (Ernst, 2016, p. 22, my emphasis)

There are three points to underline here. Firstly, in sound recordings we are dealing with an 'implicit sonicity' that is not reducible to sound but rather to the 'essential temporal nature' of sound's unfolding as a 'physical vibrational event' (*Ibid.*, pp. 23–24). With the direct acoustic link between air vibration and the human body broken, implicit sonicity is what remains. Ernst comments, '[w]ithin an electronic system, sound exists implicitly' (*Ibid.*, pp. 25-26). Sonicity is not confined to the audible, but is 'a mode of revealing modalities of temporal processuality' (*Ibid.*, p. 27). Secondly, such recordings function not at the level of *symbol*, in the manner of musical culture, but of *signal*. Here, Ernst recalls his previous argument in the essay 'Media Archaeography' that sound recordings 'contain – and thus memorize – a world of signals that operate beyond and below the cultural symbolism intended by the humans involved' (Ernst, 2013, p. 59). In signal, media archaeology engages with 'a physical layer below symbolically expressed culture' that is specific to the media apparatus and their non-discursive registration of culture. Thirdly, in the sound recording we confront not just an object in historical time, but one that constitutes its own temporality; what is reproduced is not the symbolic musical or cultural content but the transience of time itself. Ernst's concept of sonicity therefore points to the emergence in time-based media of an implicitly new relationship between technology and time.

For Ernst, sonicity opens up new modalities for dealing with the past. In a manner somewhat analogous to the way in which digital humanities are opening up novel ways of working with the textual archives, software can read and analyse time-based media archives in new ways (Ernst, 2016, p. 130). As Ernst points out, archives of recordings such as *Europeana* currently only allow searches based on title, keywords, or other metadata explicitly added by archivists. New search algorithms will eventually allow searching within the sonic 'content' of the recordings themselves where 'the search engine itself becomes an archaeologist of sonic knowledge' (Ibid., p. 134). As Ernst observes:

> Contrary to traditional musicology, which is based primarily around semantic analysis, a signal oriented archive will no longer list songs and sonic sequences according to their authors, subject time and space of recording. Instead, digital sound data banks will allow acoustic sequences to be algorithmically systematised according to genuinely sonic (i.e. wave-based) notions and computing (techno-mathematical) criteria rather than traditional musical *topoi*. Such a change reveals new insights in the non-symbolic characteristics of music as sound. (*Ibid.*, pp. 133–134)

This affords a re-structuring of both the sonic archive and the forms of knowledge derived from it. The shift from *symbol* – semantic, sono-cultural – to *signal* – implicitly sonic, non-cultural, statistical, stochastic – also represents a move away from historical musicology to 'systematic musicology'. Ernst sees *phono*-graphy as the foundation for these new ways of working with the media archaeological archive. Phonography represents a new kind of 'scriptural memory' inaugurated by the first mechanical recording devices, one which 'stood apart from alphabetic writing because of its capacity to record and replay the temporal axis itself using audio-visual signals' (*Ibid.,* p. 141). Electro-magnetic recording and digitization have greatly extended the opportunities for analysis and signal processing of recordings. However, these new forms of understanding themselves derive their insights from recording as a new time-based form of memory.

Ultimately, this new epistemology of the sonic is therefore also an ontology: the sonic archive simply embeds the past in a different way from the textual archive. It stores not only the 'cultural semantics' of musical or voice 'content', but also 'technological knowledge' of the historical materiality of its production (*Ibid.,* p. 113). What becomes audible when an early wax cylinder recording is played is not only the intentional recorded matter but also the 'noise'. This noise is itself meaningful when heard with the right media- archaeological 'ears'. It encodes the history of elecro-mechanical recording machines by allowing us to listen to the apparatus itself. Ernst even suggests that such noise is, to use Proust's term, a kind of *mémoire involontaire* (*Ibid.,* p. 114). Ultimately, this sonic memory constitutes a shortcut between one time and another, providing a sonic time machine that allows the simultaneity of one time within another. Such a simultaneity is counter-historical; that is, it runs contrary to the normal interpretative practices of history. As such, Ernst observes, '[t]he goal of media archaeology is to dig into collections of early recording machines in a non-historical way (anti-hermeneutically)' (*Ibid.,* p. 114). The sonic time machine does not just allow a new interpretation of the past, it literally brings the past back to life in a way that evades traditional notions of historical interpretation. Media archaeology of early recordings therefore, 'develops a different "hearing" of modern history, a notion of the past based on waves, simultaneous time and shifting soundscapes' (*Ibid.*).

Stiegler and the Industrial Temporal Object

In a sense, there is a remarkable parallel between Ernst's project and that which the French philosopher of technology Stiegler outlines in his multi-volume work *Technics and Time*. Stiegler similarly focuses on phonographic recording and its reorganization of temporal perception, arguing that the '*fact of recording* [...] is the phonographic revelation of the structure of all temporal objects' (Stiegler, 2011, p. 21). He sees the phonographic recording as one of a novel class of 'industrial temporal objects' that usher in a new 'industrialization of memory' (Stiegler, 2008, pp. 9, 241). But what does Stiegler mean by an 'industrial temporal object'? This concept relies heavily on a critical reading of the philosopher Edmund Husserl's phenomenological analysis of time. In Husserlian phenomenology, consciousness is intentional, that is, it is consciousness of an object. The temporal object differs from other objects of consciousness in that they are not simply 'unities in time' but also 'contain temporal extension in themselves' (Husserl, 1991, p. 24). When listening to a melody, for example, the listener must retain previous notes as well as the current note, in order for the melody to be perceived as such. What goes for the melody applies equally at the level of each tone, in the perception of its duration. The temporal object can only be perceived in the 'now' of impressional consciousness through its constant modification by what Husserl calls 'primary retention' (*Ibid.*, p. 29). Husserl, however, differentiates this primary retention from the more common understanding of memory as recollection which he regards as secondary. This secondary memory, or re-presentation, is further contrasted with image-consciousness, or, as John Brough puts it, 'the sort of awareness that comes into play when we look at a photograph, contemplate a sculpture, or view a program on television' (Husserl, 2005, p. xliv). Stiegler calls image consciousness 'tertiary memory' and argues, against Husserl, that it is constitutive in the construction of primary retention. He gives the example of repeated hearings of a gramophone record and the changing effect on the experience of melody. Stiegler argues:

> Husserl's phenomenological attitude consists of positioning consciousness as the constituter *of* the world, not something constituted *by* it. Since tertiary memory is a reality *in the world*, it cannot be constitutive of consciousness but must necessarily be derivative of a consciousness that has no real need of it. However, since the unique event of a *temporal* musical object, and the ability to repeat it technically, the link between primary and secondary retentions has become obvious: clearly, even though each time it is repeated it is the same temporal object, it produces two different musical experiences. (Stiegler, 2011, p. 21)

Both Ernst and Stiegler therefore position the advent of analogue recording as a decisive moment in the relationship between technology and time. For Stiegler, recording marks both an intensification in technics as the exteriorization of the human, but also a significant change in the technical constitution of memory, in what he calls tertiary memory, one which causes a general disorientation (Stiegler, 2008, p. 7). He contrasts analogue and digital recording with older forms of memory technology, such as orthographic (i.e. linear, alphabetic) writing. Orthographic writing was the disruptive technology of classical Greece, one which Stiegler argues, citing John M. Dodds, 'suspended the authority of traditional ethnic programmes' (*Ibid.*, p. 60). This disruption can be seen as an example of what, following Sylvain Auroux, he calls *grammatization*. Grammatization, in this context, means a process by which idiomatic differences and actions are standardized and discretized, as when, for example, out of a plethora of regional dialects a national written language is standardised. But, for Stiegler, the term grammatization applies equally to the replacement of skilled artisinal workers by a mechanical loom which standardises and discretizes the actions of weaving. Orthographic writing represents a 'decontextualizing rupture' with prior (e.g. pictographic) inscriptions, because it allows for a form of written memory that can break with its context and retain meaning. Rather than simply serve as an *aide mémoire*, 'writing has become memory itself' (Stiegler, 2008, p. 62). Paradoxically, however, the ability of orthographic writing to break with context also allows the text to be infinitely recontextualized (that is, read and reinterpreted) and lets individuals and groups differentiate themselves, or individuate themselves, through re-readings of the cultural memory preserved in it. This is a process that Stiegler calls *epochal redoubling* and, in the case of orthographic writing, it represents the evolutionary origin of what we recognize as the stable forms of Western knowledge and culture. In other words, while new forms of memory technology, which Stiegler calls *mnemotechnics*, are initially disruptive, 'suspending' ethnic groups and their traditions, they ultimately allow new forms of human culture to develop.

The techniques of analogue recording typical of twentieth-century media also represent a new form of tertiary memory. However, for Stiegler these new mnemotechnic developments, which he calls *industrial temporal objects,* are deeply troubling. This is partly because they have not (yet) been associated with a process of epochal redoubling (*Ibid.*, p. 7). These new forms of technical memory, along with the tele-technologies that disseminate them, are the source of a large-scale *disindividuation*. Through standardizing cultural memory on a global scale, they rupture existing 'programmes' of cultural memory, such as national and ethnic traditions, educational institutions, and so on. They therefore disrupt the ways in which individuals and groups have previously *individuated* themselves, to use Simondon's terminology. At the same time, they afford few opportunities for *reindividuation*; their consumers are illiterate, lacking the forms of media literacy that would be necessary for an epochal redoubling. For Stiegler, these industrial temporal objects are associated with a general societal malaise (*mal-être*), which he describes in dramatic terms:

> This loss of individuation, in which *I* persists as a yawning void, no longer moving towards a *We* who, being everything, the confusion of all possible *I*'s in an undifferentiated flux (the totalitarian model of 'community'), is condemned to dissolve into a globalised, impersonal *One*. [It] [...] leads to immense existential suffering: in the most tragic cases, this *quasi-inexistance* produces multiple personalities, and the danger of taking deadly drugs, of violence, tribal or individual, and suicide, which in France has become the second most common cause of death in adolescents and the most common in young adults. (Stiegler, 2011, p. 5)

Of course, the problem posed by these new *industrial* temporal objects is inseparable from the economic conditions under which they are produced. For Stiegler they represent nothing less that the 'industrialization of memory' (Stiegler, 2008, p. 9). He sees contemporary capitalism as not postindustrial, but rather *hyperindustrial*. The hyperindustrial era is one characterized not only by commodity production, but also by the extension of industrialization to memory, consciousness, and attention. However, the link between (hyper)industrialization and the *temporal* object is crucial here. This relationship can be best summarized by Stiegler's enigmatic assertion that the gramophone record is 'the phonographic *revelation* of the structure of *all* temporal objects' (Stiegler, 2011, p. 21, his emphasis). This assertion underlines the importance of his reading of Husserl: the gramophone record presents us – for the first time – with the potential repetition in consciousness of an identical temporal object, for example, music. What goes for the gramophone record applies equally here to other forms of recording, such as the film. The repeated audition of a record, while sonically more-or-less identical, is never exactly the same conscious experience. Stiegler argues that this demonstrates that the relationship between primary retention, secondary memory and tertiary memory (or 'image consciousness') is not as Husserl depicts it. According to Husserl, primary retention is not a representation of the mind, but gives direct experience of the temporal object: we *must* retain the immediate past in order to 'hear' the melody at all. Secondary memory, on the other hand, is selective and imaginative: I may or may not recall a tune I heard last week (Keller, 1999, pp. 73–74). Stiegler argues, on the other hand, that repeated plays of the gramophone record show that previous listenings, as 'secondary memory', *modify* primary retention, for example, perception of the temporal object that is music. The identical auditions afforded by recording technology illustrate that the *imaginative selections* of secondary memory shape primary retention itself. As Stiegler puts it, '[b]etween the two hearings, consciousness has changed because a *clearing* away has taken place: primary retention is a selection progress brought about through criteria that have been established during previous clearings away' (Stiegler, 2011, p. 19). The role of selection in primary retention undermines Husserl's apparently decisive distinction between the *direct* experience of primary retention and the imaginative selections of secondary memory. Moreover, the 'tertiary memory' of the industrial temporal object plays a crucial role in this 'phonographic revelation'. Stiegler points out that in Husserl's view 'image consciousness' (i.e. what Stiegler calls tertiary memory) is 'not a *memory* of that consciousness [...] it is an artificial memory of what was not perceived nor lived by consciousness' (*Ibid.*, p. 20). Since for Husserl only conscious *lived experience* constitutes phenomena, therefore image-consciousness or tertiary memory can only be derivative. Yet, for Stiegler the gramophone record 'reveals' the structure by which image consciousness or tertiary memory actually shapes the imaginary selections of primary and secondary memory. Far from being merely derivative, tertiary memory is, in fact, constitutive of the primary retention of the temporal object itself. For Stiegler, the phonographic revelation shows that consciousness, 'is always in some fashion a montage of overlapping primary, secondary and tertiary memories', and that 'experience' is always also composed of tertiary memories that have not in fact been lived or 'experienced' by the subject (*Ibid.*, p. 28).

Stiegler argues that the product of the industrialization of memory is, 'a flux in which absolutely unique temporal objects appear, objects whose flux coincides with the flux of the consciousness it produces' (Stiegler, 2008, p. 241). In contrast with previous forms of tertiary memory, such as orthographic memory, these industrial temporal objects decontextualize without offering any possibility of recontextualization, that is they globalize and generalize without allowing an idiomatic reappropriation at the level of the local, the community, the ethnic group.

Media Archaeology and Critical Theory of Technology

Both Stiegler and Ernst see in phonographic recording a new configuration of time and temporality. Both writers view this new configuration as marking a break with existing memory practices. But the consequences of this break are conceptualized differently by the two thinkers. My contention in this essay is that their differences illuminate the relationship between media archaeology and critical theory of technology.

One obvious difference here is the emphasis that Ernst places (and, perhaps, media archaeology more widely) on the capacity for recording technology to give rise to non-cultural, non-discursive insights. For Ernst, the recording apparatus, along with its technical manipulation in the present, grants us a new non-cultural access to the past. But does he conceptualize too cleanly here the distinction between, on the one hand, content or symbolic interpretation and, on the other, apparatus and signal processing? Does this distinction not itself suggest a dangerously simplistic opposition between culture and technology? Certainly, if one argues, as both Stiegler and Derrida do in their essentially similar yet distinctive ways, for the essential *technicity* of culture then the apparent straightforwardness of this opposition becomes problematic. In short, if culture is always technical, if everything from systems of writing through the Gutenberg press and onwards are seen as memory *technologies,* or mnemotechnics as Stiegler has it, then it becomes difficult to separate the discursive from the technological, the cultural from the non-cultural. Implicit in Ernst's insistence on the non-discursive dimension of phonographic recording is as sense that it represents a new *technological* form of memory and, therefore, can give rise to noncultural insights about the past. But for Stiegler, on the other hand, memory is always already technical. He argues that phonographic recording's novelty lies not simply in it being a memory technology but rather in the fact that it represents a new epoch within memory technology, that of the industrial temporal object.

One possible escape from this impasse would be to see the Ernst's sonic insights into audio archives not only as furnishing non-cultural insights, but rather as developing new forms of literacy in relation to the industrial temporal object. These new forms of literary would consist in new 'sonic' tools and techniques for analysing the temporal object, new techniques for reading and understanding the electro-mechanical archive. In this wider sense, one might see media archaeology as promising some of the epochal redoubling that Stiegler finds lacking in relation to twentieth-century time-based media, that is, the opportunity to reread, recontextualize and re-individuate the media object.

However, beyond his strong assertion of culture's originary technicity, Stiegler's analysis of the industrial temporal object forms part of his wider critical project, that is, a pharmacological critique of contemporary technology (Stiegler, 2013). It is his *explicit* commitment to a critical theory of technology that most clearly demarcates Stiegler from Ernst and, perhaps, beyond Ernst, media archaeology in general. My argument here is that media archaeology draws strongly on the critical theory of technology tradition, for example – as previously discussed – in its embrace of Benjamin. However its own commitment to a critical theory of technology is, at best, only *implicit*.

But what do I mean by *critical theory of technology* here? Perhaps the clearest contemporary formulation is found in the work of philosopher Andrew Feenberg who argues that it applies to theories that 'affirm human agency while rejecting the neutrality of technology' (Feenberg, 1999, p. 9). Feenberg draws particularly on Marcuse and Foucault to illustrate this position, but notes its affinity to a more general Frankfurt School claim that regards technology as 'materialized ideology' (*Ibid.*, p. 7). As we have seen, Benjamin had a keen understanding of the illusory nature of technological progress; media archaeology has drawn on this critique in order to rewrite, for example, teleological accounts of the history of cinema. Yet, is there not a risk here that Benjamin's wider critical project is reduced to simply a *method* for new forms of media study? Feenberg highlights a similar concern in rela-tion to work in the social sciences around technology. Social constructivism, for example, works to open the black box of technology and demonstrate the social nature of apparently technological developments. In doing so, as Feenberg argues, it takes inspiration from the 'left dystopianism' of the 1960s and 1970s (e.g. Marcuse and Foucault), that is, critical theory. However its 'narrow empiricism' means that, too often, its analyses simply chart how a particular technological device wins social acceptance while remaining divorced from any wider social critique. As such its insights into technology become a 'purely academic conception' (*Ibid.*, p. 12).

As Michael Goddard has commented, some forms of media archaeology share social constructivism's desire to open the black box of technology. But this desire is often motivated more by a desire to understand its 'physical workings' than to illuminate its social uses and shaping by practice (Goddard, 2014, p. 11). Goddard identifies this approach particularly with Kittler. But we can we can equally see it at work in Ernst's desire to supplant (or at least append) historical cultural interpretation with the non-discursive insights of signal processing and audio analysis. Indeed, despite Ernst's argument about the ways in which recording technology reconstitutes temporal experience he draws implications which are primarily not ontological but rather *methodological*. Sonic signal processing seeks simply to mine the riches left in audio recordings by the material properties of apparatus and medium. Ernst is more interested in how sonicity and its media archaeologi-cal exploitation will transform musicology and sound archives than in the social dimensions of this new noncultural form of memory.

Ultimately, Ernst's conception of sonicity can be seen as a new 'literacy' of temporal media. As such, it shares much in common with Stiegler's commitment to a new media literacy of the industrial temporal object, something advanced at the Centre Pompidou's Institut de Recherche et d'Innovation (IRI), where he is director, through software projects such as *Lignes de temps*, a tool for the critical analysis and annotation of films and other audiovisual media. However, whereas sonicity often simply seems to advance the new analytical possibilities latent in time-based media, Stiegler advocates a new literacy partly to counter the implicit dangers in their industrialization of memory. Without endorsing Stiegler's argument, it is clear how, despite the similarities in their way of dealing with the temporal object of recording, Ernst's approach ultimately misses this sense of media archaeology *as* critical theory of technology.

As we have seen, Ernst is excited by the recording's ability to evade history, to create a short cut between the time of the recording and the time of its audition. Stiegler, on the other hand, sees in this dimension of the industrial temporal object the crux of a problem. In orthographic recording (i.e. the text) there was a constitutive delay between text and interpretation, allowing the text to be reinscribed, recontextualized, and allowing its readers to individuate themselves through its rereading. For Stiegler, the sonic time machine's ability to provide a short cut between one time and another also risks a dangerous 'short circuit', threatening and supplanting interpretative history rather than supplementing it. It is the possibility for creative recontextualization and individuation that is lost through the 'short cut' of the industrial temporal object and its mass dissemination. In this sense, a media archaeology that remains true to Benjamin's critical project needs to rewire the temporal 'short circuit' of the sonic time machine as a 'long circuit' of critique and interpretation.

Works Cited

Louis Aragon, *Le paysan de Paris*. (Paris: Gallimard, 1926).

Stephen Bann, *Parallel Lines: Printmakers, Painters, and Photographers in Nineteenth-Century France*. (New Haven, CT: Yale University Press, 2011).

Richard Barbrook and Andy Cameron, 'The Californian Ideology', *Science as Culture* 6 (1) (1999), pp. 44–72.

John Perry Barlow, 'A Declaration of the Independence of Cyberspace', 1996, Accessed 2 June 2017, http://w2.eff.org/Censorship/Internet_censorship_bills/barlow_0296.declaration.

Roland Barthes, *Camera Lucida: Reflections on Photography.* (London: Vintage, 1993).

Walter Benjamin, *Selected Writings.* Selected writings Walter Benjamin. Michael W. Jennings, general ed. ; 4. H. Eiland and M.W. Jennings (eds.). Vol. 4: 1938–1940. (Cambridge, MA: Harvard University Press, 2003).

Walter Benjamin, *The Arcades Project.* Trans. H. Eiland & K. McLaughlin. (Cambridge, MA: Harvard University Press, 2002).

Norbert W. Bolz and W. van Reijen, *Walter Benjamin.* (Atlantic Highlands, NJ: Humanities Press, 1996).

Susan Buck-Morss, *The Dialectics of Seeing: Walter Benjamin and the Arcades Project.* (Cambridge, MA: The MIT Press, 1991).

Peter Buse *et al. Benjamin's Arcades: An Unguided Tour.* Encounters. (Manchester and New York: Manchester University Press, 2006).

Howard Caygill, *Walter Benjamin: The Colour of Experience.* (London: Routledge, 1998).

Margaret Cohen, 'Benjamin's Phantasmagoria: The Arcades Project', in D.S. Ferris (ed.) *The Cambridge Companion to Walter Benjamin.* (Cambridge: Cambridge University Press, 2004), pp. 199–220.

Thomas Elsaesser, 'Media Archaeology as Symptom', *New Review of Film and Television Studies* 14 (2) (2016), pp. 181–215.

Thomas Elsaesser, 'The New Film History as Media Archaeology', *CiNéMAS: Revue d'études cinématographiques* 14 (2–3) (2004), pp. 75–117.

Wolfgang Ernst, *Digital Memory and the Archive.* J. Parikka (ed.). (Minneapolis, MN: University of Minnesota Press, 2013).

Wolfgang Ernst, 'Let There Be Irony: Cultural History and Media Archaeology in Parallel Lines', *Art History* 28 (5) (2005), pp. 582–603.

Wolfgang Ernst, *Sonic Time Machines: Explicit Sound, Sirenic Voices, and Implicit Sonicity.* (Amsterdam: Amsterdam University Press, 2016).

Andrew Feenberg, *Questioning Technology.* (London: Routledge, 1999).

David S. Ferris, *The Cambridge Introduction to Walter Benjamin.* (Cambridge: Cambridge University Press, 2008).

Michael Goddard, 'Opening Up the Black Boxes: Media Archaeology, "Anarchaeology" and Media Materiality', *New Media & Society* 17 (11) (2014), pp.1761-1776.

Luke Harding, *The Snowden Files: The Inside Story of the World's Most Wanted Man.* (London: Guardian Books, 2014).

Erkki Huhtamo and Jussi Parikka (eds.), *Media Archaeology: Approaches, Applications, and Implications.* (Berkeley, CA.: University of California Press, 2011).

Edmund Husserl, *On the Phenomenology of the Consciousness of Internal Time.* (Dordrecht: Kluwer Academic Publishers, 1991).

Edmund Husserl, *Phantasy, Image Consciousness, and Memory, 1898–1925.* Trans. J.B. Brough. (Dordrecht: Springer, 2005).

Pierre Keller, *Husserl and Heidegger on Human Experience.* (Cambridge: Cambridge University Press, 1999).

Karen Lang and Stephen Bann, 'The Sense of the Past and the Writing of History: Stephen Bann in Conversation with Karen Lang', *The Art Bulletin* 95 (4) (2013), pp. 544–556.

Geert Lovink, *My First Recession: Critical Internet Culture in Transition.* (Amsterdam: Institute of Network Cultures, 2012).

Joshua Meyrowitz, *No Sense of Place: The Impact of Electronic Media on Social Behavior.* (New York: Oxford University Press, 1985).

Jussi Parikka, *What is Media Archaeology?* (Cambridge: Polity Press, 2012).

Jacques Rancière, 'Notes on the Photographic Image', *Radical Philosophy* 156 (2009), pp. 8–15.

Alison Ross, *Walter Benjamin's Concept of the Image.* (New York: Routledge, 2015).

Darrow Schecter, *Critical Theory in the Twenty-First Century.* (New York: Bloomsbury Academic, 2013).

Abigail Solomon-Godeau, 'Review Article: Stephen Bann's Parallel Lines', *Visual Resources* 18 (3) (2002), pp. 219–227.

Bernard Stiegler, *Technics and Time: 2. Disorientation.* Trans. S. Barker. (Stanford, CA: Stanford University Press, 2008).

Bernard Stiegler, *Technics and Time 3: Cinematic Time and the Question of Malaise.* Trans. S. Barker. (Stanford, CA: Stanford University Press, 2011).

Bernard Stiegler, *What Makes Life Worth Living: On Pharmacology.* Trans. D. Ross. (Cambridge: Polity Press, 2013).

Wanda Strauven, 'Media Archaeology: Where Film Studies, Media Art and New Media (Can) Meet', in V. Hediger *et al.* (eds.) *Preserving and Exhibiting Media Art. Challenges and Perspectives.* Amsterdam: Amsterdam University Press (2013), pp. 59–79.

About the author

Ben Roberts is Lecturer in Digital Humanities at the University of Sussex. He has published widely on philosophy of technology, particularly the work of Bernard Stiegler. He is currently completing a monograph for Manchester University Press entitled *Critical Theory and Contemporary Technology.* He is also leading an AHRC research network on automation anxiety.

Part 3

Media Archaeology at the Interface

8. The Cube: A Cinema Archaeology

Angela Piccini[1]

Abstract

Archaeologists with interests in media technologies, artefacts, networks and landscapes are seeking to apply rigorous methods from conventional archaeological practice in order to legitimize archaeological interests in the media and to distinguish archaeological approaches from those of the 'media archaeologists'. However, might there also be room for archaeologists to bring the more playful methods used in prehistoric archaeology into the media archaeology arena? In this chapter, we discuss a project undertaken at Cube Microplex, a volunteer-run arts and cinema space in Bristol, UK. In advance of major redevelopment work, we undertook an archaeology of the cinema as a collaboration between academics and the community of Cube volunteers. The aim was two-fold: to record a multi-scalar assemblage of the cinema's interior spaces and artefacts and to generate materials that could be re-assembled in future as part of an ongoing artwork to be enfolded in the cinema as part of its media heritage.

Keywords: Media Archaeology, Archaeology, Cinema, Community-involved practice, Mixed-mode research

1   While the primary author of this chapter is Angela Piccini, it was written collectively. Authors (listed alphabetically and with additional institutional affiliations) are: Laura Aish (University of Bristol), David Biddle, Esther Breithoff (University College London), James Dixon (University of Bristol), Zuleika Gregory, Paul Hanson, Graeme Hogg, David Hopkinson, Thomas Kador (University College London), Dani Landau (University of the West of England), Jamie Lindsay, Kate Maxwell, Dewi Owen (University of Bristol), Angela Piccini (University of Bristol), Kate Rich, Jelena Stanovik, Marcus Valentine, Marko Wilkinson, Chiz Williams, Alison Wills.

Roberts, B. and M. Goodall (eds.), *New Media Archaeologies*, Amsterdam Universsity Press, 2019
DOI: 10.5117/9789462982161_CH08

The Cube is a volunteer-run mixed-arts-cinema space in the Stokes Croft area of Bristol, UK. Opening in 1998 in King's Square, at the site of the former Arts Cinema (the first of the British Film Institute's Regional Film Theatres), the Cube has generated and held a diverse range of events, people, and materials during its life.[2] Since June 2015, the Cube has been involved in a collaborative contemporary archaeology project that has brought together volunteers and archaeologists to learn archaeological and heritage interpretation methods in order to investigate the human and other-than-human pasts, presents, and futures of this place. The project emerged in response to the Cube's purchase of its building and developing plans to reconfigure the interior spaces. The renovation is driven in part by regulatory pressures around health and safety, access issues, and a desire to open up the Cube more to its communities as a making and meeting space. However, the planned renovations have generated anxieties about loss: of character, of patina, of an undefined magic of place that generates the specific sense of community that Cube volunteers feel. By engaging in a range of archaeological practices, from the conventionally photogram-metric to practices of observation and performance that aim to respond to the cinema as an affective space, we – the collection of authors – felt that we could intervene in the melancholic aesthetic of loss (Freud, 1917) to consider what a media archaeology might contribute to the development of a progressive heritage.

Over the course of the project to date, we looked at the building in its landscape context, we listened to its sound environment, we explored textures and texts, we recorded materials, we photographed junk and writing on the wall. We framed the ebb and flow of things through the space and transformed event into image. We considered conducting chemical analyses of soot in order to design our own paints. We enjoyed ourselves and experienced this place anew. Importantly, we have asked: how does approaching a cinema from an archaeological perspective contribute to our understandings of place?

Film scholarship has guided readers to understandings of histori-cal cinema-going experiences through its focus on memory and on the human-centred aspects of encountering both the cinema space and the films screened. This work introduced reception studies to film schol-arship and insisted on the importance of audience in a collaborative relationship with the silver screen. Jackie Stacey (1994), Janet Staiger

---

2   The Cube is variously known as The Cube, the Cube, Cube and Cube Microplex. In this paper, we adopt 'the Cube' and 'Cube volunteers'.

(1992), and Annette Kuhn's (2002) cultural studies approaches placed the human – often female – experience of spectatorship at the centre of cinema's meaning. However, the physical, material experience of screen media has more recently emerged in the writing of scholars with interests in artists' moving image. Maeve Connolly discusses cine-material screens and structures in *The Place of Artists' Cinema* (Connolly, 2009, pp. 163–212), while Catherine Elwes writes about the role of architecture and the material specificities of the built environment of moving image installation in her recent book *Installation and the Moving Image* (Elwes, 2015, pp. 11–20). Informed by Karen Barad's agential realism (2007), Kim Knowles focuses on the material intra-activities of analogue and digital film practices to insist on the materiality of moving image processes and its role in shaping encounters with it in the cinema or gallery (Knowles, 2015, 2016). In *The Cinemas Project*, curator and writer Bridget Crone works alongside artists to respond to cinema as a site in which images appear and also as the material technology *through* which they appear (2014). In short, moving images move their audiences, take them places and also take place (after Rhodes and Gorfinkel, 2011) in terms of the locations at which they are shot and in which they are made. They are assemblages of materials that actively make place in relationships of exhibition and reception.

How might these assemblages of place, media, matter, and people be approached? In this chapter, we collectively focus on the Cube to suggest that engaging in a range of diverse collaborative archaeological practices generates thick descriptions of specific media materialities, material-social agencies, temporalities, and aesthetics that congregate within and around the volunteer-run arts space (Parikka, 2013). Put another way, by engaging in archaeological practices, we attempt to think the cinema beyond either a passive container of human activity, or an ideological determinant of human behaviour. Instead, we try to explore the co-constitution, co-production, and collaboration between human and other-than-human matters in the space that is known as the Cube. Drawing on both archaeology as such – the diverse range of multiscalar methods that seek to understand change through time by recording of material-discursivities – and the broad field of media archaeologies that are the subject of this volume we ask: what are the methodological and conceptual questions generated through a meeting between media archaeology and archaeology as a discipline and practice?

What is Archaeology? Materialities, Scale, Place

Jussi Parikka writes that media archaeology 'is not a progress story – or a story of a decline of civilizations – but is continuously written anew and branded by discontinuities' (in Ernst, 2013, p. 3). According to Geoffrey Winthrop-Young, to write this story the 'so-called German and Canadian media theories' stress 'the materialities rather than the hermeneutics of communication' in order to figure 'the routines and operations of the human psychic apparatus [...] as modeled on – and developing in feedback with – media technologies' (Winthrop-Young, 2014, p. 382). However, what methods are used to stress these materialities and write these discontinuous stories? In this chapter, we suggest that it was through a media archaeological practice that we began to understand what Karen Barad formulates as relational ontology (2007). This concept problematizes both notions of individualism (the idea that entities precede relations) and representationalism (the assumption the ideas and language exist separately from the material world and can neutrally describe it). An archaeology of the Cube therefore offers a way to manifest the intra-action of emergent, co-forming agencies and demonstrates Bernhard Siegert's argument that 'the human was always already intermixed with the nonhuman' (Sieghert, 2013, p. 53). The Cube also exemplifies Avital Ronell's (1989) essaying of the impact of the telephone on modern thought in terms of the particular assemblings of film, video, and music technologies within a specific site that structure how, as Karen Barad articulates it, the world is 'worlded' (Barad, 2007). That is, rather than the world being given, it comes into being through agential action, in which technological assemblages, such as this arts and cinema space, perform. Like the performance of Ronell's telephone in the making of new worlds, so too the techno-assemblage of the volunteer-run, open source ethos of the Cube. Its particular material discursive intra-actions produce new ways of world-making. In short, a media archaeology of the Cube models the community's radical collectivity through a methodological and philosophical commitment to the co-constitution of human and other-than-human agencies.

However, when media archaeology invokes 'archaeology', what kind of archaeology is imagined? Archaeology itself has a complex genealogy and history of use, from Sigmund Freud's reliance on the practice of archaeology for his model of mind (Thomas, 2009) to Michel Foucault's archaeologies of knowledge (Foucault, 1969). In this volume, media archaeology is, in the main, aligned with materialist media theory. In this, media archaeology has positioned itself contra archaeology *as such* due, in part, to the specific disciplinary and methodological contours of archaeology as practised in Germany. Where media archaeology and associated studies of cultural techniques explore culture as a 'humanoid-technoid hybrid' that comprises an 'actor-network that includes technical objects and chains of operations (including gestures) in equal measures' (Siegert, 2013, p. 193; see also Winthrop-Young, 2014), the archaeology practised in Germany is instead seen to eschew theoretical consideration in favour of a focus on precise excavation and finds studies (cf. Bintliff, 2011). As such, it is hardly surprising that Erkki Huhtamo and Jussi Parikka should be concerned that media archaeology not be confused with archaeology, which they suggest is a discipline that digs through 'foundations, houses and dumps' (Huhtamo and Parikka, 2001. p. 3).

Against the notion of archaeology as solely and reductively a digging practice, British, Scandinavian, North American, and Oceanic archaeology across academic and professional sectors has a deep and long-standing critical-theoretical focus on the nature and operations of its knowledge production. Discussions about archaeology as *episteme* date back at least as far as the rise of science-based, processual 'New' archaeology (Binford, 1968; Clarke, 1968). Since that time, the academic focus on 'theoretical' archaeology has sought to question what is and is not 'properly' the domain of archaeological enquiry. Bruce Trigger's *A History of Archaeological Thought* (1989) is an excellent example of the ways in which academic archaeologists have sought to problematize the discipline and to situate it as knowledge production rather than (simply) as labouring activity blindly unearthing facts. Since the publication of Michel Foucault's *The Archaeology of Knowledge*, however, archaeology-as-such has struggled to distinguish its knowledge-making practices in the public eye beyond the simply instrumentalist and methodological.

Yet, disciplinary archaeology as practised outside of the German academy is not as distinct from 'media archaeology' as some have argued (Piccini, 2015). Although some archaeologists have sought to apply technical excavation practices to media technologies (see Morgan and Perry, 2015 for their excavation of a MAD-P hard drive), it is important to hold on to and practise archaeology's various promiscuous methods. Archaeologists practise landscape archaeology, field walking, rescue archaeology, and desk-based assessment. They focus on stratigraphic superimposition and conduct meta-archaeologies of historiographic narratives. They photograph, map, draw, laser-scan, and plot. They dig, but they also touch, taste, listen, smell, and look. They measure and compare. They work with and re-work stuff, and think in terms of landscapes. They investigate assemblings and events that congeal through specific locales, yet are entangled with many different spaces and times.

Archaeology's methodological diversity is not new, however. Antiquarian William Stukeley (1740) pioneered early archaeological techniques of observation and visualization through drawing practices, transforming monuments into ink on paper. In the early twentieth century, O.G.S. Crawford realized the potential of aerial photography to illuminate archaeological approaches to understanding landscape use (1928). Landscape historian W.G. Hoskins (1955) introduced generations of archaeologists to walking the landscape as a powerful interpretative tool. Global archaeology has therefore never really been about digging in the dirt. If archaeology is about visualizing technologies and large-scale interconnected landscapes, then it is appropriate that archaeologists seek to understand media assemblages as properly archaeological. To understand these assemblages, archaeologists use the same diverse methods as the ones they use to produce all archaeological ways of knowing. Archaeology might usefully be considered both as cultural technique and as a method of exploring cultural techniques. In fact, as Greg Bailey argues in his practice-based doctoral dissertation, 'as message carrier and cultural artefact, archaeology is both transmitter and transmission' and, as such, 'media archaeology is always archaeology' (PhD thesis, 2017).

Yet, there remains a tension in the discipline of archaeology. As the discipline contracts in the wake of planning deregulation, the reduction of infrastructure projects, the impacts of global austerity on the public sector and, in 2016, the removal of archaeology from the UK's A-level curriculum, the discipline has perhaps sought its fortunes by returning to claims about its scientific legitimacy. There remains debate about the 'proper' role of archaeology in contemporary society and its methodological diversity can be restrained by normative tendencies. Archaeologists with interests in media technologies, artefacts, networks, and landscapes are seeking to apply rigorous methods from conventional archaeological practice in order to legitimize archaeological interests in the media and to distinguish archaeological approaches from those of the 'media archaeologists' (see Morgan and Perry, 2015). This is important work that makes a significant contribution to the field and is a valid and necessary position to take in the wake of ongoing critiques of contemporary archaeology. However, might there also be room for archaeologists to bring some of the more expansive methods used across archaeology (McAtackney, 2015; McFayden,

2012; Penrose, 2013) into the media archaeology arena? Might the empirical evidence base of media archaeology insist on newer methods to trouble normative archaeologies?

It is into this space, a space in which archaeology responds to media archaeology, that this chapter enters. In advance of major redevelopment work at the Cube, Angela Piccini was invited to undertake an archaeology of the cinema in collaboration with the community of Cube volunteers and colleagues James Dixon (Museum of London) and Thomas Kador (University College London). Piccini is based in the Department of Film and Television at Bristol University and is a Cube volunteer. She also has a background in archaeologies of the contemporary world and for ten years was involved in running the MA in Archaeology for Screen Media at Bristol. Over a number of years, Cube volunteers David Hopkinson, Graeme Hogg, Kate Rich, and Christopher Williams had wanted to record the Cube's features, from graffiti to architectural features original to the early twentieth-century Deaf Institute. Beyond a simple archaeological recording exercise, however, Hopkinson, Hogg, Rich, Williams and others wished to use the results to understand how the building has performed over time and also to inform its future.

The aim of this Cube project was twofold: to record a multi-scalar assemblage of the cinema's interior spaces and artefacts and to generate materials that could be re-assembled in future as part of an ongoing artwork to be enfolded in the cinema as part of its media heritage. We were interested in how to approach an ageing arts and cinema space crowded with film equipment and diverse material in terms of archaeological heritage – to embrace the intra-activity of spaces, technologies, materials, and people as media archaeology. If archaeology is one of the practices that figures the past as a sense of future possibilities (cf. Heidegger, 1962), what kinds of futures might emerge through this space and its community? In doing this collaborative project, we hoped both to contribute methodologically to the scholarly field of media archaeology and to demonstrate its potential impact beyond the academy. In this way, our cinema archaeology project is in conversation with emerging experimental media archaeologies, such as Andreas Fickers and Annie van den Oever's work on practice-based historical re-enactment (Fickers and Van den Oever, 2013). However, unlike re-enactment projects (Agnew, 2004), we are not seeking to re-perform a past through deliberate theatricality. Instead, we see we adopt the observational, inductive mode of archaeology to frame site and material culture in new ways.

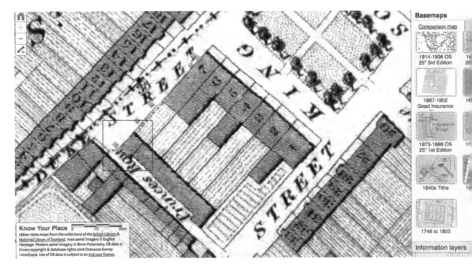

8.1 Site of Cube Cinema, on 1828 Ashmead map and contemporary view.
By permission of Bristol City Council

Archaeo-Cube

Here is a space. (Figures 8.1 and 8.2)

8.2 Cube auditorium. Photograph: Piccini

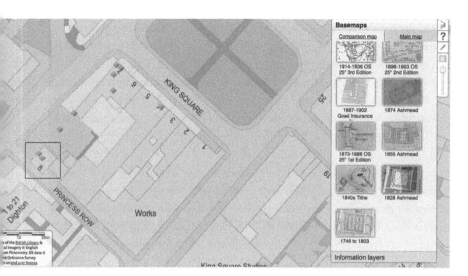

The Cube Microplex opened in 1998. It occupies Bristol's former Arts Centre Cinema (1981–1998), which had taken over the experimental Arts Centre that ran from 1964 into the very early 1980s. Together with Arnolfini Gallery, Bristol Arts Centre was a site of national importance in the development of experimental performance and video art in Britain. Until 1962, the building operated as Bristol's Centre for the Deaf, purpose-built around 1916 on what were the grounds of late eighteenth- and early nineteenth-century orchards and the grand houses of Lower Kingsdown. The Cube emerged out of Club Rombus, which was run by Graeme Hogg and Kevin Dennis from 1994–1998. Club Rombus organized 8mm and 16mm film club events in a range of settings – including the Bristol Arts Centre Cinema – using multiple projectors, music, and archive films. Hogg and Dennis worked with Julian Hollman of Bristol Film Makers Festival to take on the lease of the cinema space in order to give a more stable home to their activities. It also provided a space for makers and viewers, for people who loved analog cinema technologies and the potential for digital filmmaking, and for people who enjoyed blurring the boundaries between live art, music and the moving image. The Cube continues to operate as an entirely volunteer-run space. There is a group of directors, but hierarchies are resisted and there is a commitment to self-organization and distributed responsibility.

In 2001, a fire started in the Mayflower Chinese Restaurant, which shared its entrance with the Cube. Due to extensive smoke damage, the cinema closed for a year, the restaurant relocated to the shopping area beneath the St James Barton Roundabout in the city centre and the volunteers refurbished the Cube. The current space reflects the 2002 re-design. After raising funds to purchase the building in December 2013, the Cube was set up as an Industrial and Provident Society and Community Land Trust. The site is now protected for community use in perpetuity. Since purchasing the building, the Cube has been working with architects to imagine a new spatial-operational future. The project, called Blueprint, involved over a year of collaborating with architects to make models; workshops; visioning of a space that involved making it fully accessible; restructuring work spaces to create more rehearsal opportunity; and making it open to a wide range of community participants throughout the day and evening. As part of this process, areas of the current Cube have emerged as particularly full of memory, potential, emotion. Plans to renovate the Cube generated anxieties about loss within the volunteer community. Some of the key people involved in the Blueprint project wished to develop a range of creative approaches to involve all volunteers in the rethinking of the Cube. Archaeology was felt to offer a way to do this.

We Are All Archaeologists Now

In June 2015, we gathered on a Saturday morning for a two-day workshop on archaeological methods. We began the workshop with an introduction to archaeology and a discussion about what the temporal and methodo-logical limits of archaeology might be. We tried to trouble the notion of archaeology as merely the study of old things. Because the physical remains of the past can be spoken of only because they exist in the present, all archaeology is contemporary (see Graves-Brown, Harrison and Piccini, 2013). We linked archaeological practice with arts practices in terms of their shared attentions to the material, their attempts to exhaust material potential, their focus on assemblage (Harrison, 2011), their considerations of scale (Edgeworth, 2013) and their interests in troubling relationships between event and document (Shanks and Pearson, 2001; Allegue, Jones, Kershaw and Piccini, 2009). Archaeology is also always a visualizing practice. From antiquarian drawings of Stonehenge to early aerial photography to current work with Geographical Information Systems to computer-aided visualization, archaeology transforms human practices of looking and measuring into visual media forms. In short, we focused on the ways in which archaeology is itself a promiscuous disposition, entangled with the media technologies that it attempts to describe.

In terms of beginning to create an archaeology of the Cube, we discussed the importance of the built environment, the way in which the building's corners, hidden spaces, layers of grime and graffiti all shape the human activities that take place there. The Cube has frequently turned to its archaeology and its history, through the practices of many of its volunteers and its various film projects and events. The Cube is invoked as sacred myth, as ritual space, bound up in its own archaeological imaginings. An example of this would be the November 2015 KLF: Chaos, Magic and The Band Who Burned a Million Pounds event. There, David Hopkinson produced an archive film of his own and others' video documentation of the band The KLF, which wove the history of the Cube in with that of the group, and the evening ended with ritual money burning facilitated by Jonathan Harris.[3] These are the more playful edges of media archaeology that respond to the spirit and practice of the cinema, that use the building, its old technologies, and its own archive as source materials for new work.

We talked about how we might transform elements of the Cube into other kinds of material such as drawings, pictures, video, instruments, notes. We considered how the Cube might want to archive itself. Did we wish to make a cabinet of curiosities? A box of tricks? A card catalogue? A vetrine? Perform a ritual burial? Transform everything into a single, dense cube? All or none of the above? We decided to set up a folder on the Cube server and a cardboard box for non-digital materials. We seemed to agree that whatever we did with the Archaeo-Cube project, we needed to be producing things that were physically accessible so that people could make new works from these materials. While there was no interest in a conservative preservation approach to the Cube's heritage, we desired a baseline snapshot of the space and its technical assemblages in order to keep open and elastic possibilities for future work.

James Dixon moved us out of this conversational/seminar space to lead the first workshop, which focused on non-recording techniques. We began the weekend with non-conventional techniques because we did not wish to reproduce the popular belief that there is a 'proper' archaeology or that participants necessarily required specialist skills to conduct archaeological survey. Moreover, by beginning with a refusal to privilege the transformation of the archaeology into another form of material record we insisted on the primacy of observational practices and the eventness of archaeological interpretation.

3   Known as 'Money Burning Man', Accessed 2 June 2017, https://medium.com/@jonone100/
money-burning-ritual-at-f23-fc7e256e920a#.91a9kr6t2.

We organized ourselves into pairs and spent the rest of the morning looking and listening. Each pair followed one of these five instructions:

1. Explore the exterior of the Cube from different positions in order to explore its situation in a landscape context
2. Observe ways in which text operates
3. Listen to the Cube's various soundscapes
4. Collect rubbish
5. Follow the interior structure

When we reconvened in the Cube car park, James Dixon announced to us that because we had completed our first non-recording surveying task, we were all archaeologists now (pace Holtorf, 2005, p. 160). He then asked us to describe to the group what we had done and what we had found.

Group 1 spoke about taking the decision to explore how far we could walk from the Cube while still keeping it in sight. Although this may echo the psychogeographical practices developed by Guy Debord and the Situationists International, it is also an established landscape archaeology method, mixing the early work of W.G. Hoskins (1955) with 1960s phenomenology, psychogeography, and experimental land art practice. We began by walking the perimeter of the building to explore its architectural context. Starting from the parking lot, we walked up to Dove Street, which appears on the 1828 Ashmead map as Duke Street, and then walked south-west to the corner of Princess Row (see Figure 8.1). We walked south-east along Princess Row, tracing the rear wall of the Cube along the narrow cobbled lane, until we reached the junction with Dighton Street, where the Cube's rear exterior becomes obscured by Llewellin's Gears, a specialist engineering company opened in 1833 on King's Square. We then retraced our steps up to Dove Street and decided to ascend into Kingsdown, the hilly residential area to the north and north-west of the Cube. Gaining height by following a pedestrian walkway from the lower loop of Dove Street to its upper loop behind the Carolina House block of flats, we stopped at various points to look back at the Cube and to discuss how the early twentieth-century building sits within its mixed-use and multi-period urban landscape setting. We were struck by how the bird's-eye view produces a sense of the Cube as sitting within a small enclave of Georgian houses and gardens, that although the building is early twentieth-century, its proportions and setting place it within a Georgian context rather than the other surrounding contemporary architecture. Adopting a landscape archaeology approach highlighted the multi-period nature of the city as viewed from this point and brought the importance of scale to the fore such that the Cube appears very

8.3 *The Cube,* photographed from Carolina House. Photograph: Dixon and Gregory

differently whether looked at within its immediate surroundings, within a 1km radius or with the visible horizon as the limit point. Looked at in this way, the Cube becomes a reference point for understanding the rest of the city.

There is not the space in this chapter to describe each of the other groups' tasks in detail. However, Group 2 led us into the men's toilets to discuss the texts found in the form of graffiti and to compare the graffiti there with that in the women's toilets. Group 3 led us into the bar area and showed us the range of sound sources in the room. Two 1200 series Technics turntables, a sound mixer, a CD player, and ceiling-mounted speakers were the most obvious sound producers. However, two Casio SE-G1 cash registers and a glitter ball also produce both percussive and ambient electronic sound. Glasses clink and crisp packets rustle. The motorized glitter ball about the bar produces an underlying mechanical whirr as it rotates. And the low ceiling and oak parquet flooring create a particular sonic environment that shapes how we hear things. Group 4 then led us into the cinema auditorium for a conversation about the things collected from the floors. We talked about how difficult it was to decide whether some things were on the floor because they were forgotten or because they were lost or because they were no longer needed. This fed into a broader conversation about the nature of rubbish and how, through practice, we determine what is to be considered waste and what is to be retained. We also discussed the spatial distribution of material on the floor and how the larger and smaller items concentrate in different areas, from floor centre to periphery.

Finally, Group 5 took us on a walk through the Cube to look at different structural and decorative features. Inside the cupboard to the right of the stairs that leads into the auditorium from the bar is a feature that is potentially original to the Deaf Institute. Shining a flashlight up into the interior of the space, about 2m above floor height, a line of wooden beading is visible, which runs for approximately 1m until it hits the back of the wall of the cinema auditorium. The beading is a decorative feature and marks the remains of an interior wall, arguably of a space that would have seen some collective use rather than a private room. We explored the sound booth at the back of the cinema auditorium and found that beneath the plaster is a section of wall built in rough stone rather than brick.

Our buildings expert, James Dixon, suggested that this wall predates the Deaf Institute. As it looks like a nineteenth-century feature, it is possibly the remains of an outbuilding from the house that once stood on this site and is visible on the 1858 Ashmead map. We then walked through the projection booth at the back of the auditorium, with its 35mm projector and DCP set up, its monitor stacks and trays of microphones, xlr leads, empty 35mm film take-up reels, amps, envelopes, and empty DVD cases. We exited onto a roof level to see the wooden-louvered lantern that sits on the top of the Cube before walking to the rear entrance of the cinema, to look at a range of now-bricked-in gaps that run along the rear exterior wall. These bricked-in features tell of past doors and windows and the past spatial relations of the building.

8.4 Remains of the wall. Photograph: Dixon and Gregory

8.5 Projection room. Photograph: Piccini

As the final group ended its account, Dixon announced that we were 'all heritage interpreters now'. The first phase of our archaeological training was complete.

Experience and Record

On Day 2, we began with an introduction to the idea of conventional archaeological recording. Dixon's non-recording archaeological methods from the previous day were discussed in the context of their proximity to the range of artistic practices represented by Cube volunteers. As volunteers, we found playful and experiential methods of engaging with the cinema's multi-scalar materialities familiar, yet we also expressed a desire to learn more conventional methods. This was in part due to our need to engage knowledgeably with architects and planners and also a sense of legacy: what we could leave behind as a legible archive. This stimulated a conversation about mark-making and the recording of marks, with a focus on the camera as writing tool and the connections between the cinematic sense of the *camera stylo* (Astruc, 1948) and the ways in which recording technologies produce the archaeological (Lucas, 2012; Wickstead, 2013).

Thomas Kador introduced the practice of photogrammetry. In archaeology, photogrammetry involves producing a systematic and methodical series of overlapping photographs of objects or surfaces and processing those images through software to create a stitched-together image. Frequently used to produce 3D models of objects, photogrammetry is also used to generate high fidelity, detailed surface maps of features. Kador demonstrated the principles of photogrammetry before proceeding to map the Cube's interior graffiti wall, which is located in the corridor that links the rear access to the office and the bar space.

The richness of graffiti in the Cube has been valued by the volunteer community over many years and provides a focal point both for emotional attachment to the space and its perceived heritage value by volunteers and Cube visitors. The women's toilets had been a site of special heritage interest in the graffiti since the 1998 opening, but the stall walls were painted and papered over in the late 2000s. However, the extant graffiti at that time was photographed and printed out and used as wallpaper as part of a decorative tidying up effort. This 'tidying' has itself produced tension and various users of the toilets have expressed their unhappiness with the effective erasure of significant elements of women's textual histories in the Cube. Since the Cube's refurbishment following the 2001 fire, the rear corridor has also become a site of multiple inscriptions, including a 2005 marking of Angela Piccini's height, at the age of 37, alongside friends and her son, Milo Piccini Noble, at the age of five. Although some of this graffiti can tend towards the scatological – 'Laura's bum' – this long corridor primarily engages with the domestic practice of marking family members' heights within the home and

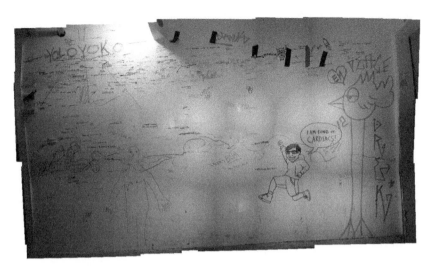

8.6 *Cube* graffiti. Photograph: Kador

evidences claims that Cube volunteers make about the community being an alternative family form.

Following the introduction to conventional photographic recording of archaeological features we returned to work in pairs to focus on particular aspects of the Cube that interested us, using whichever combinations of methods we desired. A key site in the Cube that was of interest to a number of people was the doorway frame that separates the the office from the serving bar area. During the same short period that saw the corridor graffiti emerge, extensive markings were drawn onto the door frame. We filmed it, photographed it and transcribed the text:

Ali [...] Needs me [...] he doesn't know it
I need her too but he needs me

Lucy is a lagoon
Lucy is lurvely
violence
MyckMy, Let me suck it! Please!

Chiz is cheesy
Chiz's colour is
Julian is Joy [...]
Julian's Joke

[...] hole it hurts and much curry

Cube Please don't go
The Cube (like a dice, only more so) Graz.oo
Tonight was v. good

Let's take this board

[...] is hilarious
Kari is kinky
Kari is [...]

Murty

Miss Laura Leigh heats it up!

$\sqrt{34.4}$ 14.2÷10 + Log.225

Spell Reftniereey
is Debbie Definite, Debbie is defined, Debbie is dirty, Debbie is bear
Adam doesn't understand that

Belief cannot be de-bunked
Nor can my briefs

Bruce is benevolent
Hogge is a tomato
Julian is a [...]

Chiz is a badass
Jack is a peach
Ben is a man that goes
Laura is a woman
Debbie is an avalanche
Cathey is a nectarine
Lucy is a blackberry

Level of my belly button
Kari is a clementine
Heath is a kiwi

Marianne is a grapefruit
Jean is grapes with slime
Rod is a pea
Bruce is a plum
Graham is a black grape

Tom Cusak

A drunken I love you
Was a shock in itself
Like a shove in the heart
A knock on the block
I had a sneaking suspicion
You wouldn't speaking
Those words in the
Queue for the loo
Had you not been drinking
Which set me to thinking
Am I falling in love with you

Mark is Burt Lancaster
Chiz is Charles Bronson
Hogge is Steve McQueen
Julian is Oliver Reed
Ben is Woody Allen
Debbie is Vanessa Redgrave
Kari is Ingrid Bergman Julie Andrews
Jean is Jean-Paul Belmondo
Bruce is Arnold Schwarzenegger
Nicky is Alison Steadman
Tim is Ian McKellan
Rod is Mel Gibson
Laura is Diana Dors
Heath is [...]
Marianne is Mia
Lucy is Juliet Lewis
Cathey is Emily Watson
Graham is Terence Stamp

The insistent '[name] is' marks an archival present on this 'back office' working space of the Cube. The doorway is a pinch point on busy evenings as volunteers slide past one another to move from Front of House to bar to fridge through to the kitchen and office area to wash glasses and grab packets of crisps. It is also a social space for volunteers at the end of an event evening. The names listed alongside volunteers are familiar from film history but are rendered ridiculous when juxtaposed with the fruit comparisons and the knowing sexual innuendo.

Findings and Analysis

At the end of Day 2, we gathered to share our recordings and our attempts to produce an initial media archaeology of the Cube.

Dani and Esther had spent the day working on an archaeology of a drum that they found backstage. They began by looking at various bodges at the Cube done with different kinds of tape. They were interested in what they could find out about what people did from the objects in the spaces. While looking at the different kinds of tape, they were soon distracted by a note taped to the bottom of a drum. The note was a set list from Mike Heron and the Trembling Bells from December 2014, with the writing facing up so that the drummer could read through the transparent drum surface to see the list of song titles as they played. Dani and Esther were struck by the dents on the striking surface of the drum as indexical marks of the songs played. They took photographs of the tape on the drum and made a book, which takes the reader on a journey from macro to micro scale of the various practices at the Cube. The Cube is unusual in that the people who do things there sometimes do not physically meet. Or, rather, the only ways in which people and things encounter each other is through the collisions and encounters with and across things.

Zuleika and Jim talked about their attempts to create a chronology from the outside in. They looked for little spaces that would tell stories of change. They looked at the auditorium walls where the plaster had been removed. As a buildings archaeologist, Jim thought they were mid-nineteenth century. They also looked at the modern Princess Row wall of the fly tower, made from reclaimed brick. Jim said that it was 'the cheapest sort of wall you could build with any kind of stability'. For them, the story of the 1916 Deaf Institute build was the archaeology that was disappearing as it was very difficult to see its material traces. They then went looking for the future, for accidents waiting to happen.

8.7 Tape Recorder. Photograph: Piccini

David produced a tape recorder, which is now in the Archaeo-Cube Archive. He went on a search for tape around the Cube. Tape is on a range of surfaces, from equipment to walls. He removed the tape, stuck it in the tape recorder and made notes about where it was found and any stories associated with it. This remains as an open-ended archive and all Cube volunteers are invited to record tape in the tape recorder, providing they carefully note date, exact location and any narrative and/or material associations.

Jamie recorded nineteen separate dust zones and collected dust into little bags, which are now archived. He thinks there might be an interesting project in chemically analysing the dust and turning it into different paints for the renovated Cube. The dust find locations were noted on sticky labels that were stuck on the bags but there was no attempt to be systematic in this practice. The aim was to take archaeology's clichéd forensic obsession and transform it into something playful where the aim was not to find an accurate past but to produce options for the future.

Monica and Laura took rubbings of non-slip surfaces and explored patterns and tiles in the lounge area of the Cube. They produced rubbings of the areas where different materials and patterns cross over in order to focus on spaces of work and emotion. Laura filmed outside of the projection room and experimented with connecting up different spaces, which eventually resulted in her HyperCube tour.[4] Alison and Jo attempted to produce rubbings of the micro marks on the tiles in the toilets, but found that this was not possible with the materials that they had to hand. Instead, Alison

4   (Accessed 2 June 2017) https://www.youtube.com/watch?v=Y1eYMaLoyu0.

worked with the constraints of the paper, charcoal, and colours to explore how best to respond to the patina of place, informed by Jo's consideration of textures, assemblages and markings. All four recombined the spaces to create idealized maps of the Cube.

Finally, Kate Maxwell took 35mm film photographs. She intended to work with older celluloid technologies to respond to the building. She wrote 2 poems: to the projection room and to the auditorium and made archaeological drawings of different spaces. Her main focus, however, came about through these practices of attention. It was only through engaging with the finer grain of the Cube through writing and imaging that she was able to 'see' aspects of the space that seemed to confound rational operation. For example, her archaeological practice prompted her to ask why we would need both a bell and a horn in the main bar area. Rather than use photography to record the building's features or extant artefacts, she used the photographs as an active form of essaying space.

Conclusion

Following the June 2015 workshop, we gathered again in September to pursue our developing practices and interests in order to produce a more data-rich contribution to the archive. Then, in October 2015, we presented our activities and findings at the Rebox event where, together with the architects and designers, we shared with the audience our thinking about the future of this space. This was in advance of being informed that our Arts Council England funding application had not been successful. However, rather than this being paralyzing news, the lack of public funding has freed up the possibilities for the Cube. Over spring and summer 2016, we have been renovating many of the spaces and electrical and digital infrastructures. Lack of external funding has resulted in a greater sense of communal responsibility for the space and its transformations.

It appears clear to us that any archaeology of the Cube Microplex needs to be multi-scalar and demands an assemblage-, rather than artefact-level approach to working through the human and non-human entanglements of technology, body, site, and archive that constitute this art cinema. A site such as the Cube offers the potential to explore the interpolations of Vismann's files (2008) and Ernst's zombie media (2013). We are highly aware of the entanglement of our media practices and those of the development, production, post-production, and screening of the films that we show with wider global forces and their deleterious environmental impacts. A site-based archaeology *as such* enables the presencing and mobilization of the multiple, diverse agencies of media. Practising archaeology invites us to attend to space and material culture in unusual and productive ways.

Archaeo-Cube is an ongoing collaborative project that will shift over time in response to funding applications and the amount of unscheduled time that participants can devote to it. The space is continually in flux and the photographs we produced in summer of 2015 are, on the one hand, simple snapshots of objects that flow in and out of the spaces in unpredictable ways. Yet, both disciplinary archaeological recording practices and the practices of media archaeology engage with synchronic and diachronic approaches to material. Our attempts to conduct a complex, site-based archaeology of the Cube were not intended to produce a genealogy of the technologies at site, although that kind of granular level analysis is the next step for this project. Instead, the impact of undertaking this form of multi-scalar, assemblage-focused archaeology has been to transform the ways in which we, as Cube volunteers, have understood the working environment. The agencies of architecture, of surface, of depth, of assemblage and of technological infrastructure have been manifested through the three events held so far. The Cube gathers multiple cultural techniques (Siegert, 2013; Winthrop-Young, 2014) and is, as a volunteer-run art and cinema space, its own form of cultural technique.

Undertaking a contemporary archaeology of the Cube, using the full range of promiscuous methods developed and practised by both academic and developer-funded archaeologists, manifests the ways in which a range of these techniques intersect. Where Fickers and Van den Oever (2013) adopt re-enactment-based experimental archaeology as a method of conducting media archaeology, in our project we pursued multi-modal, landscape-based site survey in order to expand media archaeology methods to include those approaches that attend to the 'networkyness' of technological assemblages. The outcomes of our contemporary media archaeology are geared towards creating a polyphonic archaeology that addresses the otherwiseness of place and technology, which generates source materials from which further media work may emerge and that throws a new light on the ways in which the techno-media assemblage of the art-and-cinema space produces new ways of worlding the world. Contemporary archaeological methods open out multiple understandings of media as material culture and landscape while situating the study of media as 'properly' archaeological.

The Cube community wishes to continue this work and there is potential for designing a longer-term project that develops the nascent findings of the first workshops. Combining synchronic and diachronic approaches to the Cube as site, as landscape, as assemblage will inform a greater understanding of the performative role of media in the production of sociabilities and modes of making at the Cube. The Cube's material-discursive practices world the world in specific ways that only contemporary archaeological methods begin to frame. Mixed archaeological methods add empirical ground and complexity to media archaeology and we anticipate continuing to contribute to this expanded field.

Works Cited

Vanessa Agnew, What is Re-enactment? *Criticism* 46 (3) (2004), pp. 327–339.

Ludivine Allegue, Simon Jones, Baz Kershaw and Piccini, Angela (eds.), *Practice-as-Research in Performance and Screen.* (London: Palgrave Macmillan, 2009).

Alexandre Astruc, 'The Birth of a New Avant-Garde: La Caméra Stylo', in Peter Graham (ed.) *The New Wave*, Trans. from *Ecran Français* 144 (Secker & Waurburg 1968).

Karen Barad, *Meeting the Universe Halfway.* (Durham, NC: Duke University Press, 2007).

Lewis R. Binford, *New Perspectives in Archaeology.* (Chicago, IL: Aldine Publishing Company, 1968).

John Bintliff, 'Does German Archaeology have a Future? Some Reflections on the Esslingen EAA Session'. In A. Gramsch and U Sommer (eds.), *A History of Central European Archaeology: Theory, Methods and Politics.* (Budapest: Archaeolingua, 2011), pp. 169–176.

David L. Clarke, *Analytical Archaeology.* (London: Methuen, 1968).

Maeve Connolly, *The Place of Artists' Cinema* (London: Intellect, 2009).

O.G.S. Crawford, *Air Survey and Archaeology.* (Ordnance Survey, 1928).

Bridget Crone (ed.) *The Cinemas Project.* Melbourne: National Exhibitions Touring Support (NETS) Victoria (2014).

Matt Edgeworth, 'Scale'. In P. Graves-Brown, R. Harrison and A. Piccini (eds.), *The Oxford Handbook of the Archaeology of the Contemporary World.* (Oxford: Oxford University Press, 2013), pp. 379–391.

Catherine Elwes, *Installation and the Moving Image.* (New York: Columbia University Press, 2015).

Wolfgang Ernst, *Digital Memory and the Archive.* (Minneapolis, MN: University of Minnesota Press, 2013).

Andreas Fickers and Annie van den Oever, 'Experimental Media Archaeology: A Plea for New Directions'. In A. van den Oever (ed.) *Téchne/Technology: Researching Cinema and Media Technologies, their Development, Use and Impact*. (Amsterdam: Amsterdam University Press, 2013), pp. 272–278.

Michel Foucault, *Archaeologies of Knowledge*. (Paris: Éditions Gallimard, 1969).

Sigmund Freud, 'Mourning and Melancholia'. In *The Standard Edition of the Complete Psychological Works of Sigmund Freud, Volume XIV (1914–1916): On the History of the Psycho-Analytic Movement, Papers on Metapsychology and Other Works*, (London: Hogarth Press, 1917), pp. 237–258.

Rodney Harrison, 'Surface Assemblages: Towards an Archaeology *in* and *of* the Present'. *Archaeological Dialogues* 18(2) (2011), pp. 141–161.

Martin Heidegger, *Being and Time*. Tr. John Macquarie and Edward Robinson. (London: HarperCollins, 1962).

Cornelius Holtorf, *From Stonehenge to Las Vegas: Archaeology as Popular Culture*. (Lanham, MD: Altamira Press, 2005).

W.G. Hoskins, *The Making of the English Landscape*. (London: Hodder and Staughton, 1955).

Erkki Huhtamo and Jussi Parikka, *Media Archaeology: Approaches, Applications, and Implications*. Berkeley, CA: University of California Press, 2001).

Kim Knowles, 'Locating Vintage'. *NECSUS – European Journal of Media Studies* 4(2) (2015), pp. 73–84.

Kim Knowles, 'Slow, Methodical and Mulled Over: Analog Film Practice in the Age of the Digital'. *Cinema Journal* 55(2) (2016), pp. 146–151.

Annette Kuhn, *An Everyday Magic: Cinema and Cultural Memory*. (London: I.B. Tauris, 2002).

Gavin Lucas, *Understanding the Archaeological Record*. (Cambridge: Cambridge University Press, 2012).

Laura McAtackney, 'Memorials and Marching: Archaeological Insights into Segregation in Contemporary Northern Ireland'. *Historical Archaeology* 49(3) (2015), pp. 110–125.

Leslie McFadyen, 'Practice, Drawing, Writing and Object', in T. Ingold (ed.), *Redrawing Anthropology*. (London: Ashgate Press, 2012), pp. 33–44.

Colleeen Morgan and Sara Perry, 'Materializing Media Archaeologies: The MAD-P Hard Drive Excavation'. *Journal of Contemporary Archaeology* 2(1) (2015), pp. 94–104.

Sefryn Penrose, 'The charter'd Thames', in Gonzalez-Ruibal, A. (ed.), *Reclaiming Archaeology: Beyond the Tropes of Modernity*. (Abingdon & New York: Routledge 2013), pp. 272–285.

Angela Piccini, 'Media Archaeologies: An Invitation'. *Journal of Contemporary Archaeology* 2(1) (2015), pp. 1–8.

John David Rhodes and Elena Gorfinkel (eds.), *Taking Place: Location and the Moving Image*. (Minneapolis, MN: University of Minnesota Press, 2011).

Avital Ronell, *The Telephone Book: Technology, Schizophrenia, Electric Speech*. (Lincoln, NE: University of Nebraska Press, 1989).

Michael Shanks and Mike Pearson, *Theatre/Archaeology*. (London: Routledge, 2001).

Bernhard Siegert, 'Cultural Techniques, or, the End of the Intellectual Postwar Era in German Media Theory', translated by Geoffrey Winthrop-Young. *Theory, Culture, and Society* 30 (6) (2013), pp. 48–65.

Jackie Stacey, *Star Gazing: Hollywood Cinema and Female Spectatorship*. (London: Routledge, 1994).

Janet Staiger, *Interpreting Films: Studies in the Historical Reception of American Cinema*. (Princeton, NJ: Princeton University Press, 1992).

William Stukeley, *Stonehenge, A Temple Restor'd to the British Druids*. (London: W. Innnys and R. Maney, 1740).

Julian Thomas, 'Sigmund Freud's Archaeological Metaphor and Archaeology's Self-Understanding', in Cornelius Holtorf and Angela Piccini (eds.), *Contemporary Archaeologies: Excavating Now*. (London: Peter Lang 2009), pp. 33–45.

Bruce Trigger, *A History of Archaeological Thought*. Cambridge: (Cambridge: Cambridge University Press, 1989).

Cornelia Vismann, *Files: Law and Media Technology*, trans. by Geoffrey Winthrop-Young. (Stanford, CA: Stanford University Press, 2008).

Helen Wickstead, 'Between the Lines: Drawing Archaeology', in Paul Graves-Brown, Rodney Harrison and Angela Piccini (eds.), *The Oxford Handbook of the Archaeology of the Contemporary World*. (Oxford: Oxford University Press, 2013), pp. 549–564.

Geoffrey Winthrop-Young, 'The Kulture of Cultural Techniques'. *Cultural Politics* 10 (3) (2014), pp. 376–388.

About the author

Angela Piccini is Reader in Screen Media at the University of Bristol. Her research and teaching are focused on the moving image and its intersections with place, space and materiality. From 2002-2013, she co-directed the MA in Archaeology for Screen Media, which was an industrial partnership with Channel 4's Time Team series. She is co-founder of Contemporary and Historical Archaeology in Theory (2003-date). She recently published 'Media Archaeologies of the Olympic City' in *Public* (2016) and was guest editor of the Media Archaeologies Forum in the *Journal of*

Contemporary Archaeology (2015). She is currently co-editing *Imagining Regulation Differently: Co-creating Regulation for Engagement* (Policy Press, 2019) and writing *City Screen Archaeologies: Materialities of the Moving Image* (Palgrave Macmillan, 2020).

9. Inventing Pasts and Futures

Speculative Design and Media Archaeology

Jussi Parikka

Abstract

This chapter aims to put imaginary media research and speculative design in conversation; what does it mean to think of media archaeological and imaginary media projects in the context of speculative design? This earlier missing discussing of the two parallel fields sets out to investigate critical methods in speculative practices across media and design with a special angle to imaginary pasts. Both speculative design and imaginary media research are interested in how alternative worlds might be created and how both temporal, social, and technological tabulations situate coordinates of past-future in alternative ways. The chapter addresses different art and design projects, cross-fertilising the two traditions of media and design theory and practice, and aims to elaborate ways how media archaeology could contribute to speculative design and hence contemporary issues in critical design.

Keywords: Imaginary media, speculative design, design fiction, art practice, practice-based research

Introduction: Imaginary Media as Impossible Yet Necessary Techniques

To be able to start with the non-existent, sometimes even the absurd, is a skill in itself. It can be a methodological way of approaching reality not as ready-made and finished, but as produced and open to further variations, potential, and a temporality that includes the possibility of something else. Like with all methods, the skill of thinking the non-existent needs practicing. It also needs institutional contexts that are able to support such an odd task that seems devoid of actual truth-value and easily dismissed as

Roberts, B. and M. Goodall (eds.), *New Media Archaeologies*, Amsterdam Universsity Press, 2019
DOI: 10.5117/9789462982161_CH09

not incorporating the epistemological seriousness required of the academic subjects.

Despite the difficulty of giving a good one-liner definition that could cover all aspects of different traditions of media archaeology, it is safe to say that it has been able to create an identity as a field interested in the *speculative*. This has meant many things from mobilisation of media history executed by way of surprising connections across art, design, technology, and architecture to acknowledging the unacknowledged, a sort of a search and rescue-operation for devices, stories, narratives, uses, and misuses left out of the earlier registry. Archaeology has been sometimes used as a general term for the way in which we investigate the conditions of existence of media culture, and the media technical conditions of existence of cultural practices – two things that are closely connected, with the two aspects in co-determining relations: media technology and cultural practices. And it also bends our notions of history and time itself. As Thomas Elsaesser (2016, p. 201) puts it, it is a symptom of a very different sort of a relation to the past: 'on the one hand, it suggests a freeing up of historical inevitability in favour of a database logic, and on the other hand, it turns the past into a self-service counter for all manner of appropriations'.

Already, early on, imaginary media was one part of the media archaeological body of research. It had the clear aim of reminding scholars and artists that media technological reality was not to be restricted to what actually is. It was not to be contained by the histories of technological achievement but meant to relate to the broader cultural and artistic history, which technology can be imagined, and where it returns as imaginary attachments to values, affects, aspirations and dreams. Eric Kluitenberg (2011) articulates that such shifts seem at times almost seamless, a theme rather prescient in the marketing discourses of digital culture. We feel constantly affectively attached to dream devices of corporations, carefully framed by their sales pitches as part of a wider infrastructure of desire. While such an attachment is odd enough, broadly speaking the discourses of imaginary connections constitute also our cultural topoi (Huhtamo, 2011a), which then become the environment for recursive dreaming that characterizes consumer culture and production of reality.

But how insufficient and narrow it would be to restrict oneself to what is actual. A variantology of imaginary media, as Kluitenberg puts it (2011, p. 57) can address theological discourses, aliens and the dead, to things untrue and yet so impactful for any account of cultural history. Such imaginations are ways to rethink the usual coordinates of time and space – the time of not merely a past-that-was, but a past-that-could-have been; a future imagined as one recurring fantasy of rejigging the time we are in now.

These are the places that are not only distant but sometimes impossible. How liberating this feels instead of buying into the ready-made dreams. No wonder such strategies can be connected to a wider political imaginary that includes geographical, racialized and gendered others. Artists such as Zoe Beloff have set scenes for alternative media histories through the silent mediums – female protagonists, written into the stories. Furthermore, Kluitenberg points to afrofuturism as another interesting political imaginary. As the director John Akomfrah puts it in an interview with Kluitenberg, afrofuturism and other imaginary media practices are not mental refuge. They produce and sustain new cultural practices and spaces in which black science fiction carves its collective existence but also facilitates relations with, for example, gay and women's movement including in the science fiction of Octavia Butler and Samuel Delaney. What is being approached is a black techno-cultural imagination where also music plays a key role in how pasts, presents, and futures co-determine each other in new ways: 'Black science-fiction culture, especially music, figures the past in the present by matching the quest for 'outer' space with new journals into the inner "technological tape" space of black sound itself via the digital utopias of jungle and techno.' (Kluitenberg and Akomfrah 2006, p. 293). Even if also imaginary media is at times defined as 'untimely'[1] (Zielinski, 2006, p. 30; Kluitenberg, 2011, pp. 56–57), it functions as an interesting situated practice that is aware of geographies and can challenge the Eurocentric focus of some of the speculative design discourse and practice (see Parikka, 2018). Hence, the more interesting of such fabulations function as situated imaginaries that play with the Deleuzian theme of Erewhon (of Samuel Butler's imaginary places with connotations of Nowhere) transformed into NowHere. In some recent work, afrofuturism has also been connected to issues of cultural heritage as a project between speculative futures and records of the past (see Nowviskie, 2016).[2]

1   Zielinski (2006, p. 30) list the various ways in which imaginary media works in the context of historical examples: '*Untimely media/apparatus/*machines. Media devised and designed either much too late or much too early, realised in technical and media practice either centuries before or centuries after being invented'.
'*Conceptual media/apparatus/machines.* Artefacts that were only ever sketched as models or drafted as concrete ideas on paper, but never actually built'.
'*Impossible media/apparatus/machines.* Imaginary media in the true sense, by which I mean hermetic or hermeneutic machines, that is machines that signify something, but where the initial design or sketch makes they cannot actually be built and whose implied meanings nonetheless have an impact on the factual world of media'.
2   In general, methodologies of speculative design have been discussed also in our AHRC-funded research project Internet of Cultural Things (2016), where we worked with the British Library and

So what does it mean to think of media archaeological and imaginary media projects in the context of speculative design? The question itself acts as a conceptual probe that searches for specific practices in both media and design. Furthermore, it is also a probe that scans the disciplinary relations of two sets of discourses about the past and the future. As two parallel fields with not much contact in the past, speculative design and imaginary media research are interested in how alternative worlds might be created and how temporal, social, and technological fabulations situate coordinates of past-future in alternative ways. I will discuss different art and design projects, cross-fertilizing the two traditions of media and design theory and practice, and aim to elaborate how media archaeology could contribute to speculative design and to some contemporary issues in critical design. There are some earlier ideas that have suggested how this might work. For example, Bruce Sterling's idea of 'paleo-futures' as 'the reserve of historical ideas, visions and projections of the future – a historical futurity of that prospective' (Hales, 2013, p. 7) is one example of the shared suitably complex time-scales of overlapping design and media archaeological imaginations, but this chapter teases out further contexts for this methodology.

Speculative Pasts

The term *speculative* has enjoyed quite the popularity over the past years. There are different versions of how the speculative is manifested from global financial markets to non-human philosophy (speculative realism), and it seems a very apt word to summarize the cultural situation of metastability we are surrounded by. As Benjamin Bratton (2016) argues, it is not in any way marginal to the core processes of contemporary culture and economics – the speculative *is* the core.

In the context of design education and practice, speculative design emerges primarily at the Royal College of Art, and Fiona Raby and Anthony Dunne's practice in critical design in the age of digital culture. It is not

an artist in residence (Richard Wright) to creatively assess what it means to consider cultural institutions as data institutions and in the context of discussions such as Internet of Things and big data as the future-horizons of cultural heritage. Wright designed the Elastic System (2016) as a sort of a media archaeological alternative interface through which to visually browse some of British Library's collections, which are not otherwise accessible to the general public. The art project borrows its name from the librarian Thomas Watts's elastic system of storage from 1838 and mobilized as an intervention into current debates related to data and digital libraries.

merely a term or practice tied to one institution, the RCA, but has started to resonate with other institutions (not least through the new Speculative Design undergraduate major at UCSD, led by Benjamin Bratton). As a technique or a method, it has already always been in close proximity with a range of related themes such as design fiction. Referring to the usual preference to discuss real world problems – or more specifically things – design discourse and practice attaches and reproduces certain ontological preferences, as Dunne and Raby (2013) argue. They propose speculative design as an intervention in this field. This intervention becomes both an idea of how to engage with design education and also how to understand the function of reality production as exactly a *production* of what we consider as real and actual, which then also implies what is potential as an open ended variation of what *could* be:

> This form of design thrives on imagination and aims to open up new perspectives on what are sometimes called wicked problems, to create spaces for discussion and debate about alternative ways of being, and to inspire and encourage people's imaginations to flow freely. Design speculations can act as a catalyst for collectively redefining our relationship to reality. (Dunne and Raby, 2013, p. 2)

Some of the foundational ideas in speculative design attach it to a multidisciplinary field of investigations, including cinema and other media. The design methodology becomes linked to discursive methods too: 'fictional worlds, cautionary tales, what-if scenarios, thought experiments, counterfactuals, reductio ad absurdum experiments, prefigurative futures, and so on' (*Ibid.*, p. 3). It is important to realize that the ideas relate to a bundle of terms and affiliated work that shares some similar values related to prototyping, speculation, and new critical stances that at least seem to try to avoid the commercial market as the only focus of design; examples include critical making, reflective design, near futures-design fiction, adversial design and even critical engineering (as represented by Julian Oliver, Gordan Savičić, and Danja Vasiliev's work) (Hertz, 2016, p. 8). In any case, it is fair to point out the multiple ways in which speculative design is meant to work as a way to reinvigorate certain aspects of practice and design education as well as to think of alternative social macro-perspectives, to follow ideas suggested by Ramia Mazé (quoted in Mitrović, 2015, p. 11. See also Bratton, 2016.)

A lot of the work focuses on design fiction and powers of the narrative to create such alternative worlds. As Lindley (2015) has argued, design fiction works at least through three different approaches;

1. Intentional design fictions – artefacts that are created as a design fiction.
2. Incidental design fictions – artefacts that can be interpreted as a design fiction.
3. Vapor fictions – usually marketing materials that resemble design fictions.

But *fiction* is quickly reminded to also include physical objects: design fictions are real material media objects that 'are deeply implicated in the ecology of the media situation, that they cannot be untangled from that milieu' (Hales, 2013, p. 7). Fiction is understood as material vehicles expressed through prototyping 'speculative design props' that are 'physical synecdoches' and 'designed to prompt speculation in the viewer about the world these objects belong to' (Dunne and Raby, 2013, p. 92). One can also call this diegetic prototyping (Kirby, 2010). What is constantly emphasized is that this is not part of the epistemology of modelling, but a different attitude towards the future that works by synecdoche; an object might stand for a wider alternative reality, a speculative environment, a strangeness that gets drawn into our current situations by triggers of relative familiarity. Bruce Sterling writes:

> It's the deliberate use of diegetic prototypes to suspend disbelief about change. That's the best definition we've come up with. The important word there is *diegetic*. It means you're thinking very seriously about potential objects and services and trying to get people to concentrate on those rather than entire worlds or political trends or geopolitical strategies. It's not a kind of fiction. It's a kind of design. It tells worlds rather than stories. (Bosch, 2012)

Hence, it is important to realize what is at stake in the mobilisation of design fiction as a critical gesture. Beside the obvious rather discursive stance, there is still a possibility to think of it as a creation of worlds, as Sterling briefly hints. In terms of design, it relates to how artefacts can act as such diversions from the assumed values of design practice. For example, as Wakkary *et al.* (2015, p. 102) put it: 'In interaction design, counterfactual artefacts can also be seen to gain a perch in this critical inquiry space of consequential propositions rather than matters of functionality or consumption.' It is clearly useful to develop theoretical positions, references and vocabulary that do not only refer to the meaning-creating or discursive structures, but also take into account how we might want to address the entanglement of design strategies and their material practices producing objects.

The recurring reference is to science fiction; design fiction as a core drive of speculative design has a proximity with the poetic powers of science fiction. However, perhaps this is where the reference points could be also extended to a range of material as well as media-specific fields of knowledge, including media archaeology and imaginary media, evidenced in the range of research over the years but also artistic and design work. Bruce Sterling (2009) raises the question of whether one could even speak of a broader 'speculative culture' and in this way he recognizes the valorization of speculation for a range of contemporary practices. Sterling's list of examples includes the scientific experiment, futurist scenario work, observations, storyboards, and storytelling, as well as techniques such as flowcharts and analytical software, brainstorms, and mashups. There's a proximity with a lot of things that resonate with the corporate and business focus on speculation, including the interest in start-up culture. Furthermore, this necessitates to ask whether there are other contexts that are slightly less corporate that could work to restore critical and material issues in speculative design. As Bratton (2016) presents, the historical emergence of speculative emergence could be also situated as part of what he calls the 'material palette' of modern design: mass society based on availability of steel, plastics, the various products emerging from the chemical revolution over the past 100 years or so, etc. So, while in some accounts, speculative design is seen emerging as part of the 1960s architectural discourse (such as Archigram's hypothetical projects) as well as in general the Cold War period synthesis of disciplinary fields expressed in Buckminster Fuller's work, it is also an attachment to the availability and use of new materials that drives the possibilities of design methodologies. In other words, it refers to design in and with materialities that then force to think issues of scale and hence also temporality in particular ways (Bratton, 2016).

To state perhaps the obvious, what is constantly present in speculative design discourse and prototyping is the temporal perspective of the future. This comes out in many of the definitions and is manifested in statements such as when architect Liam Young defines speculative design as 'a space between design, fiction and future' (Duyar and Andreotti, 2015). It is useful in this context to continued developing how the core ideas of speculative design overlap, incorporate, but also could be complemented with media archaeological and especially imaginary media-themed research and art/ design projects. What if we could then also expand to the spaces between design, fiction and the pasts – alternative, imaginary, recreated, and impacting on alternative presents too? So, if following Mitrović (2015, p. 19) we can justifiably say that '[s]peculative practice is related to two basic concepts: speculation on possible futures and the design of an alternative present', it might be as interesting to expand towards a speculation about possible pasts, retroactive futures, and design of alternative presents by different time-based design briefs. This could relate to design in and of deep times (Bratton, 2016), but also design that emerges aware of the media archaeological time of interactions of media-art-science (Zielinski, 2006) and imaginary media (Kluitenberg, 2011) both as a historical targeting of earlier practices of speculation and as ways to mobilize those into consideration of new scales, new temporalities in which design takes a new temporal turn.

Next, I want to turn to discussions of some media archaeological angles to both 'material speculations' (Wakkary *et al.*, 2015) and imaginary media.

Speculative Conglomerations

As already briefly mentioned, media archaeological art has dealt with issues that seem intuitively close to some of the methods in speculative design, design fiction, and even what Sterling flags as speculative culture. It has also resonated on a level of a broader attitude: speculative timescales that are brought back to bear upon the otherwise seemingly stable present. There is a political side to this sort of fabulation that has been recognized as part of speculative design's task in a reshuffling of the disciplinary field of design (Mitrović, 2015). However, the emphasis is different both in terms of the institutional contexts – media archaeology has not penetrated design courses and institutions so strongly as it has done with fine art/media art – and the temporal interest. For media archaeology, inventing an imaginary past, the search for lost ideas and forgotten themes has been more important than the framing of a possible *future* even if it is not necessarily very useful to entirely separate these two.

Some of the work and methodologies in critical design did, however, include a strong relation to media archaeological theories. Paul Demarinis' approach to historical worlds and technologies of media has become a recurring inspiration for experiments with media archaeological material and named aptly as 'thinkering' by Erkki Huhtamo (2011b). In some installations, this included creating immersive environments of past media solutions that in their imaginary quality were well positioned for the speculative take: a good example is the award-winning *The Messenger* (1998) that is a reimagining of the Catalan scientist Don Francisco Salvá i Campillo's (1751–1828) early ideas concerning telegraphic communications systems.

A recent version of engaging with the media archaeological past in a Maker Lab type of a setting is found in places such as the Critical Media Lab (University of Waterloo) and the Maker Lab in the Humanities (MLab) at the University of Victoria (UVic). The latter of the two is led by Jentery Sayers, and it defines the work of design as prototyping 'the past by proto-typing absences in the historical record' (Sayers and Chan, 2016). Clearly inspired by critical theories of technology and work that comes close to media archaeology, it is still a site of activity that has a particularly clearly expressed relation to media history but through iterative design processes employing '3-D modeling, fabrication, physical computing' (*Ibid.*) and more. Media history becomes framed through a test-drive that is interested in remaking: a good example is the 'Early Wearables Kit'.[3] But the focus is not merely on technological reconstruction but how such prototyping triggers critical questions about the social contexts in which such early technologies worked. To quote Sayers and Tiffany Chan:

> The technologies we prototype are dated anywhere between the 1850s and 1950s, which give us a sense of media history prior to personal computing but after early feedback control and related mechanics. These prototypes usually inform present-day technologies – wearables, cloud comput-ing, and optical character recognition, for example – by giving them a sense of texture and change. How did these technologies become those technologies? Who contributed? Who got credit? Who was ignored? What materials were used, and when? Who or what was deemed innovative or obsolete, and under what assumptions? Did old stuff actually work how people said it did? How might we better understand materials such as early patents, illustrations, advertisements, journals, and even fictions by remaking objects depicted in them? (*Ibid.*)

Garnet Hertz's Concept Lab has also been one of the key reference points where the different traditions of media theory and design have met and been elaborated. This has resulted in media archaeology articulated in relation to design practice – including speculative methods – and design being able to utilize the past, historical sources, archival inspiration and found-objects. Similarly, as Sterling (2006) was already interested early on in the material

3   See online here: (Accessed 2 June 2017) https://github.com/uvicmakerlab/earlyWearablesKit

cultures of dead media – the things fallen out of use as the long backlog of technological culture – Hertz has built on DIY, circuit bending, hardware hacking, and other practices of design in relation to media cultural materials and documents. This has resulted in several projects, some prototypes and some in other ways challenging ideas of functionality and usefulness. But it also included a different sort of a temporal horizon of alternative design models: an implied continuation of critical design methodologies based on the 'bizarre, farfetched and unlikely' (Sterling, 2006, p. 60) aspects of what one could dig from dead media archives.

Consider some of Hertz's ideas in this light. 'Experiments in Galvanism' from 2002 restaged the spectacles of scientific experiments for the public.[4] Another relevant – and undeniably quirkily great example – is the Outrun mod. It is a modification of the 8-bit arcade game turned into an actual physical automobile where the simulation of reality of driving is transformed back into a contemporary version of reality of simulation: 'the windshield of the system features custom software that transforms the real world into an 8-bit video game, enabling the user to have limitless gameplay opportunities while driving'. (Hertz, 2012). Retro-nostalgia of 8-bit 1980s computer culture is remediated but not on new platforms as in retrogaming (Suominen, 2008). Instead, it works as a retro-mediation: driving simulation harks back to the old-fashioned media of cars (even if an electric one) (Hertz, 2012). It is not so much a speculative future but a different sort of a material artefact that becomes the trigger in the experimental work. Sometimes it works even as part of the diegetic fabulation.

Retro cultural practices relate to a mobilization of already existing, abandoned, sometimes broken and in general obsolete sources and materials for design. With Hertz, our collaborative work referred to this as 'zombie media' that is a conceptual tweak to Sterling's dead media: instead of death, we were interested in practices that revive and reanimate obsolete materials and technologies (Hertz and Parikka, 2012). In other ways, this parallels other experimental media archaeological practices that mobilize re-enactments of historical use situations but with an imaginary bent: in the film studies context, at the International Orphan Film Symposium 2014 the performance 'Staging the Amateur Film Dispositif' showed a re-enactment of past media

---

4   Luigi Galvani's eighteenth-century experiments with animal electricity were remediated as part of network culture where the trigger was not merely a public showing how electricity animates an animal body but how 'small implantable web servers' can 'trigger physical activity in the bodies of worm and frog specimens, updating galvanism's electricity with network activity' (Hertz, 2002) and webcast directly from the lab to the social media audience.

situations. As Andreas Fickers (2015) explains, the performative elaborates not only the apparatuses in the technical sense (8 mm home film, the video camera, etc.) but also speculates in relation to the imaginary worlds of living and experience in which subjectivities take place as part of such dispositifs. This *explorative speculation* as Fickers calls it is not so much about reconstruction in regards to authenticity but a creation of a sensibility to the complex interplay between semantic aspects and the material design cultures of the past, a proximity with technical apparatuses but as hands-on reflexivity.

In a different context, this relates to the materially grounded speculative practices (Wakkary *et al.* 2015). Continuing the work of speculative approaches and design fiction, it flags an interest in materially grounded 'actual artefacts', which are already situated or resituated objects in the everyday. It could be seen as a sort of a reality tweak by way of design, where with subtle shifts the material speculation attaches to a present temporal horizon. Building on the literature in speculative design and design fiction, the writers aim to elaborate counterfactual artefacts as the starting point of a situated material speculation. Besides a short elaboration of 'possible worlds', as it is discussed in analytical philosophy (such as Saul Kripke), there are also other influences: 'Eco viewed a literary text as "a machine for producing possible worlds" and in this sense we view a counterfactual artefact as a "machine" for producing possible worlds.' (*Ibid.*, p. 102). Such a generative notion of material speculation engages with not only the cognitive reality of possible vs. actual world – a discussion that should in another context be related to the alternative Deleuzian pairing of virtual and actual – but also to the idea of reality production. Instead of cognitive contemplation, reality is being produced by way of material interventions.

The showcased projects are able to shed some light into how design methods are made use of. Among the various ideas they discuss is the Inaccessible Digital Camera, packed inside a concrete casing into a form of inaccessible, unusable piece of media; it becomes one way of commenting on the various layers of the seemingly soft digital technologies, which however prevent tinkering and opening up the machine in multiple other ways than what are preconfigured for the user. Even the digital service industries are built on various layers of hardware nested inside various layers of legal conventions and code. The project with most media archaeological connotations is the simple Photobox machine: 'The Photobox is a domestic technology embodied in the form of a well-worn antique chest that prints four or five randomly selected photos from the owner's Flickr collection at random intervals each month' (*Ibid.*, p. 104). The Photobox sits as traditional technological design – when technologies were to be hidden inside doors and panels – and as a sort of an algorithmically determined slowing down of user patterns. It also is speculative design that establishes relations than merely presenting objects; it articulates social media (Flickr archive), print technology, old-stylized wooden box design at the crossroads of different materials and networks. As such, it is hard to pinpoint it on a map of new or old, future or the past, as it is more of a constellation of multiple overlapping times. Hertz has in another context spoken of *speculative conglomerations* to refer to this sort of a multi-temporal perspective to living media history. It attempts to avoid both the reference to dead media and to future, being a design or art method attached to 'a blend of dead media from the past that are not replicas of an exact time and location, but a speculative conglomeration of lost forms of communication from the history of computing' (Hertz, 2009, p. 127). It involves multiple materialities and multiple temporalities, which in Hertz's analysis stem from his reading of Tom Jennings' *Story Teller*, art installation/experimental narrative about Alan Turing. It can be addressed as as a sort of a media archaeological version of counter-factual objects as 'a hybrid blend of obsolescence where unfamiliar time periods are layered into a functional system that is almost impossible to differentiate from an actual historical artifact from the 1950s' (*Ibid.*) The narrativization of Turing is supported by an assemblage of (obsolete) technologies to underline multitemporality of the various devices 'thinkered' together: perforated paper tape, teletype, phoneme-speech, glowing phosphors, and ink-on-paper.

Such counter-factual devices and installations become design strategies for alternative experiential realities that are not attached to just one temporal perspective. In other words, speculations with the past have a sort of a possibility of prescribing also the past – as visible in archival material, obsolete technologies, and forgotten ideas, media that imaginary media research has been interested in – as open ended, not fixed. This is a sort of a media theoretical versioning of William Faulkner's often quoted words 'the past is never dead. It's not even past.' In practices such as the earlier mentioned MLab this comes out probably clearest, while the other examples cited above are also contributions to the continuum across media theory and design.

One can also find other individual projects that resonate with the already mentioned ones. This sort of a seriality between projects is what I argue as defining a speculative design in a media archaeological, imaginary media context. One often mentioned example is Gebhard Sengmüller's *A Parallel Image* installation. The installation is an alternative, partly imaginary, partly once-existing patent of a transmission system. It offers, however, a break from the adopted, normal transmission systems that work by way of serial transmission (an image broken down into signals serially transmitted to the receiving end) and conceives a parallel image transmission with every image element (or pixel) connected to the receiving end simultaneously. The system of 2500 cables then offers an imagined and built alternative media world to that of Maurice Leblanc's serial transmission that stems from 1880. What if things, circa 1879, had proceeded differently, and the contemporary global sphere had been formed around this rather alternative sort of technical image culture? It fabulates with the history of HCI before computational culture, relating to alternative interfaces, but also the speculative worlds in which such systems might be viable (or, in fact, bracketing viability and preferring the speculative stance). *A Parallel Image* is not the only speculative media system that is part imaginary part real constructed by Sengmüller. His VinylVideo system created an alternative media entertainment discourse around the possibility of recording video on vinyl records. Similarly, some of the other works revolve around different transmission and expression systems that mix lineages of audiovisual media development as well as scales of perception (such as the Very Slow Scan Television-experiment of a bubble wrap CRT screen with a frame rate of one per day).

Diego Trujillo's *This Tape Will Self Destruct* also plays with historical narratives and connotations that fabricate an imaginary device that relate to Cold War narratives. With an honorary mention in the Prix Ars Electronica, the device looks at the intersection of SigInt and HumInt – signal intelligence and human intelligence. Spy narratives conglomerate with a technical device that 'prints self destructing documents'. As Trujillo explains:

> *This Tape Will Self Destruct* explores the intersection between our current techno-political status and Cold War spy fiction. The project consists of an electronic device that prints self destructing documents. The documents are a mixture of images and texts extracted from Cold War fictions paired up with excerpts from current secret documents, resulting in an amalgam that blurs the line between present reality and past fiction. A short amount of time after leaving the machine the documents burst into fire and their content is forever erased as the flames consume the paper. Making the iconic self destructing document real through a functional machine revalidates Cold War fictions in the context of our contemporary values surrounding secrecy. (Trujillo, 2015)

One can see where it fits in both in relation to media archaeology (an investigation of real and imaginary narratives and devices of the technical media of the Cold War with a dose of Thomas Pynchon-styled rhetoric) and to speculative design. It operates as a work of physical fiction (Dunne and Raby, 2013, p. 89). The material nature of such fiction was of course underlined in many of the examples in design fiction but undertheorized in terms of what sort of fiction and textuality is at play. One might wonder whether this sort of speculative stance also attaches to material specificities in the manner of not just alternative cognitive worlds of meaning but mixed semiotics and a-signification. Hence, just to briefly address this other sort of thinking about the nature of signs in such a design fiction that is materially specific one can turn to Félix Guattari. By detaching the work of signs from signification and instead approaching them as material signs that have effects in the world, we start to understand how signs change matter by way of assembling and undoing, to paraphrase Genosko (2009, p. 94). This view concerning language is not merely about a fabulation of possible worlds as a set of already existing possibilities – but one that is interested in which ways material signs, objects, etc. can operate as part of a world that is not predetermined; it is instead, performed and in operation as mutating matter. Signs have an impact with a material force that is not returnable to merely operations of signification (*Ibid.*, pp. 94–95). To understand the full impact of this version of alternative linguistics would need much more elaboration in the context of this chapter, but the main takeaway is to understand how instead of thinking the speculative materialities merely as illustrating a piece of narrative design fiction we can underline that there is a material force in such design strategies and their milieus of objects that surpasses the representational content. They are vectors to an alternative, already situated and yet imaginary possibility that work through a combination of methods of fiction and methods committed to material impact. This impact, then, can also link with change and transformation: reality producing and inducing fictions.

Dramaturgies of Difference

Moving back and forth between media archaeological art and speculative/ critical design projects, one also has to be rather acutely aware of the range of criticism that have been raised. In terms of speculative design, the issues of (cognitive) fabulation and work of fiction have been accused of being constrained by attachment to the White Cube format of the gallery and museum-exhibition styled visual curating of objects with design trying to imitate the institutional prestige of fine art. Such design practices come close to the expanded possibilities of expression that art methods have enjoyed over the twentieth century, and yet also are constrained by similar reasons and spatial settings that are seen as socially and geographically exclusive. In some cases, this has led to the questioning of the viability of such projects as critique: whether 'novels, films, games, and theme parks are better platforms for critical and speculative design than galleries and museums will ever likely be' (Laranjo, 2015; see Russell, 2015). However, many of the projects have actually employed the widespread use of media like film/audiovisual as the mode of expression in order to reach wider audiences.

A more detailed criticism can be found in Cameron Tonkinwise's review of Dunne and Raby's work. The critique raises the need to consider the wider institutional context in which speculative design is being mobilized. Tonkinwise (2014) argues there are several shortcomings in the projects and the methodology. He continues to outline that these include the implicit modernist spirit of technological objects as design leadership, aimed for an audience for which the pieces are created as stylish and admirable and which then might trigger certain cognitive and affective feelings. But he also argues that there is a radical lack of diversity in the geographical contexts and ethical constituency of how the speculation is situated. For speculative design to claim to address an existing lack of imaginaries implies that only specific kinds of situated practices were in the first place accredited as interesting enough to be 'speculative'. This might then relate to for example a different set of coordinates for what counts as the temporality of the speculative and for example how different regions and practices e.g. in the Global South presents have a different sense of the future/present/past. The design practices of speculation remain too easily a mere market diversification that is still rather presentist in its assumed audience than committed to specified politically significant goals. In such a case, politics risks becoming merely a liberal horizon of choice between different options. As Tonkinwise suggests, perhaps there is an unrecognized danger that despite the criticality, some of this sort of methodology actually mirrors the normalized design discourse as well as its Eurocentric underpinnings when it comes to what sort of design methodologies are employed and what sort of imaginaries are being produced. (On speculative design and feminism, see also Martins, 2014). I will return later to the alternative temporalities and alternative modernities that might facilitate developing ideas in Speculative Design and broaden the scope towards a wider set of geographies and situated imaginations.

As some have warned, also speculative historical practices such as media archaeology have to address the tendency that it would succumb to being 'mere rediscovery of the forgotten, the establishment of oddball paleontologies, of idiosyncractic genealogies, uncertain lineages, the excavation of antique technologies or images, the account of erratic technical developments' (Druckrey, 2006, p. ix) and so on. To continue this argument, some artistic practices are important to keep in mind as ways of articulating the continuation of the textual form of theory by way of other means of expression (Fickers, 2015). I argue that some work in gender studies and feminist theory, and also post-colonial studies can point out interesting tentative resonances that could address some existing issues that are not, of course, restricted only to speculative design. It is also an interesting way to tackle the mantra that media archaeology is not political or that it is overly focused on technologies, which is sometimes a claim left underdeveloped or articulated in passing without much critical in-depth debate as well as ignoring existing important work in gender and other political contexts.

Zoe Beloff's audiovisual practices engage in early and pre-cinematic era often with a rather emphasized gender perspective. As examples of design fiction by way of audio-visual and media archaeological art practice, her projects and installations engage in alternative worlds but, as she emphasizes, are not merely interesting as forms of media historical fiction but aware of the material media conditions of the scene.

> [T]he apparatus is always a part of the storytelling process – part of the experience of understanding media – whether people are aware of it or not. I had the idea that, to conjure up the past, it was not enough just to work with historical imagery or archival footage; one must think also about projection apparatuses of an earlier era. (Beloff and Parikka, 2011)

Especially in some of her work, such as *Charming Augustine*, the gendered conditions of a 'medium' become central. The piece addresses practices of medial treatment of hysteria, and the female patients as objects of photographs. Here, the female body becomes an essential part of the media situation, not merely the male photographers Paul Régnard and Albert Londe. In Beloff's world that summons past imaginaries of media:

> Too often it is simply the technologists who go down in the history books not those who created the desire for the apparatus, the reason for its existence. In this sense Elizabeth d'Esperance and Augustine were also important to the invention of the moving image. It was women like them

who opened up a space of desire, of possibility that the moving image apparatus could come into existence (*Ibid.*).

Here, conditions of media are not merely technological but work through the social networks in which gendered subjectivities, institutional contexts, medical practices, media techniques, discourses of madness and more interact. The apparatus plays part in this assemblage alongside other social forces. One can see some similarities with other work that address the past worlds – part real, part imaginary and speculative – through media archaeological methods such as Aura Satz's audiovisual art. *Joan the Woman – With a Voice* (2013) takes scenes from Cecile B. deMille's silent feature 'Joan the Woman' (1916) and uses them in the light box installation. As a reminder of the labour of colour in early film, Satz narrates that this media historical trait is not merely about technological capacities that was then automated – originally '[t]he repetitive, menial and dexterous task of adding colour frame by frame was mostly relegated to female labour, and some film factories such as the Pathe laboratory in Vincennes employed hundreds of women for colour printing' (Satz, 2013). Not so much imaginary media, but through artistic methods illuminating a forgotten side of media history, it allows a different sort of awareness of reality production to emerge: hand tinted worlds of colour with issues of gendered labour framed as more central than the narrative of technological progress and enhanced verisimilitude. Fabulation 'backwards' in time instead of towards the future is efficient as well in illuminating politically important themes relating to what often gets side-tracked as one variable in speculative work.

In artist Peter Blegvad's three-part division, media appear as remembered, observed and imagined (Kluitenberg, 2011, p. 55); the past and present of media as actual things is complemented by the persistence of what can be imagined as media. One can start to see how many media archaeological art projects are designing the objects, which *could have been* as well as such aspects of media realities, which have not been acknowledged as part of the discursive or physical spaces. Hence, issues of gender are articulated into the picture not merely as imaginaries but necessary corrections to established historical narratives. They are also one expression of a political method of 'thinking as intervention' (Brecht, quoted in Zielinski, 2006a, p. 259) into the supposedly real but working through the impact of also the potential worlds. We can perhaps also talk of design as intervention. Somewhere in the interstitial spaces between the remembered, the present and the imaginary these shadow realities re-appear by way of ghosts unseen in the first place. Indeed, this is not so much the category of impossible media, or conceptual or even timely media (Zielinski, 2006b, p. 30), but an alternative reality of media culture's actors, objects, processes, discourses, and aesthetic-political themes. It resonates with the theme of variantology that is partly driving some part of the conceptualization of imaginary media: to resist the drive of normalisation and engage in 'cultivating dramaturgies of difference' (Zielinski, 2006a, p. 259) as a way to question issues of progress.

Gender issues have not featured strongly in the existing work in variantol-ogy but it has given good clues as to where theory is situated as embodied knowledge and as geography. Zielinski recognizes the primacy of narratives of invention in 'Berlin, London, New York, and Paris' (*Ibid.*, p. 261), but also flags all that has been geographically excluded. Or perhaps this could be even called geopolitics of media history-cum-media archaeology: to articulate both when are media, but also where are media. The current centrality of many regions in Asia – such as Japan and China – are among the discursive vehicles through which to 'advocate a two-fold shift of geographic attention: from the North to the South and from the West to the East' (*Ibid.*). Such new cartographies are according to Zielinski more accurate descriptions of the travels of innovations and devices. They are also correctives to the usual linear stories of media history. Without developing the link to post-colonial theory it does however flag the possibilities of thinking the Global South in the context of speculative practices and media archaeology. This includes both the ignored real histories as well as imaginary possibilities that can impact the dominant narratives of innovation as well as issues of gender in the non-Western context too.

In other words, the speculative geographies are linked to what I already briefly flagged at the beginning. The situated imaginaries that emerge since the 1970s in the form of Afrofuturism describe different sorts of vari-ations of future and past that do not merely reproduce the social relations of normalized technoutopias. Of course, they are not entirely devoid of the usual references which however take a different shape, sometimes in playful ways too. Transport and departure takes place through trope of the spaceship, perhaps most famously articulated by Sun Ra. But it is also the context where, as Akomfrah articulates, science fiction meets a reflection on the trans-Atlantic as the seascape of racial, colonial violence that is the historical reference of the enduring presence of the past as persistence of the experienced injustice:

> A series of thinkers starting with Samuel Delaney have in different ways teased out a suggestive connection between extraterritoriality and the new world slave sublime, the kind of alienation that science-fiction writers

try to explore through various genre devices – transporting someone from the past into the future, thrusting someone into an alien culture, on another planet, where he has to confront alien ways of being. All of these devices reiterate the conditions of being black in the New World [...]. (Kluitenberg and Akomfrah, 2006, p. 290)

But this context then clearly articulates a wider space of cultural practices that combine real issues in social movement with the discovery of important texts, historical layers, and theoretical references. As Akomfrah narrates, it becomes a space for 'an inventory of black techno-arcania' (*Ibid.*). The variantological ideas that are allowed space in some media archaeological publications have also links to the possibilities of such an excavation of historical, politically important tropes (Kluitenberg, 2011). In either case, it also relates to a different sort of an institutional situation than much of speculative design (see also Martins, 2014). My point is not so much to accuse speculative design of elitism (*Ibid.*) while staying aware of limitations and shortcomings that need to be addressed, as well as expand the temporal horizon of practice. Next, I want to continue on this topic by way of some media archaeologically-inspired experiments that bring relevant points in educational contexts to the fore.

Speculative (Media Archaeology) Design as Briefs

In addition to theoretical discussions, the implications for design and art education are interesting. The MLab, and some other labs that are not thoroughly discussed in this chapter, presented an institutional site for speculative prototyping that engages with media history; it can be seen as a sort of a spatialisation of media archaeological work in design contexts. Besides what has already been discussed, I want to refer to one particular brief at Winchester School of Art, my home institution. As part of Fine Art's undergraduate Sculpture and Print pathways, the second- and third-year students under the supervision of Ian Dawson and Louisa Minkin were to create a collective piece of work, a reconstruction of the 1860s Francois Willeme photosculpture-machine. Willeme's original piece has been briefly mentioned in some histories of photography as a curiosity from the 1860s Paris and patented in 1864 in the US (Patent: US43822 A): a photographic studio and apparatus that works by multiple parallel cameras set from different angles to produce a 3-D image of the model that then was worked into a sculpture with the help of a pantograph and a cutter. The 24 images set at a 15-degree angle in that specific photographic space are the data capture feeding the visual information for the print/sculpting phase. It can be seen as a financially unsuccessful attempt at 'reconstructing spatial information' (Schröter, 2014, p.109) through multiplanar images, and as a pre-digital attempt at virtual optics (*Ibid.*, p.108) and rapid prototyping as a design technique.

We can also approach contemporary practices of 3-D imaging as later remediations of the idea and this speculative proposition was picked up in the student project through a collaboration with the University's digital humanities scholars in Archaeology and their expertise in 3-D modelling (see Beale *et al.*, 2013). The project produced the contained space where the cameras were operated by participants. The model sat in the middle of the constructed 'room' and the multiple images were later reworked into a sculpture. What is most interesting is the challenge how to integrate media archaeological thinking into a speculative, yet historically grounded project that also needs to work as an educational brief. Was the most interesting idea whether the apparatus 'worked'? The functionality of combination of the studio and fabrication was limited. The end results of 3-D sculptures were clearly more akin to prototypes, but they performed a speculation with past material that had been left outside the mainstream development of photography. Perhaps it was exactly this sort of combination of design fiction together with material art practices (in the context of sculpture and print) that held the most promise as an experiment in educational practices (that then also toured to Central Saint Martins in London as a featured student/art project). I am also keen to stress its potential as an alternative temporality for speculative projects where the archival material and the media archaeological methodology were some reference points together with the new and emerging technologies of 3-D modelling and printing. The material practice, re-enactment performed the work in a way that was not merely about a historical reconstruction. It also provided a way to imagine how differently 3-D technologies look like from the past perspective. And indeed, it was also one way of featuring experimental media archaeology (Fickers, 2015): staging experimental situations by way of artistic methods and in resonance with design fiction, describing an alternative world where photosculpture had become the mainstream way of producing portraiture (perhaps pre-empting current practices of 3-D printing selfies!).

Another approach to mobilizing speculative design in the context of media archaeology is part of a brief we jointly designed with my collaborator, designer and writer Ayhan Aytes.[5] The brief was tested at the 3rd Istanbul Design Biennale in November 2016 with designers, artists, and students. The workshop attendants were tasked to offer initial design blueprints or scenarios for speculative devices/fiction worlds resting on the assumption that 'the Arab-Islamic Renaissance of 800-1300' of technological automata and other inventions triggered an earlier wave of technological modernity. This geopolitical shift in the usual story of emergence of modern scientific societies from Europe to the Middle East was to function as a reminder of the roots of some technological innovations and also to spark a context of design fiction: a *what if* speculative design brief that picks up on ideas that branded steampunk in the 1990s to an 'islampunk' of Baghdad, and the Middle-East: from the design fiction worlds of Victorian era as the start of the computer culture as William Gibson and Bruce Sterling pitched in 1990 (in the midst of the massively invested discussions about emerging Digital and Network Culture) to about a thousand years earlier and in a different socio-religious context.

The brief benefited from the ZKM exhibition Allah's Automata, which exhibited and discussed 'Artefacts of the Arab-Islamic Renaissance (800-1200)' in Karlsruhe in 2015 and the spring of 2016. With Aytes as a special advisor on the project that was led by Peter Weibel and Siegfried Zielinski, we had an insider view to the construction of the exhibition that featured Al-Jazari's work, *Banū Mūsā* brothers' *'Treatise on Music'* and programmable music automaton, and other examples. It included a replica of the famous Elephant Clock with its various references: not only Arabia (the falcons) but also China (dragons), India (the elephant itself), Persia (the carpet), Greece (the construction of the mechanics and movement), Mesopotamia (the scribe sitting on top), Egypt (Phoenix), and, of course, Alexandria (with the hydraulic mechanism). (Zielinski, 2015, p. 15; see in general Zielinski and Weibel, 2015). Visual and design cultures were condensed in the example of the Elephant clock, which also featured a key technology in the sense we usually ascribed to European modernities and the Christian habits of the everyday: time-keeping and clocks as public ways of communicating organized life of periodic rhythms, and in some cases, even communication with God (as Kluitenberg 2011 articulates in relation to the medieval mystic Heinrich Suso, and something that also features in Allah's Automata – the audiovisual worlds of minareths as unifying time and sound based environments).

---

5   Aytes (2020) is also preparing a book manuscript on *A History of Intelligent Automata from the Middle East to China*. This book is contracted with Amsterdam University Press, in the Recursions-series.

Allah's Automata was primarily based on the importance of the translational work that define the centrality of Muslim cultures as part of the history of technology. It offered a sort of a media-archaeological entry into the conditions of existence of European renaissance by looking at Arab, Persian, Indian, and Chinese contexts, although focusing mostly on the Abassid Empire and its 'thirst for knowledge and scholarship' (Weibel, 2015, p. 7). The understanding of technology was expanded to include the systematization of fields of knowledge, including astronomy as well as chemistry, and to be included as part of considerations of technology – what could be more natural for our age as well than to focus for example on the bioengineering challenges as utopian moments of design briefs of a very fundamental kind?

The exhibition painted an image of an audiovisual universe that was technologically advanced. Hence, in this alternative geography of media, Constantinople/Istanbul, Baghdad, Kurdistan, and many other places start to play a new, deterritorializing role that is pitched as the challenge to a design imagination of a media archaeological kind. This project was clearly inspired by variantology (Zielinski, 2006a; Zielinski and Furlus, 2010); the enthusiasm that is expressed in variantological research writes important corrections and additions to the assumptions of the primacy of the Greek-European lineage of technology and science; the manuscripts and designs for automata by *Banū Mūsā* are part of this narrative of rare artefacts from the mentioned Arab-Islamic Renaissance, with the Book of Ingenious Devices from ca. 850 being one of the precious objects mentioned. The conditions of existence of the core European technological culture were in this case argued to be preceded historically and geographically by something else – by the Muslim cultures hundreds of years earlier, a theme discussed in historical scholarship earlier: 'The hardware is virtually identical to the revolving cylinders with pins that were used 500 years later in the European glockenspiel of the late Middle Ages, even later in the mechanical organs of the Renaissance, and for writing automata and automatic music instruments in the Age of Enlightenment' (Zielinski and Furlus, 2010, p. 10).

Besides this historical work included in Allah's Automata, which inspired our smaller exhibition element at the Istanbul Design Biennale 2016, the references became a resource for the speculative design engagement that included this empirical angle to artefacts and manuscripts. But it was also meant to perform subtle sorts of tweaks of the geopolitical definitions of advanced technologies. Through speculative practices of imaginary times of past and futures we wanted to ask: can we shift the understanding of sites of technology and their cultural markers from the usual stories of the US and

Europe to these other locations, including in relation to the much-debated discussion relating to Muslim cultures in the current context of security fears and deliberately mobilized islamophobia used as a tool of xenophobic politics? How are we able to pitch alternative frames for the infrastructures of technology that define the contemporary geopolitical condition including urban development in current geopolitically central metropolises such as, for example, Istanbul where the religiously conservative government and policies meet with massive corporate investment into technological constructions with questionable environmental consequences?

In other words, we wanted to interface historical discourse and archival research with design practices that touch contemporary political issues. Such have to do with the particular ways in which history is mobilized in current social contexts such as in Turkey through fabulations of Ottoman histories to justify policy decisions and the geopolitical manoeuvring of the current AKP-government. And it has to do with the wider global geopolitical situation post-9/11 with the increase in anti-Muslim sentiment, the Middle Eastern crisis with wars in Iraq and Syria, and the refugee movements through Turkey to European Union as one crucial line of renegotiation of several political issues from border (control) to religious identities including debates about the veil. In other words, aware of the rather different focus of many speculative design projects, we wanted to develop a brief that even in subtle ways carries with it this rather urgent and sensitive set of political conditions in a media archaeological context.

Conclusions

Garnet Hertz summed up many of the potentials in media archaeological art and design practices some time ago. It is a well-known quote but worth reprinting again as it can now be read in the context of this discussion of speculative design and imaginary media too:

> The history of obsolete information technology is fruitful ground for unearthing innovative projects that floundered due to a mismatch between technology and socioeconomic contexts. Because social and economic variables continually shift through time, forgotten histories and archaeologies of media provide a wealth of useful ideas for contemporary development. In other words, the history of technological obsolescence is cheap R&D that offers fascinating seeds of development for those willing to dig through it. (Hertz, 2009)

Work with historical materials – both related to discourses of the imaginary and to issues previously ignored, forgotten – can drive interesting ways to think about design and art practices. Archives and historical examples, both familiar and more obscure ones, can provide radically new ways to think not only objects, but also relations that are not, exclusively, history in the narrative sense of the term. The specific future-oriented nature of speculative design can in this sense be expanded to a broader set of imaginaries and temporalities that are not attached to 'future' only. This is not to downplay the importance of such ideas, but to offer a broader perspective as to how any speculation can be rerouted through past-futures and how the past can become a way of pitching alternative worlds. Paleo-futures and dead media discourse was one attempt at this direction, as Hales (2013, p. 7) summarizes well: 'Sterling's entanglement of fiction with the technological culture of the retrospective, with the retromanic and the imagined, provide an interesting point of convergence with design fictions and archaeologies of imaginary media. If we can say that the actually-futuristic are partly real, then the paleo-futuristic are partly imagined.' Such descriptions, but also the actual projects over the years, should offer good impetus to move away from even the linear past-present-future timescales to something else. Media archaeology has always been very good at pitching alternative temporal frameworks as integral to its various methodologies, from recurring topoi (Huhtamo) to time-criticality and microtemporalities (Ernst) to deep times (Zielinski). When Benjamin Bratton (2016) voices that speculative design occupies a good position to redesign the twentieth-century design culture, he is speaking of a radical brief to rethink not only objects, but also the scope of material relations involved from subjectivities to planetary systems. Indeed, speculative design functions also as such a metanarrative that might facilitate a self-reflexive moment although not merely for the sake of self-reflexivity but for developing it as a critical methodology that needs to sustain its complexity and be aware of its blind spots. This is not merely a task of futurity in the narrow sense, but can clearly adopt a complexity of time at its core: pasts and presents, alternative realities and imaginary pasts, non-human times of planetary duration or bacteria millions years old; a repository of dead media alive again.

On a broader note, I am interested in how media archaeological methods, themes and discourses can be employed in practice-based research and education. This implies that media archaeology has a lot of promise for art and design education, and, in this case, much to contribute to speculative design and design fiction. In other ways, perhaps this modest suggestion featured in this chapter is also useful for speculative design? Critics have flagged the shortcomings of some of the practices: it has remained attached to a Modernist appreciation of practice; it is elitist; it is committed to a rather narrow idea of future; it fails to ascribe to a stronger sense of politics. Whether or not all of the critique is justified, especially considering how differently speculative design is employed in so many institutional contexts, even hackerspaces (see Eriksson, 2011), the critiques are important issues to deal with and take into account in future iterations. The issues brought to the fore by feminist theory and post-colonialism are important ways to open up the situated nature of the imaginaries. As such, they can also be brought to new contexts in which the media-enabled imaginaries function. In either case, the guiding questions have to relate to the politics of the imaginaries produced and also how they reproduce or might help to improve the practices of education in which they function. In my perspective, for both practice-based fields and in the spirit of transdiscplinarity the question becomes: how does one engage in such design fictions and speculations that are impactful of a situated change, recognizing the crucial planetary issues and are fabulating in ways that don't merely repeat the same but produce variations? This refers to a variantology, which is not merely for the sake of sheer amazement, but a geopolitically tuned awareness of where theoretical and practice-based work functions.

Acknowledgements

Warm thanks to Ayhan Aytes, Jane Birkin, James Branch, Ian Dawson, Louisa Minkin, and Eda Sancakdar for the ideas and feedback that facilitated writing this chapter.

Works Cited

Ayhan Aytes, *Difference Engines: A History of Intelligent Automata from the Middle East to China*. (Amsterdam: Amsterdam University Press, forthcoming).

Nicole Beale, Gareth Beale, Ian Dawson, and Louisa Minkin, 'Making Digital: Visual Approaches to the Digital Humanities', in, *EVA 2013: Electronic Visualisation* and the Arts, London, GB, 29–31 July 2013. BCS, pp. 240–247.

Torie Bosch, 'Sci-Fi Writer Bruce Sterling Explains the Intriguing New Concept of Design Fiction' *Future Tense*, 2 March 2012, Accessed 2 June 2017, http://www. slate.com/blogs/future_tense/2012/03/02/bruce_sterling_on_design_fictions_. html.

Benjamin Bratton, 'A Theory and History of Speculative Design': A Talk at the Alternative Models and Modernities: The Past, Present and Futures of Speculative Design Event, UCSD, 10 February 2016, online at (Accessed 2 June 2017) https:// www.youtube.com/watch?v=fbyIiX5mw_Y.

Zoe Beloff and Jussi Parikka, '"With each project I find myself reimagining what cinema might be": An Interview with Zoe Beloff', *Electronic Book Review*, 24 October 2011, Accessed 2 June 2017, http://www.electronicbookreview.com/ thread/imagenarrative/numerous.

Anthony Dunne and Fiona Raby, *Speculative Everything: Design, Fiction, and Social Dreaming*. (Cambridge, MA: MIT Press, 2013).

Yunus Emre Duyar and Alessia Andreotti, 'Liam Young on Speculative Architecture and Engineering the Future', In *NextNature.net*, 2015, Accessed 2 June 2017, http://www.nextnature.net/2015/03/interview-liam-young-on-speculative-architecture-and-engineering-the-future.

Thomas Elsaesser, 'Media Archaeology as Symptom' *New Review of Film and Television Studies,* 14 (2), 2016, pp. 181–215.

Andreas Fickers, 'Hands-on! Plädoyer für eine experimentelle Medienarchäologie' *Journal Technikgeschichte*, 82 (2015), p. 1.

Derek Hales, 'Design Fictions. An Introduction and Provisional Taxonomy.' *Digital Creativity*, 24 (1), 2013, pp. 1–10.

Garnet Hertz, 'Experiments in Galvanism: Neutral Ground Webcasts', 2002, Accessed 2 June 2017, http://www.conceptlab.com/galvanism/.

Garnet Hertz, Dead Media Research Lab-web page, 2009, Accessed 2 June 2017, http://www.conceptlab.com/deadmedia/.

Garnet Hertz, Outrun project web page, 2012, Accessed 2 June 2017, http://www. conceptlab.com/outrun/.

Garnet Hertz, 'Garnet Hertz Interview.' *Neural*, 54, 2016, pp. 8–11.

Garnet Hertz and Jussi Parikka, 'Zombie Media. Circuit Bending Media Archaeology into an Art Method.' *Leonardo*, 45 (5), pp. 424–430.

Erkki Huhtamo, 'Dismantling the Fairy Engine: Media Archaeology as Topos Study' in *Media Archaeology: Approaches, Applications and Implications*, Erkki Huhtamo and Jussi Parikka (eds.) (Berkeley, CA: University of California Press, 2011a), pp. 27–47.

Erkki Huhtamo, 'Thinkering with Media: On the Art of Paul DeMarinis', in Paul DeMarinis, *Buried in Noise*. (Heidelberg: Kehrer Verlag, 2011b), pp. 33–39.

David Kirby, 'The Future is Now: Diegetic Prototypes and the Role of Popular Films in Generating Real-world Technological Development' *Social Studies of Science*, 40 (1) (February 2010), pp. 41–70.

Eric Kluitenberg, 'On the Archaeology of Imaginary Media' in *Media Archaeology: Approaches, Applications and Implications*, Erkki Huhtamo and Jussi Parikka (eds.) (Berkeley, CA: University of California Press, 2011), pp. 48–69.

Eric Kluitenberg and John Akomfrah, 'Mother Ship Connections. An Imaginary Conversation with John Akomfrah' in *Book of Imaginary Media*, Eric Kluitenberg (ed.) (Amsterdam: debalie, NAi Publishers, 2006), pp. 280–295.

Magnus Eriksson, Labbet utan egenskaper Master's Thesis. (Lund: Lund Universitet, 2010).

Ivica Mitrović, 'Introduction to Speculative Design Practice', in: *Introduction to Speculative Design Practice*. Eutropia, A Case Study. (Zagreb/Split: HDD & DVK UMAS, 2015), pp. 8–23.

Bethanie Nowviskie, 'Everywhere, every when' A talk at the Insuetude: Conversations in Technological Discard and Archaeological Recuperation conference, Columbia University, 28–29 April 2016. Online at (Accessed 2 June 2017) http://nowviskie.org/2016/everywhere-every-when/.

Matt Ratto, 'Critical Making: Conceptual and Material Studies in Technology and Social Life.' *The Information Society*, 27 (2011), pp. 252–260.

Gillian Russell, 'United Micro Kingdoms (UmK): A Design Fiction' Design and Culture: *The Journal of the Design Studies Forum*, 7 (1), (2015), pp. 129–132.

Jentery Sayers and Tiffany Chan, 'Prototyping the Past: The Maker Lab in the Humanities at the University of Victoria. An Interview with Jentery Sayers and Tiffany Chan by Darren Wershler', *What is a Media Lab?*, Accessed 2 June 2017, http://whatisamedialab.com/2016/05/10/prototyping-the-past-the-maker-lab-in-the-humanities-at-the-university-of-victoria/.

Jens Schröter, *3D. History, Theory and Aesthetics of the Transplane Image*. (London: Bloomsbury, 2014).

Bruce Sterling, 'Media Paleontology', in *Book of Imaginary Media*, Eric Kluitenberg (ed.) (Amsterdam: debalie, NAi Publishers, 2006), pp. 56–73.

Bruce Sterling, 'Icon Minds: Tony Dunne/Fiona Raby/Bruce Sterling on Design Fiction'. A public conversation organized by Icon Magazine, London, 14 October 2009. Notes from the conversation are available at (Accessed 2 June 2017) https://magicalnihilism.com/2009/10/14/icon-minds-tony-dunne-fiona-raby-bruce-sterling-on-design-fiction/.

Jaakko Suominen, 'The Past as the Future? Nostalgia and Retrogaming in Digital Culture' *Fibreculture*, 11, 2008, Accessed 2 June 2017, http://eleven.fibreculture-journal.org/.

Cameron Tonkinwise, 'How We Intend to Future: Review of Anthony Dunne and Fiona Raby, Speculative Everything: Design, Fiction, and Social Dreaming', *Design Philosophy Papers*, 12 (2), 2014, pp. 169–187.

Diego Trujillo, 'This Tape Will Self Destruct'-project webpage, 2015, Accessed
    2 June 2017, http://trujillodiego.com/work/ttwsd.html.

Ron Wakkary, William Odom, Sabrina Hauser, Garnet Hertz, and Henry Lin,
    'Material Speculation: Actual Artefacts for Critical Inquiry', 5th Decennial
    Aarhus Conference on Critical Alternatives, 17–21 August 2015, Aarhus Denmark.

Peter Weibel, 'How Did the Knowledge of the Ancient Greeks Reach Medieval
    Europe?' in *Allah's Automata. Artefacts of the Arab-Islamic Renaissance (800-1200)*
    Zielinski and Weibel (eds.) (Ostfildern: Hatje Cantz, 2015), pp. 6–11.

Siegfried Zielinski, *Deep Time of the Media. Toward an Archaeology of Hearing
    and Seeing by Technical Means.* Trans. Gloria Custance. (Cambridge, MA: MIT
    Press, 2006a).

Siegfried Zielinski, 'Modelling Media for Ignatius Loyol. A Case Study on Athanius
    Kircher's World of Apparatus between the Imaginary and the Real' in *Book of
    Imaginary Media*, ed. Eric Kluitenberg. (Amsterdam: debalie, NAi Publishers,
    2006b) pp. 28–55.

Siegfried Zielinski and Eckhard Furlus, 'Introduction: Ex Oriente Lux' in *Vari-
    antology 4. On Deep Time Relations of Arts, Sciences and Technologies in the
    Arabic-Islamic World and Beyond*, Siegfried Zielinski and Eckhard Furlus (eds.)
    (Cologne: Walther König, 2010), pp. 7–18.

Siegfried Zielinski, 'Allah's Automata. Where Ancient Oriental Learning Intersects
    with Early Modern Europe. A Media-Archaeological Miniature by Way of
    Introduction' in *Allah's Automata. Artefacts of the Arab-Islamic Renaissance
    (800–1200)*, Zielinski and Weibel (eds.) (Ostfildern: Hatje Cantz, 2015), pp. 12–27.

Siegfried Zielinski and Peter Weibel (eds.), *Allah's Automata: Artefacts of the Arab-
    Islamic Renaissance (800–1200)*. (Ostfildern: Hatje Cantz, 2015).

About the author

Jussi Parikka is Professor of Technological Culture & Aesthetics at the Winchester School of Art (University of Southampton). His work has addressed
media archaeological theory and the historical contexts of network culture.
The books include the media ecology-trilogy *Digital Contagions* (Peter Lang
2007, 2016 2nd ed.), *Insect Media* (2010) and most recently, *A Geology of Media*
(University of Minnesota Press, 2015), which addresses the environmental
contexts of technical media culture. In addition, Parikka has published
such books as *What is Media Archaeology* (Polity, 2012) and edited various
books, most recently *Writing and Unwriting (Media) Art History* (MIT Press,
2015, with Joasia Krysa) on the Finnish media art pioneer Erkki Kurenniemi.
Parikka's website/blog is at http://jussiparikka.net.

Index